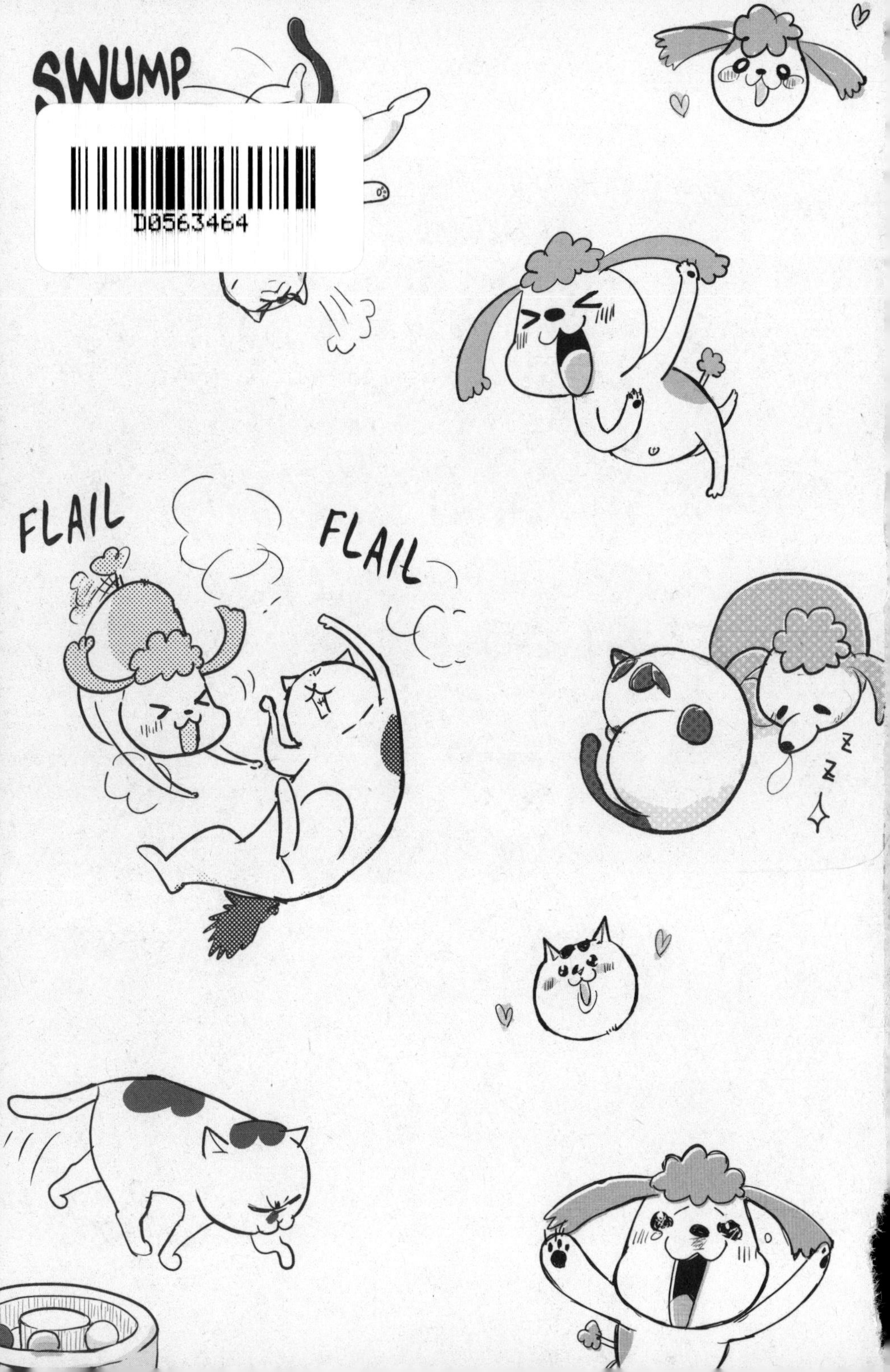
SWUMP
FLAIL
FLAIL
Z
Z

Thanks to you,
my dog and cat manga
has now become a book.
Neither of them know
they're now in a book,
and they're both sleeping
peacefully and unaware.
They're sleeping like crazy.

Hidekichi Matsumoto

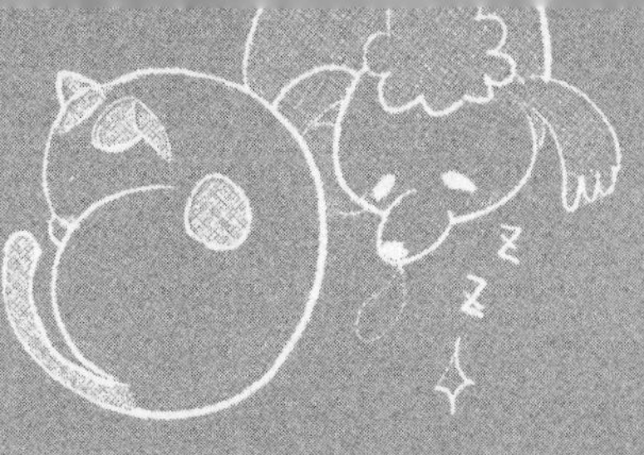

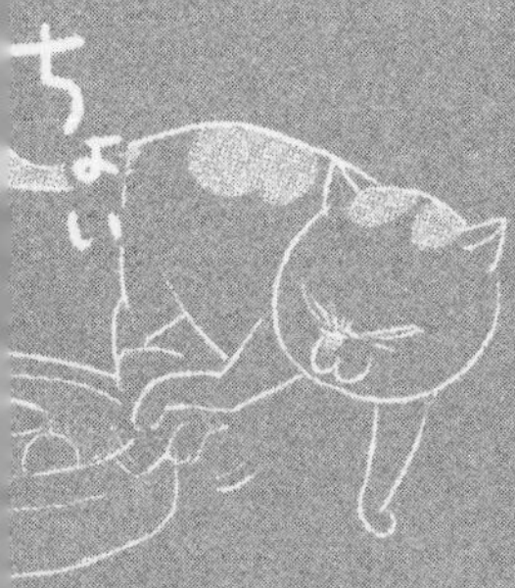
ちょい

With a Dog AND a Cat, Every Day is Fun

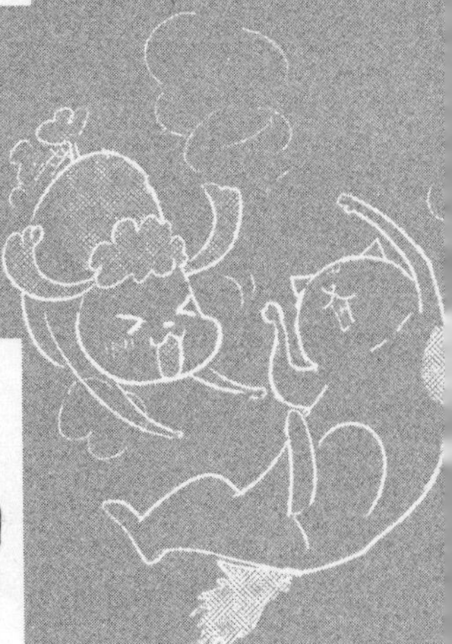

1

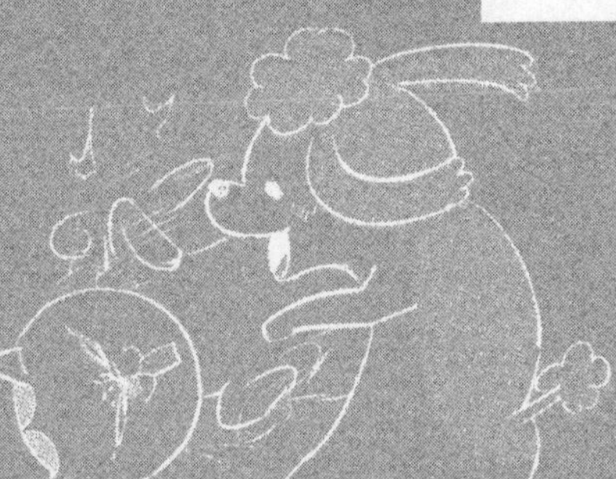

Hidekichi Matsumoto

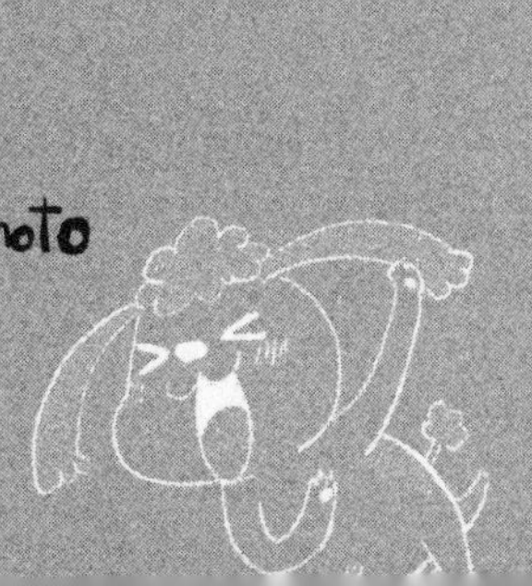

CAST

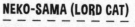

INU-KUN (MR. DOG)

Loves Neko. Even when he doesn't like something, if you sing and dance, he soon forgets about it.

NEKO-SAMA (LORD CAT)

A fearsome face. A cool customer. His passion for theft is staggering.

HIDEKICHI MATSUMOTO

Manga artist. Loves animals.

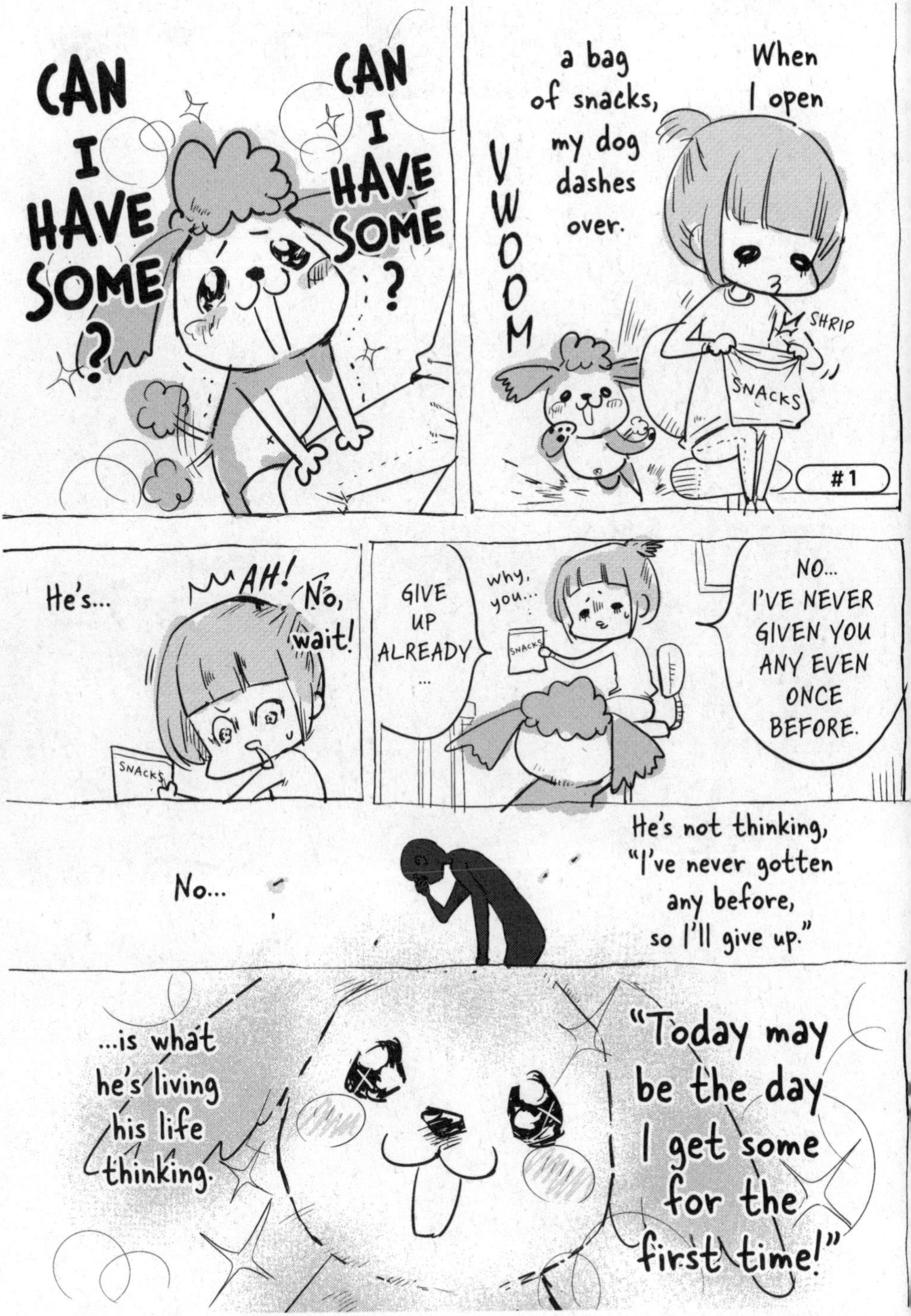
#1
When I open a bag of snacks, my dog dashes over.
VWOOM
SHRIP
SNACKS
CAN I HAVE SOME?
CAN I HAVE SOME?
NO... I'VE NEVER GIVEN YOU ANY EVEN ONCE BEFORE.
why, you...
GIVE UP ALREADY...
SNACKS
AH! No, wait!
He's...
SNACKS
He's not thinking, "I've never gotten any before, so I'll give up."
No...
"Today may be the day I get some for the first time!"
...is what he's living his life thinking.

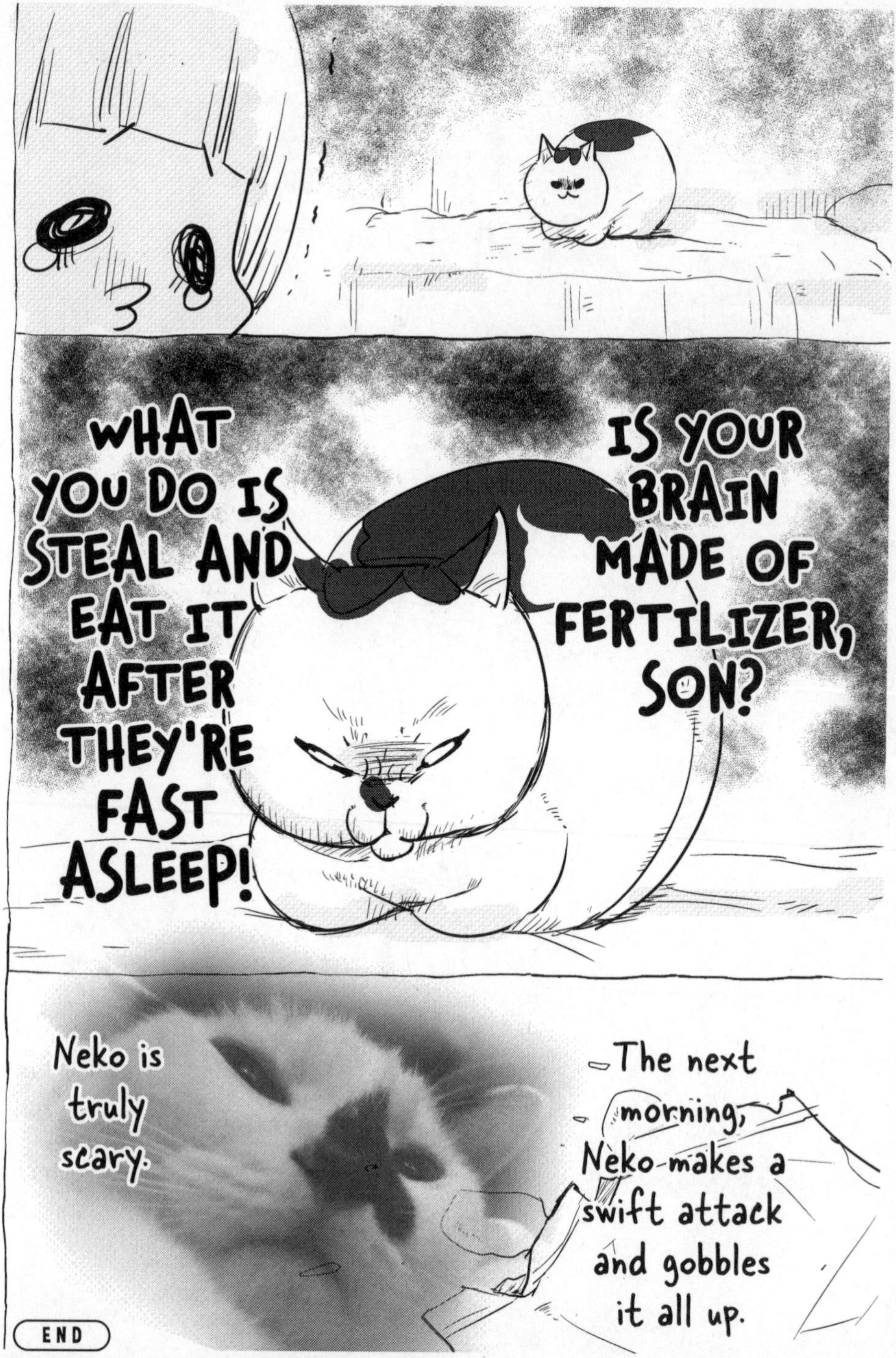
IS YOUR BRAIN MADE OF FERTILIZER, SON?
WHAT YOU DO IS STEAL AND EAT IT AFTER THEY'RE FAST ASLEEP!
The next morning, Neko makes a swift attack and gobbles it all up.
Neko is truly scary.
END

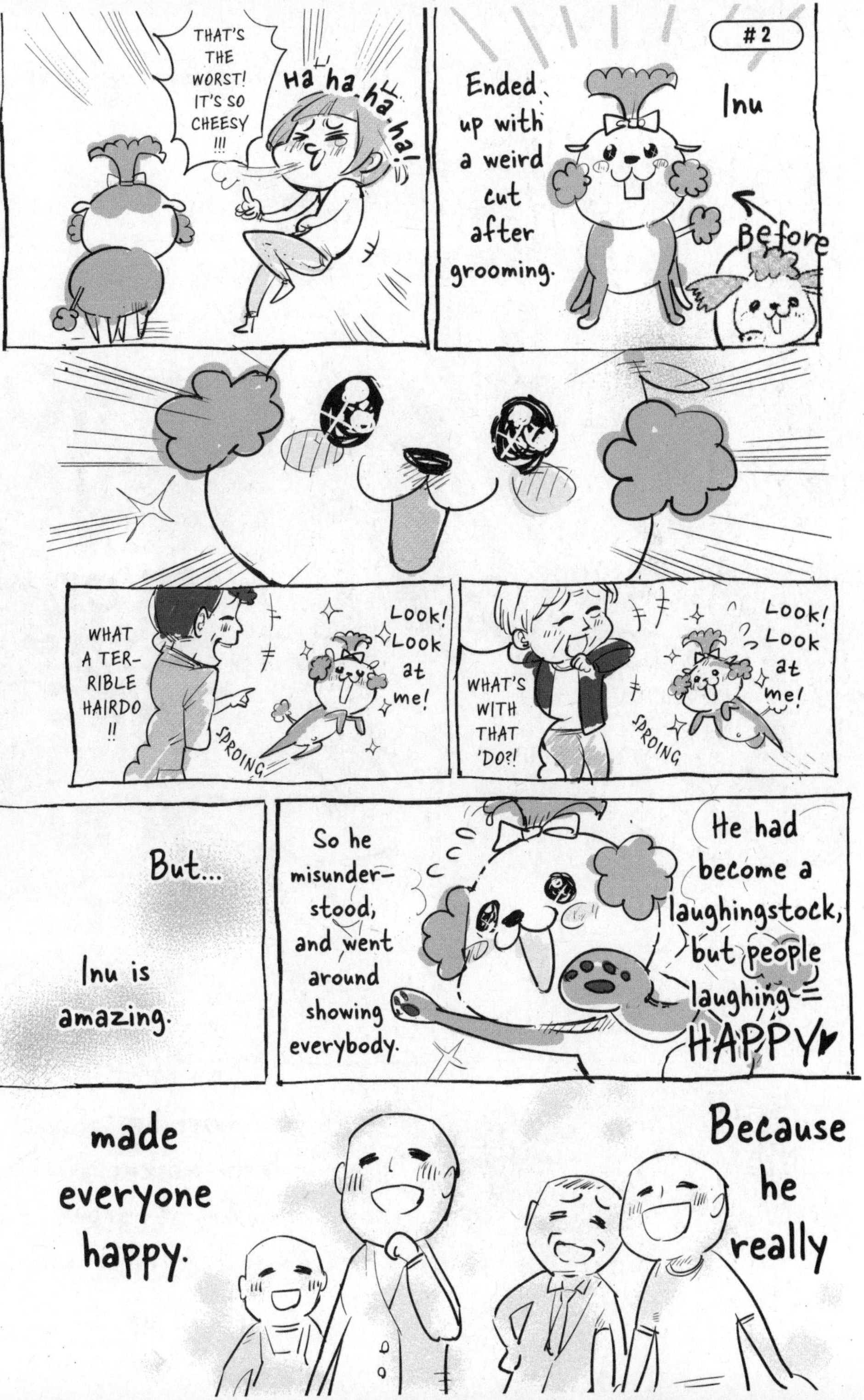
#2
Ended up with a weird cut after grooming.
Inu
Before
THAT'S THE WORST! IT'S SO CHEESY !!!
Ha ha ha ha ha!
LOOK! LOOK at me!
WHAT'S WITH THAT 'DO?!
SPROING
LOOK! LOOK at me!
WHAT A TERRIBLE HAIRDO !!
SPROING
He had become a laughingstock, but people laughing = HAPPY
So he misunderstood, and went around showing everybody.
But...
Inu is amazing.
Because he really
made everyone happy.

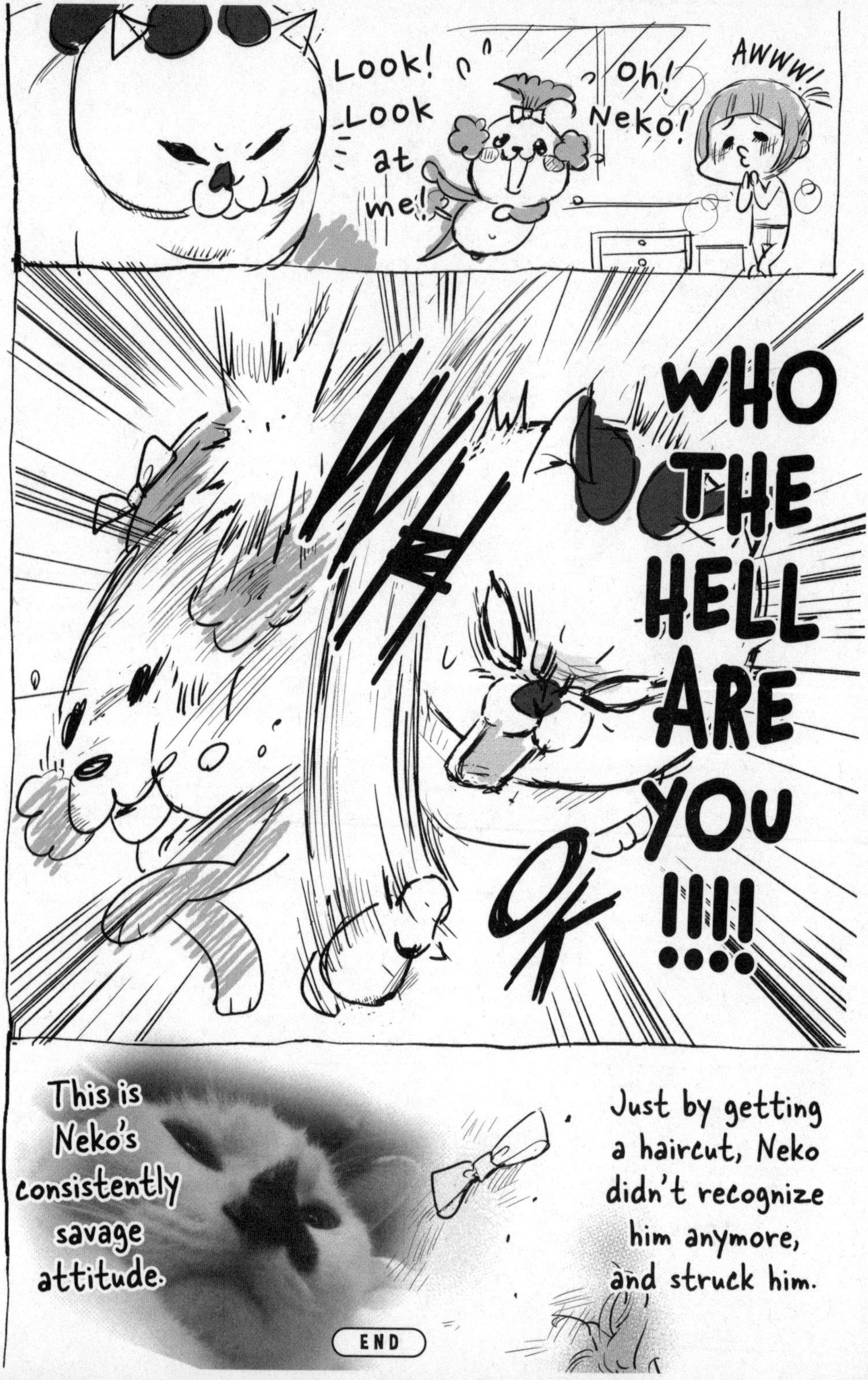
AWWW!
Oh! Neko!
Look! Look at me!
WHO THE HELL ARE YOU!!!!
Just by getting a haircut, Neko didn't recognize him anymore, and struck him.
This is Neko's consistently savage attitude.
END

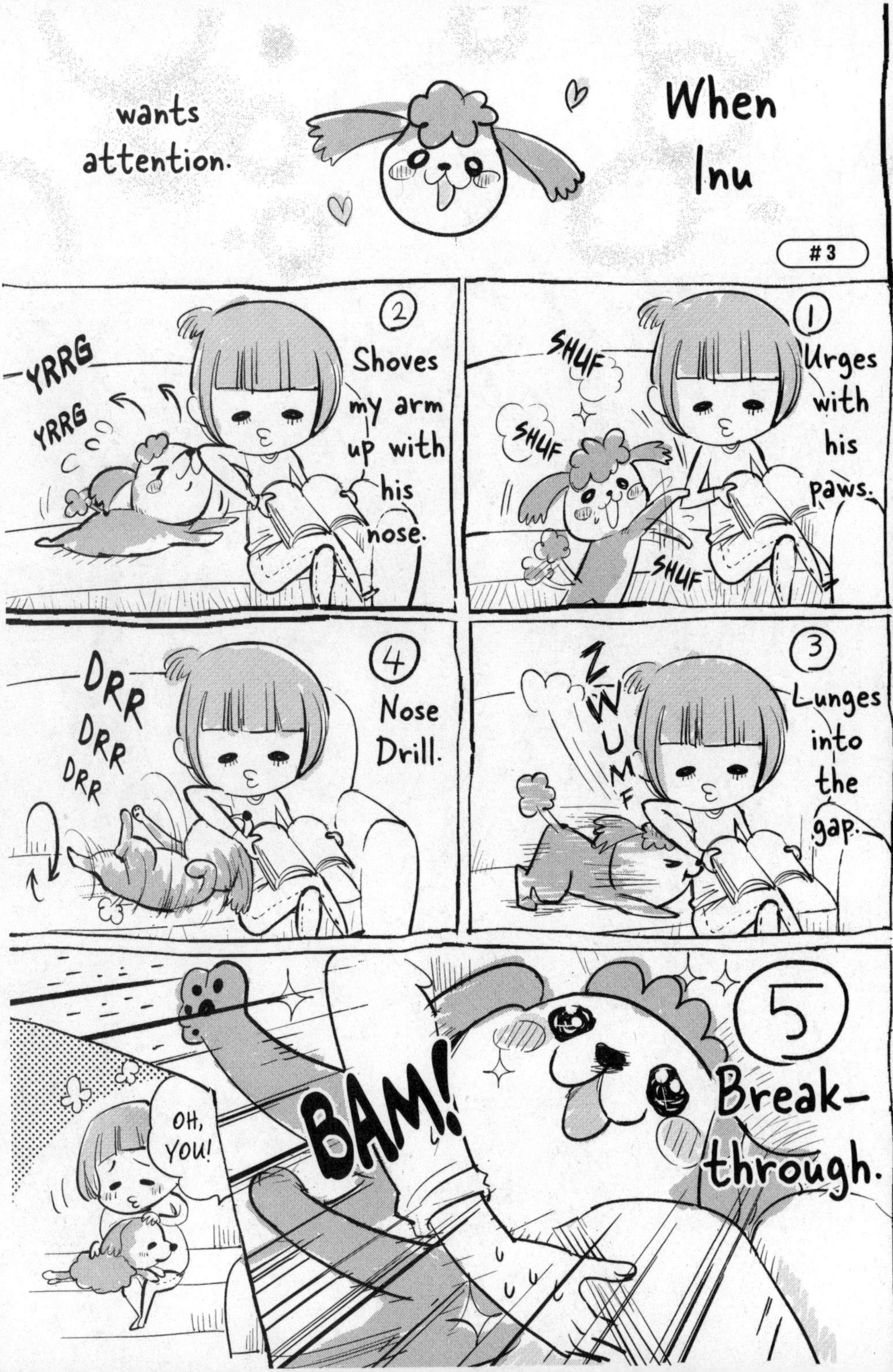
When Inu
wants attention.
#3
1
Urges with his paws.
SHUF
SHUF
SHUF
2
Shoves my arm up with his nose.
YRRG
YRRG
3
Lunges into the gap.
ZWUMF
4
Nose Drill.
DRR
DRR
DRR
5
Break-through.
BAM!
OH, YOU!

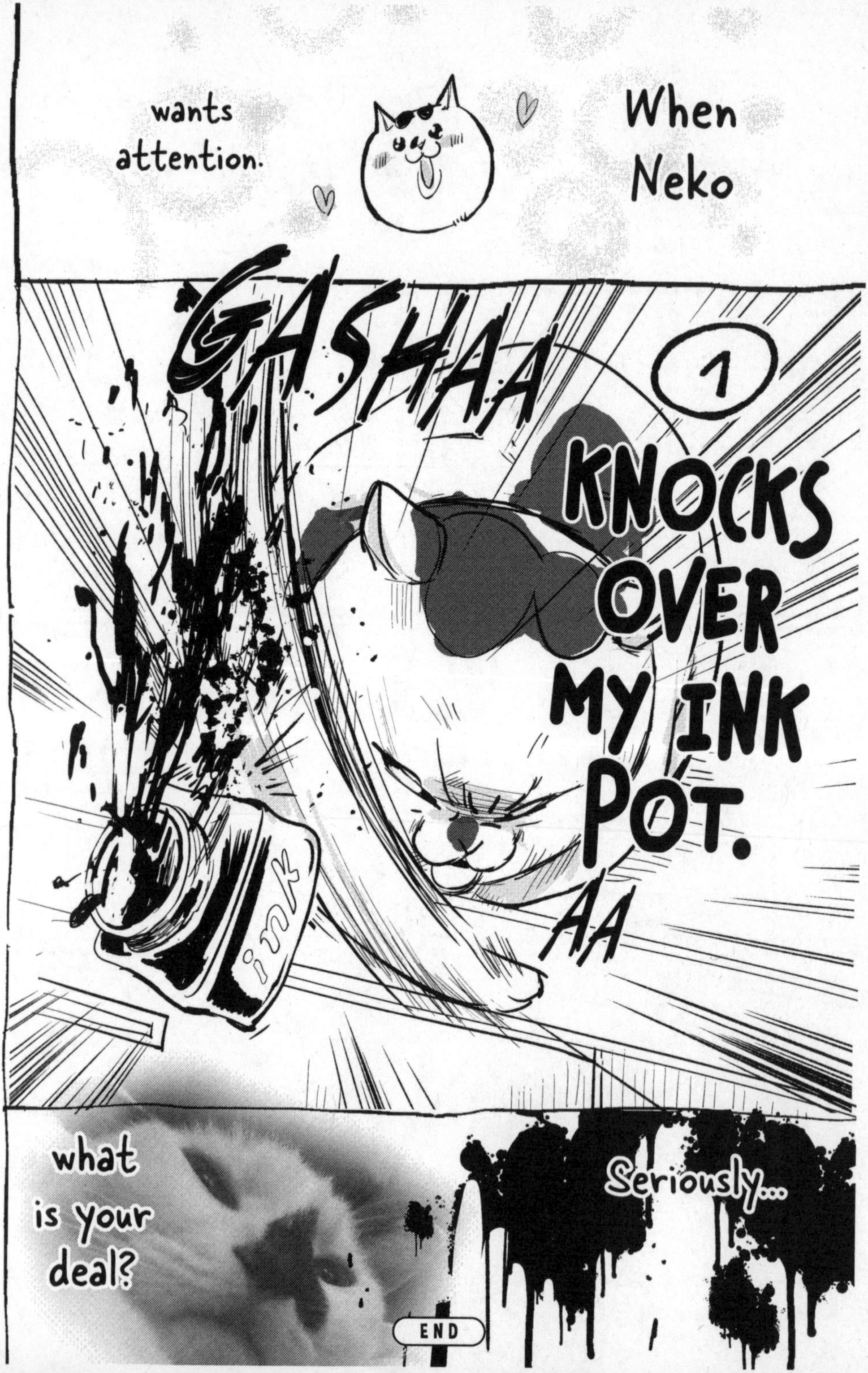
When Neko
wants attention.
GASHAA
1
KNOCKS OVER MY INK POT.
AA
ink
Seriously...
what is your deal?
END

Inu's happy-looking face.

Newly-Drawn 4-Panel Strip

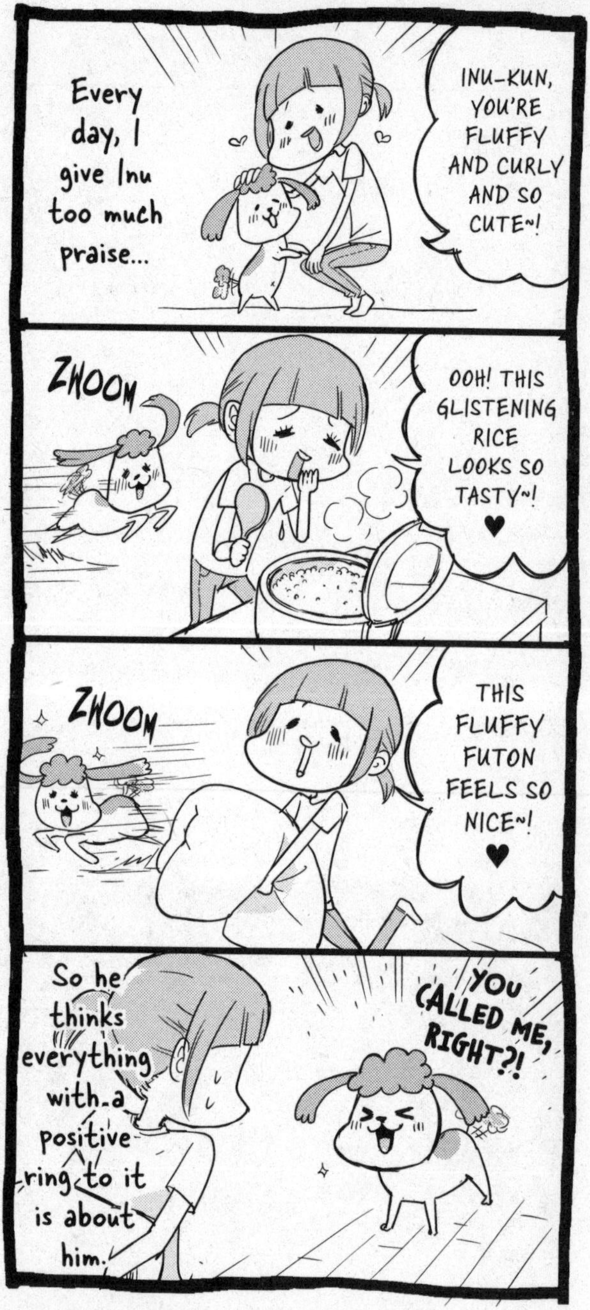

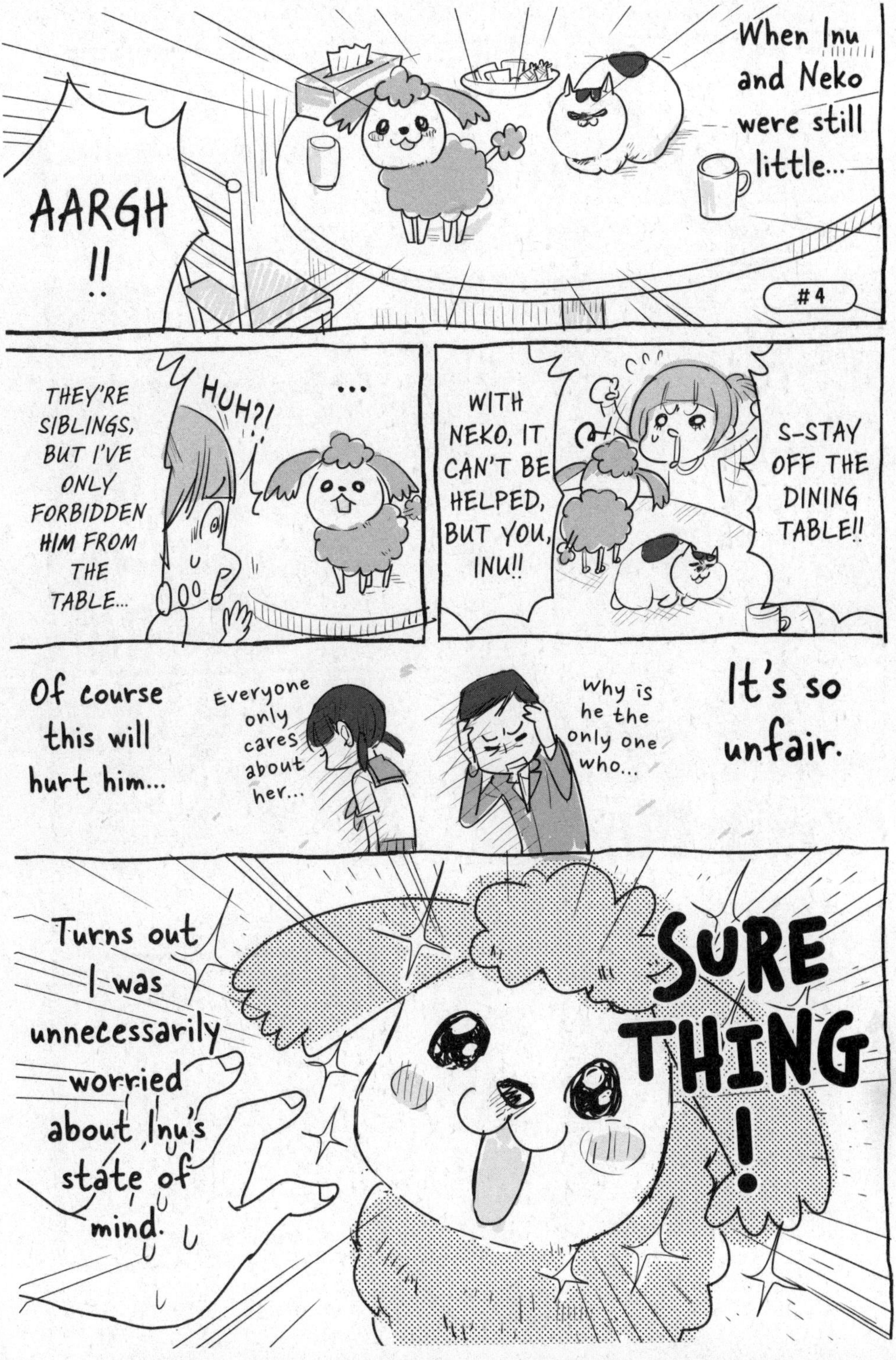

When Inu and Neko were still little...
AARGH!!
#4
S-STAY OFF THE DINING TABLE!!
WITH NEKO, IT CAN'T BE HELPED, BUT YOU, INU!!
...
HUH?!
THEY'RE SIBLINGS, BUT I'VE ONLY FORBIDDEN HIM FROM THE TABLE...
It's so unfair.
Why is he the only one who...
Everyone only cares about her...
Of course this will hurt him...
SURE THING!
Turns out I was unnecessarily worried about Inu's state of mind.

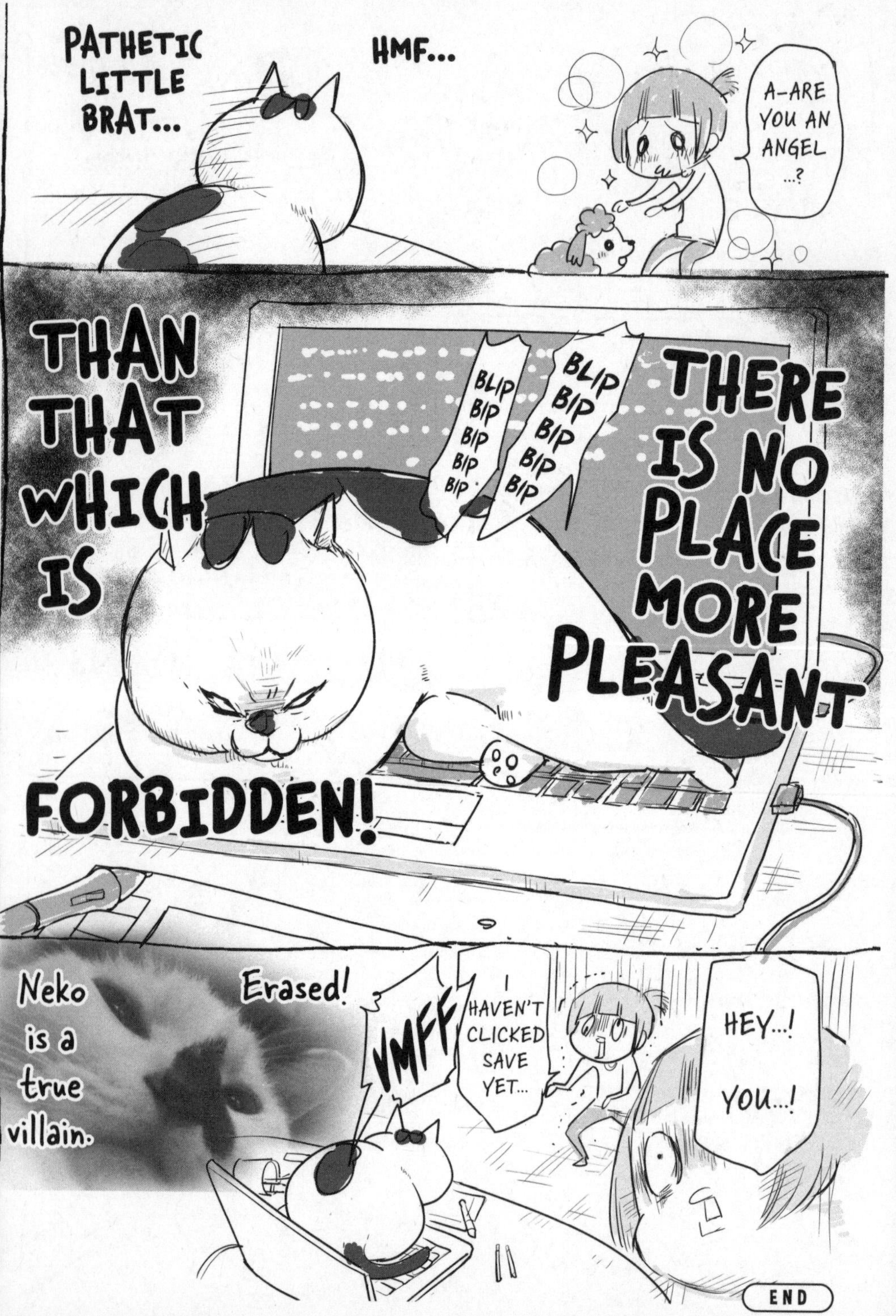
A-ARE YOU AN ANGEL ...?
HMF...
PATHETIC LITTLE BRAT...
THERE IS NO PLACE MORE PLEASANT
BLIP BIP BIP BIP BIP
BLIP BIP BIP BIP BIP
THAN THAT WHICH IS FORBIDDEN!
HEY...! YOU...!
I HAVEN'T CLICKED SAVE YET...
VMFF
Erased!
Neko is a true villain.
END

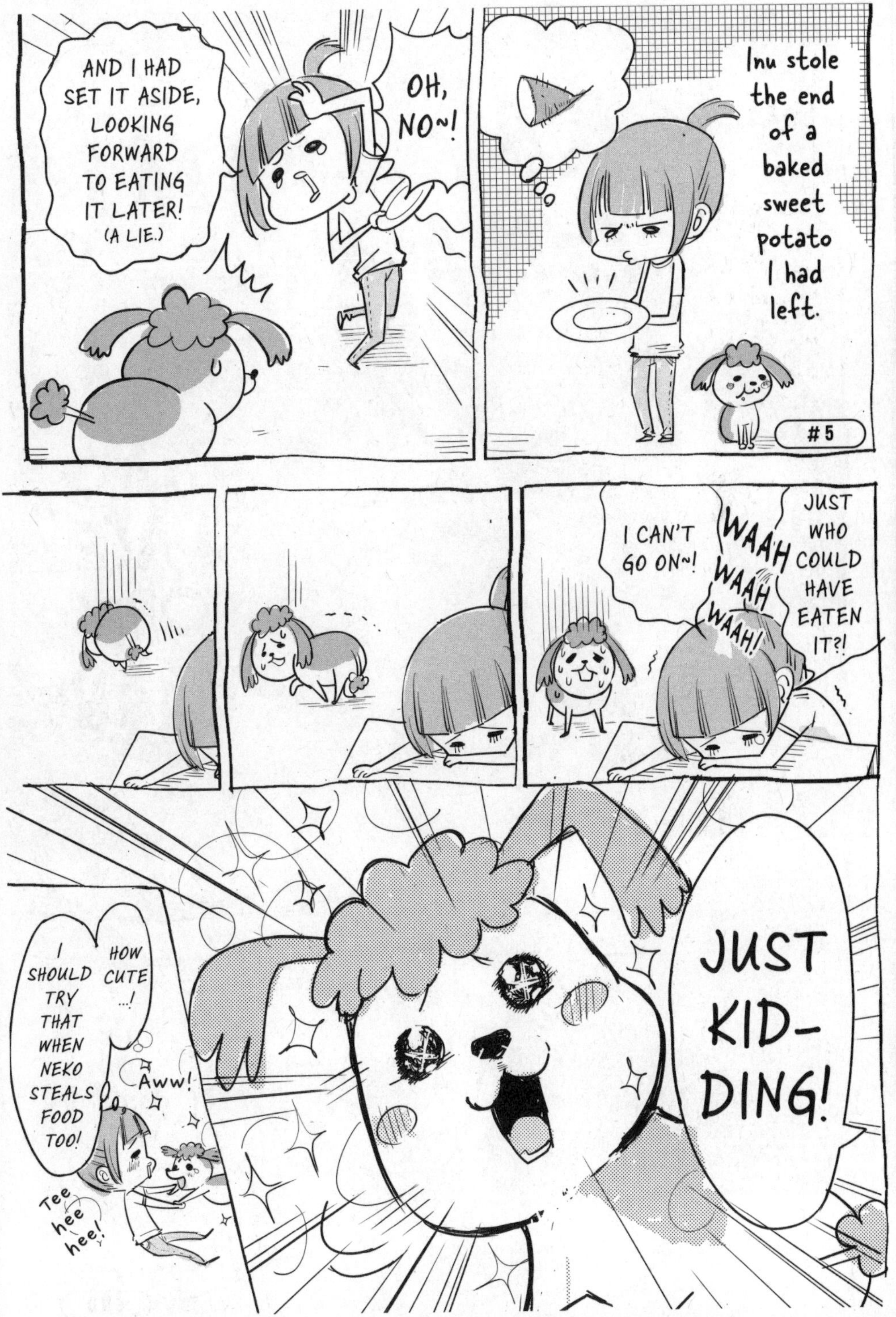
Inu stole the end of a baked sweet potato I had left.
#5
OH, NO~!
AND I HAD SET IT ASIDE, LOOKING FORWARD TO EATING IT LATER! (A LIE.)
JUST WHO COULD HAVE EATEN IT?!
WAAH WAAH WAAH!
I CAN'T GO ON~!
JUST KID-DING!
HOW CUTE ...!
I SHOULD TRY THAT WHEN NEKO STEALS FOOD TOO!
Aww!
Tee hee hee!

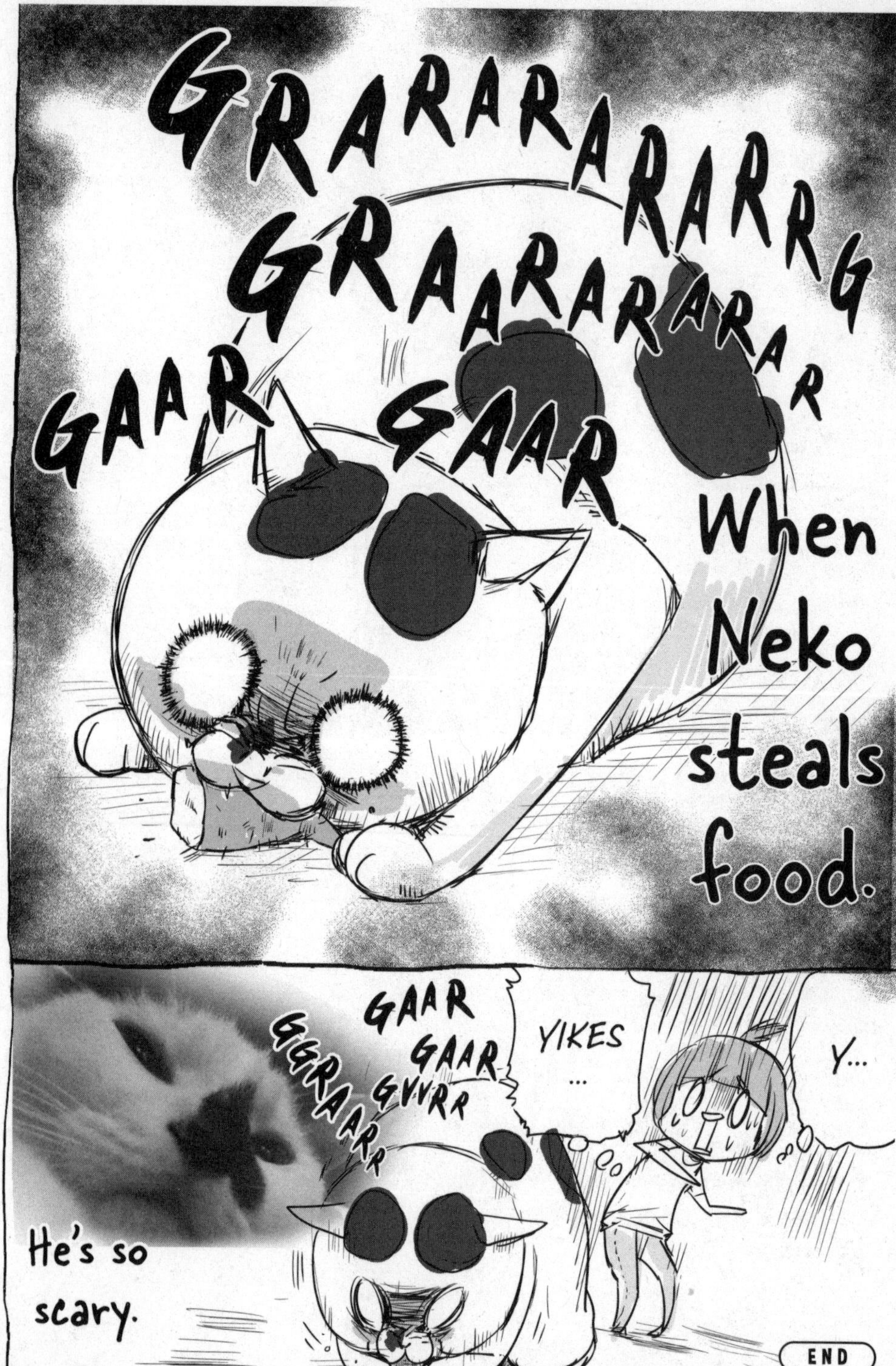
GRARARARARRG
GRAARARARAR
GAAR
GAAR
When Neko steals food.
Y...
YIKES ...
GAAR GAAR GVVRR
GGRAAARRR
He's so scary.
END

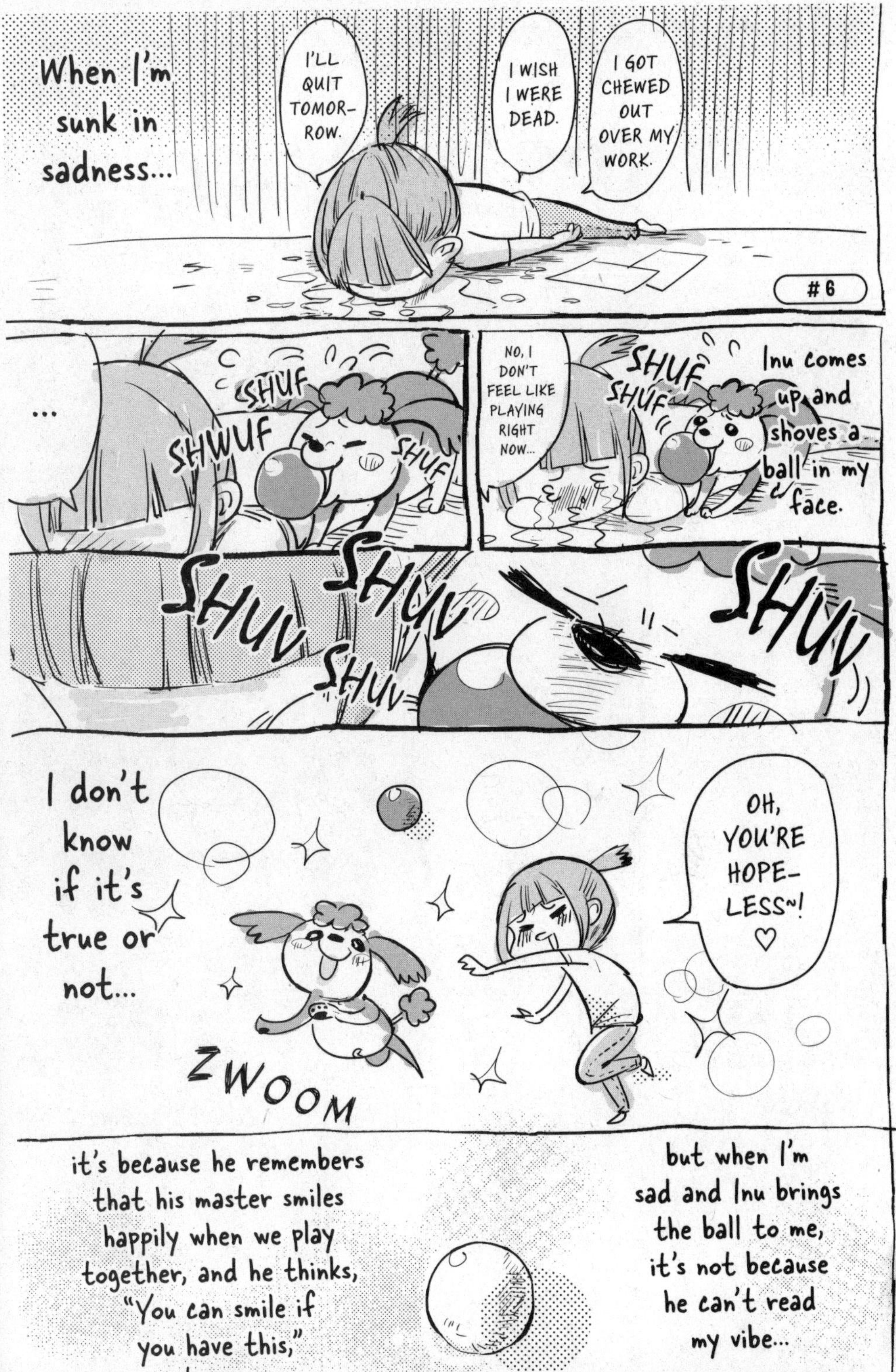
I GOT CHEWED OUT OVER MY WORK.
I WISH I WERE DEAD.
I'LL QUIT TOMOR-ROW.
When I'm sunk in sadness...
#6
Inu comes up and shoves a ball in my face.
SHUF
SHUF
NO, I DON'T FEEL LIKE PLAYING RIGHT NOW...
SHUF
SHUF
SHWUF
...
SHUV
SHUV
SHUV
SHUV
OH, YOU'RE HOPE-LESS~! ♡
I don't know if it's true or not...
ZWOOM
but when I'm sad and Inu brings the ball to me, it's not because he can't read my vibe...
it's because he remembers that his master smiles happily when we play together, and he thinks, "You can smile if you have this," I guess...

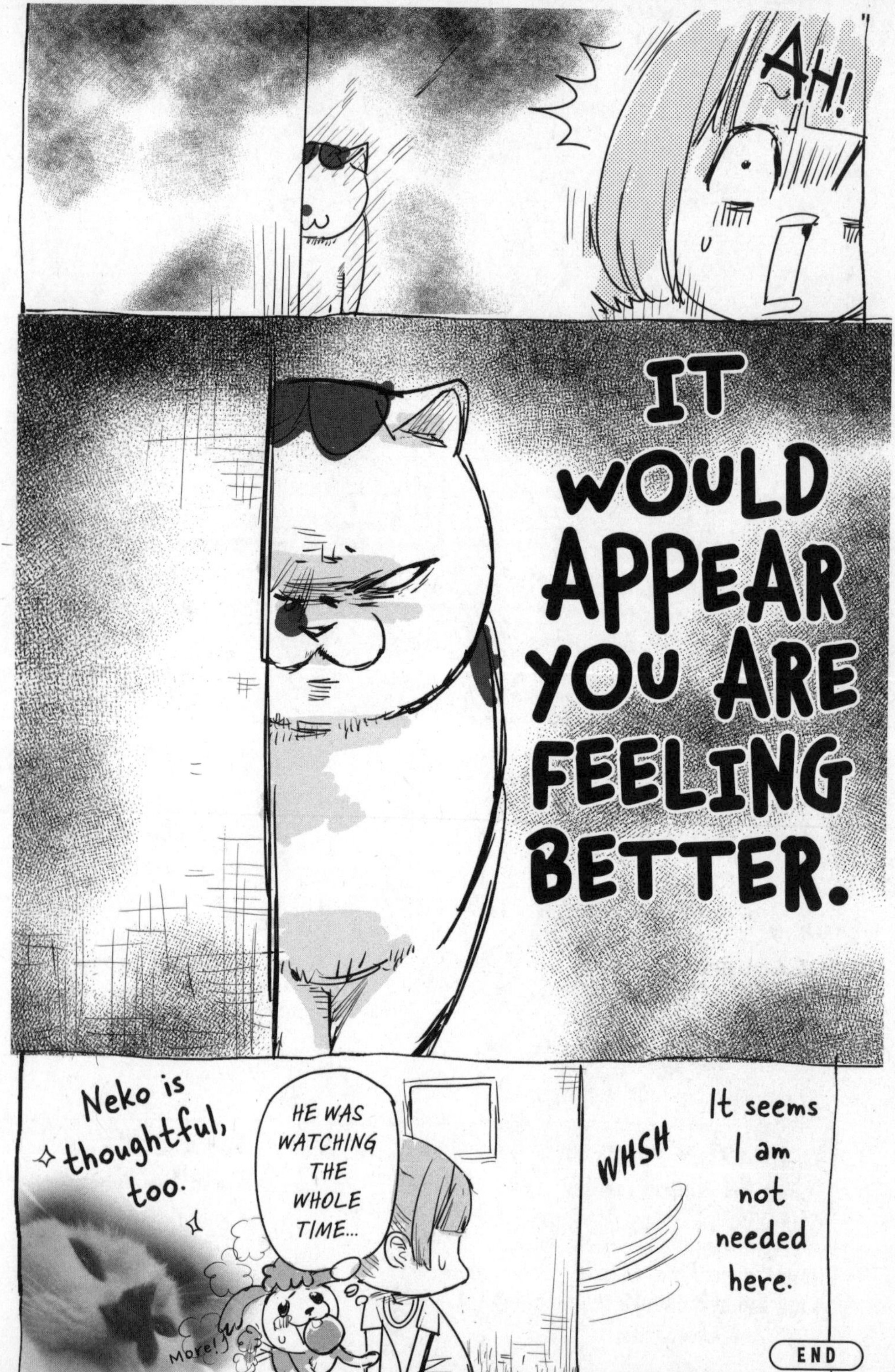
AH!
IT WOULD APPEAR YOU ARE FEELING BETTER.
It seems I am not needed here.
WHSH
HE WAS WATCHING THE WHOLE TIME...
Neko is thoughtful, too.
More!
END

When I'm working, he sometimes climbs up
on my lap and checks my manuscript.

Newly-Drawn 4-Panel Strip

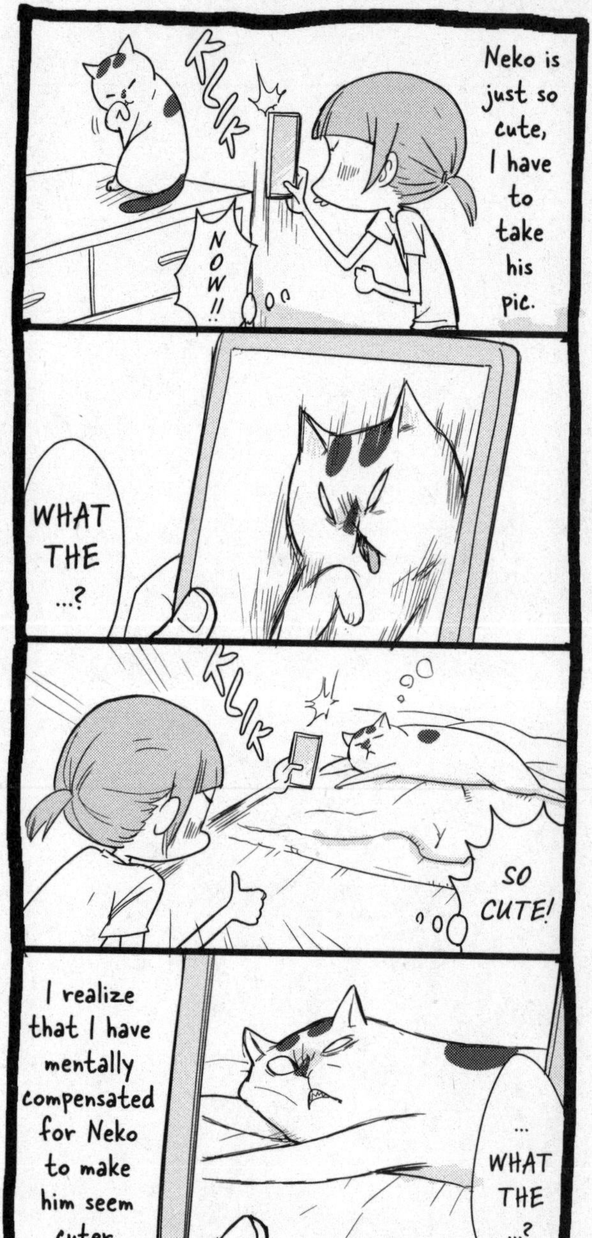

Hello and Nice to Meet You.

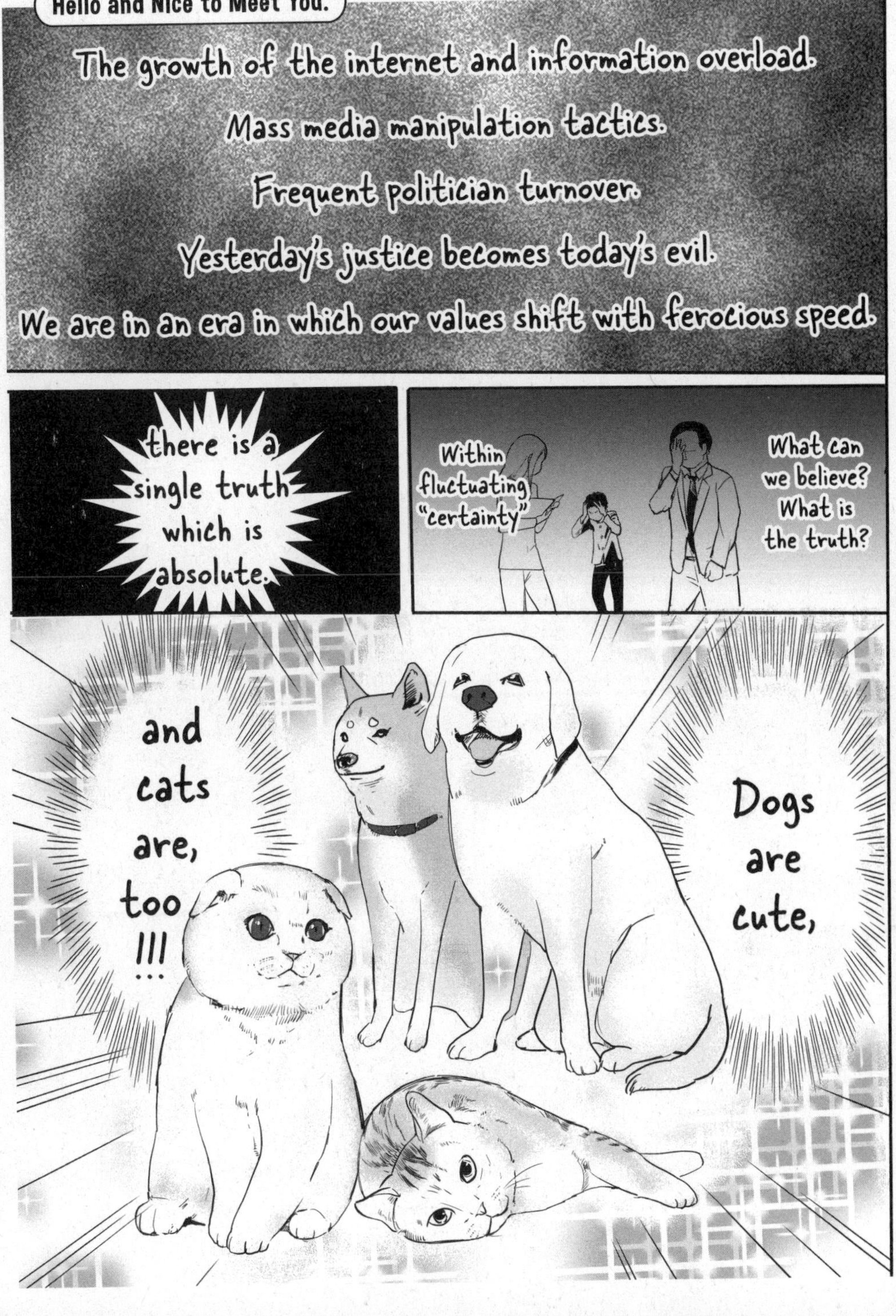
The growth of the internet and information overload.
Mass media manipulation tactics.
Frequent politician turnover.
Yesterday's justice becomes today's evil.
We are in an era in which our values shift with ferocious speed.
What can we believe? What is the truth?
Within fluctuating "certainty"
there is a single truth which is absolute.
Dogs are cute,
and cats are, too!!!...

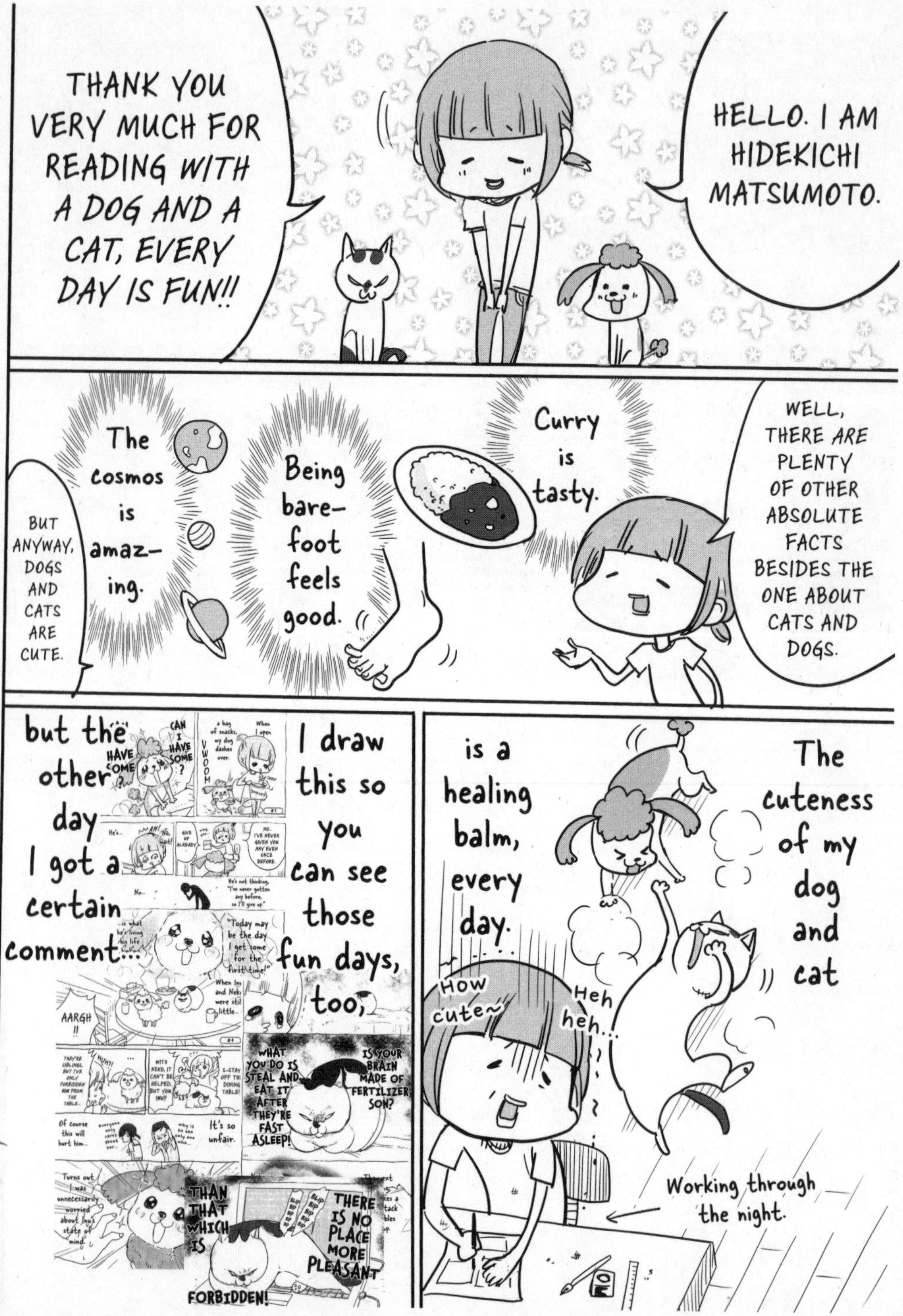
HELLO. I AM HIDEKICHI MATSUMOTO.
THANK YOU VERY MUCH FOR READING WITH A DOG AND A CAT, EVERY DAY IS FUN!!
WELL, THERE ARE PLENTY OF OTHER ABSOLUTE FACTS BESIDES THE ONE ABOUT CATS AND DOGS.
Curry is tasty.
Being barefoot feels good.
The cosmos is amazing.
BUT ANYWAY, DOGS AND CATS ARE CUTE.
The cuteness of my dog and cat
is a healing balm, every day.
Heh heh...
How cute~
Working through the night.
I draw this so you can see those fun days, too,
but the other day I got a certain comment...
IS YOUR BRAIN MADE OF FERTILIZER, SON?
WHAT YOU DO IS STEAL AND EAT IT AFTER THEY'RE FAST ASLEEP!
THERE IS NO PLACE MORE PLEASANT
THAN THAT WHICH IS FORBIDDEN!

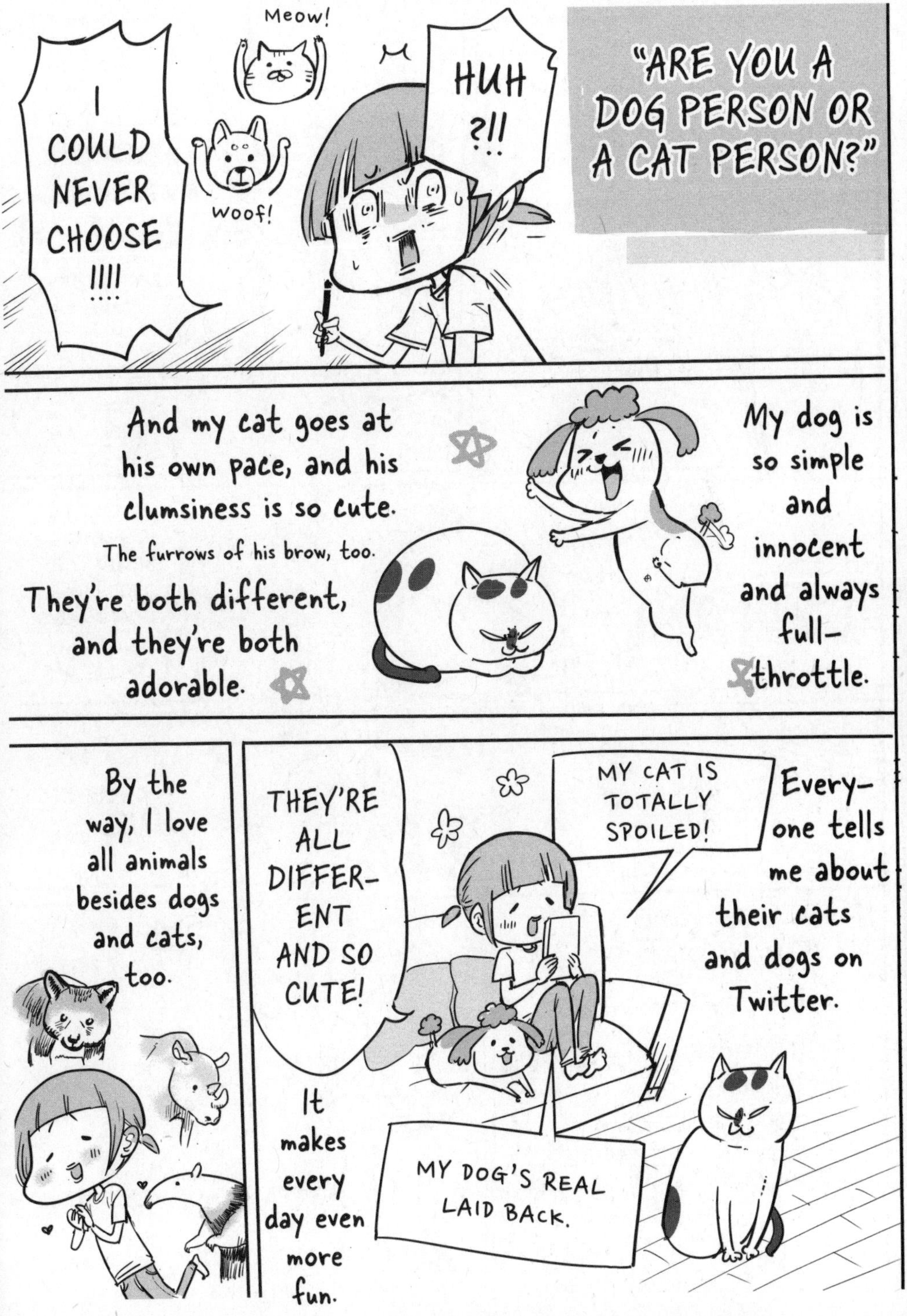
"ARE YOU A DOG PERSON OR A CAT PERSON?"
HUH ?!!...
Meow!
woof!
I COULD NEVER CHOOSE !!!!....
My dog is so simple and innocent and always full-throttle.
And my cat goes at his own pace, and his clumsiness is so cute.
The furrows of his brow, too.
They're both different, and they're both adorable.
Every-one tells me about their cats and dogs on Twitter.
MY CAT IS TOTALLY SPOILED!
MY DOG'S REAL LAID BACK.
THEY'RE ALL DIFFER-ENT AND SO CUTE!
It makes every day even more fun.
By the way, I love all animals besides dogs and cats, too.

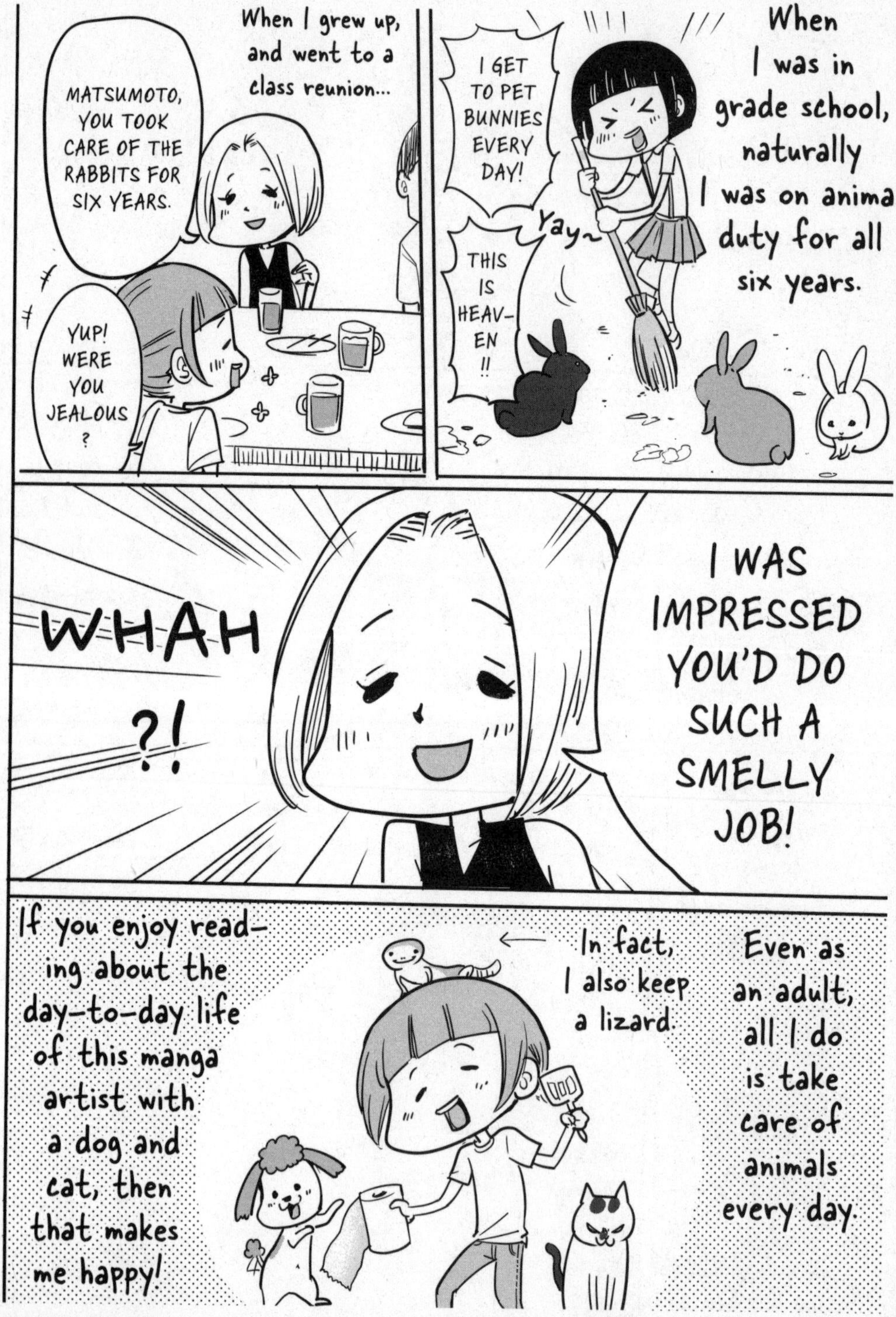
When I was in grade school, naturally I was on animal duty for all six years.
I GET TO PET BUNNIES EVERY DAY!
Yay~
THIS IS HEAV-EN!!
When I grew up, and went to a class reunion...
MATSUMOTO, YOU TOOK CARE OF THE RABBITS FOR SIX YEARS.
YUP! WERE YOU JEALOUS?
I WAS IMPRESSED YOU'D DO SUCH A SMELLY JOB!
WHAH
?!
Even as an adult, all I do is take care of animals every day.
In fact, I also keep a lizard.
If you enjoy read-ing about the day-to-day life of this manga artist with a dog and cat, then that makes me happy!

Inu-kun has big paw pads.

Newly-Drawn 4-Panel Strip

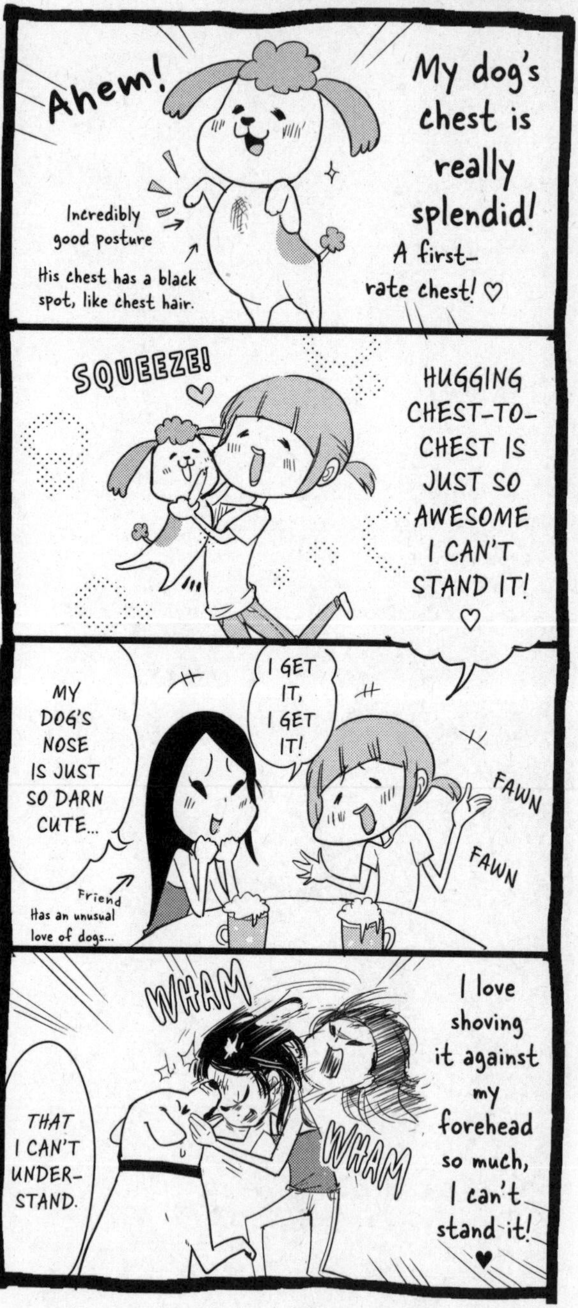
My dog's chest is really splendid!
Ahem!
A first-rate chest! ♡
Incredibly good posture
His chest has a black spot, like chest hair.
HUGGING CHEST-TO-CHEST IS JUST SO AWESOME I CAN'T STAND IT! ♡
SQUEEZE! ♡
FAWN
FAWN
I GET IT, I GET IT!
MY DOG'S NOSE IS JUST SO DARN CUTE...
Friend
Has an unusual love of dogs...
I love shoving it against my forehead so much, I can't stand it! ♥
WHAM
WHAM
THAT I CAN'T UNDER-STAND.

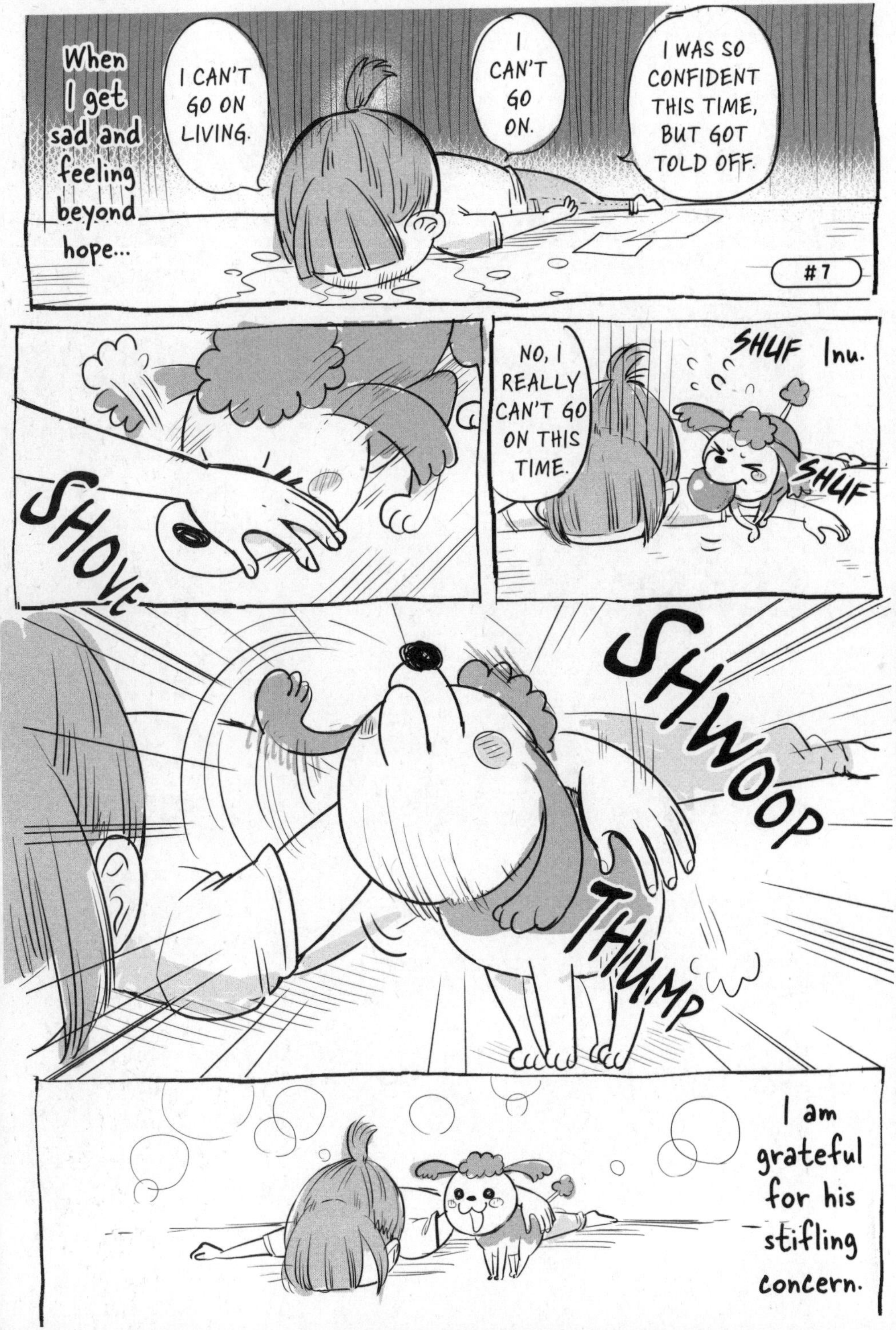
I WAS SO CONFIDENT THIS TIME, BUT GOT TOLD OFF.
I CAN'T GO ON.
I CAN'T GO ON LIVING.
When I get sad and feeling beyond hope...
#7
SHUF
Inu.
NO, I REALLY CAN'T GO ON THIS TIME.
SHUF
SHOVE
SHWOOP
THUMP
I am grateful for his stifling concern.

GAH !!
ZWOMP
Neko:
DIDN'T NOTICE IN THE LEAST.
OH, DEAR ME. I DIDN'T EVEN REALIZE YOU WERE THERE.
Also, he's heavy.
I'LL DO MY BEST AT WORK.
So be it. You can pet me if you want.
I am grateful for his tactless concern.
END

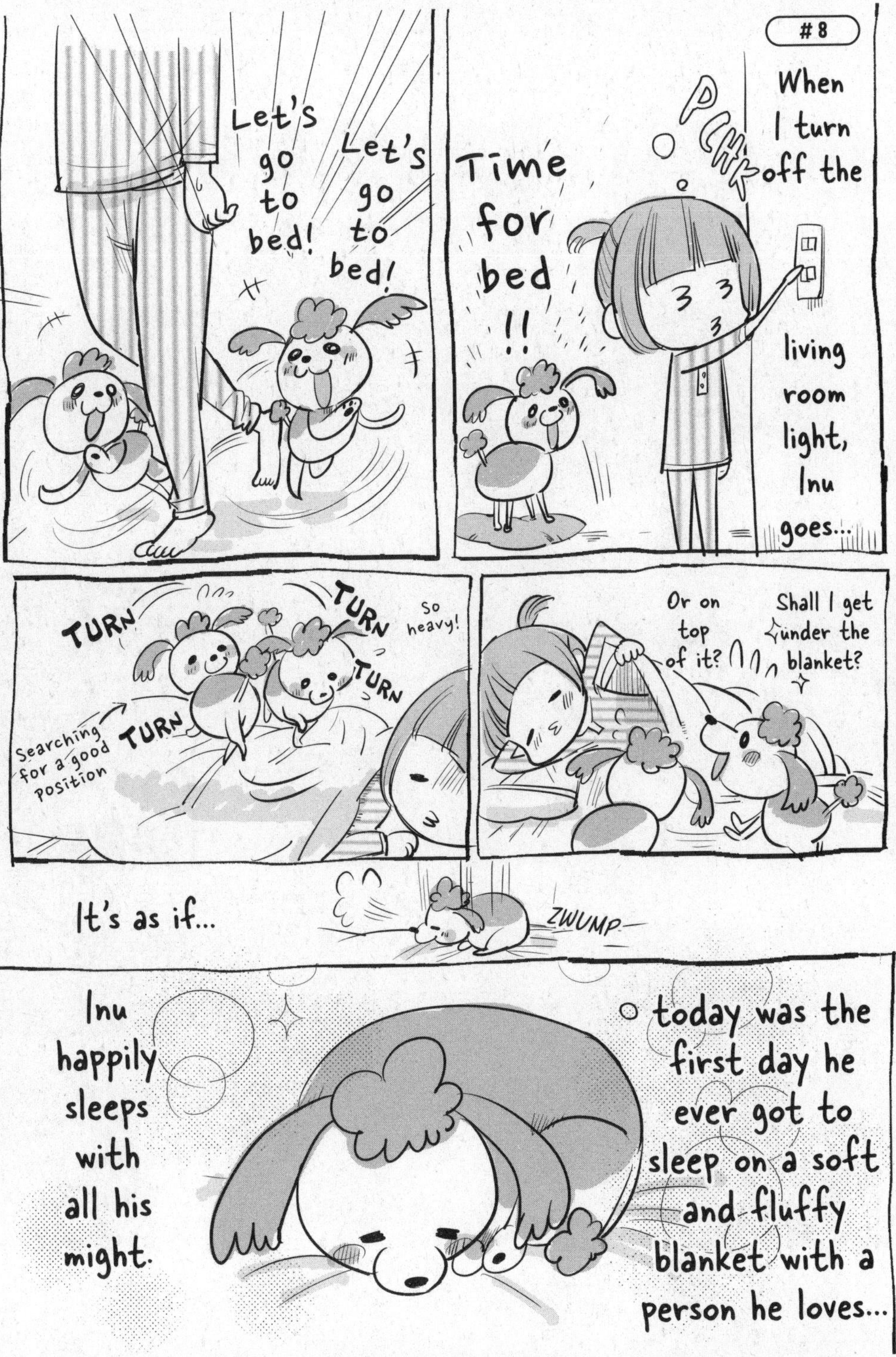
#8
When I turn off the living room light, Inu goes...
PCHK
Time for bed!!
Let's go to bed!
Let's go to bed!
Shall I get under the blanket?
Or on top of it?
So heavy!
TURN
TURN
TURN
TURN
Searching for a good position
ZWUMP
It's as if...
today was the first day he ever got to sleep on a soft and fluffy blanket with a person he loves...
Inu happily sleeps with all his might.

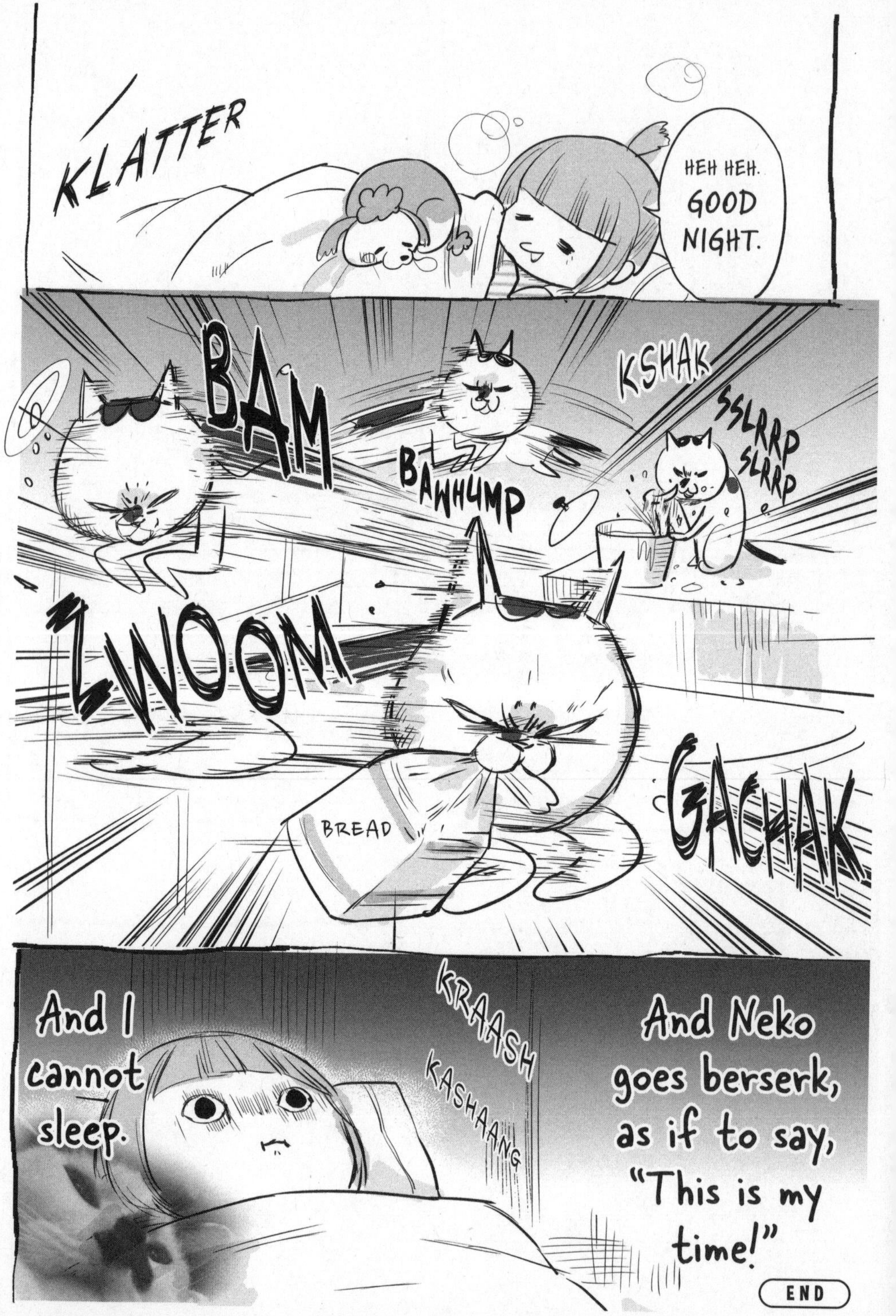
HEH HEH. GOOD NIGHT.
KLATTER
KSHAK
SSLRRP SLRRP
BAM
BAWHUMP
GACHAK
ZWOOM
BREAD
And Neko goes berserk, as if to say, "This is my time!"
KRAASH
KASHAANG
And I cannot sleep.
END

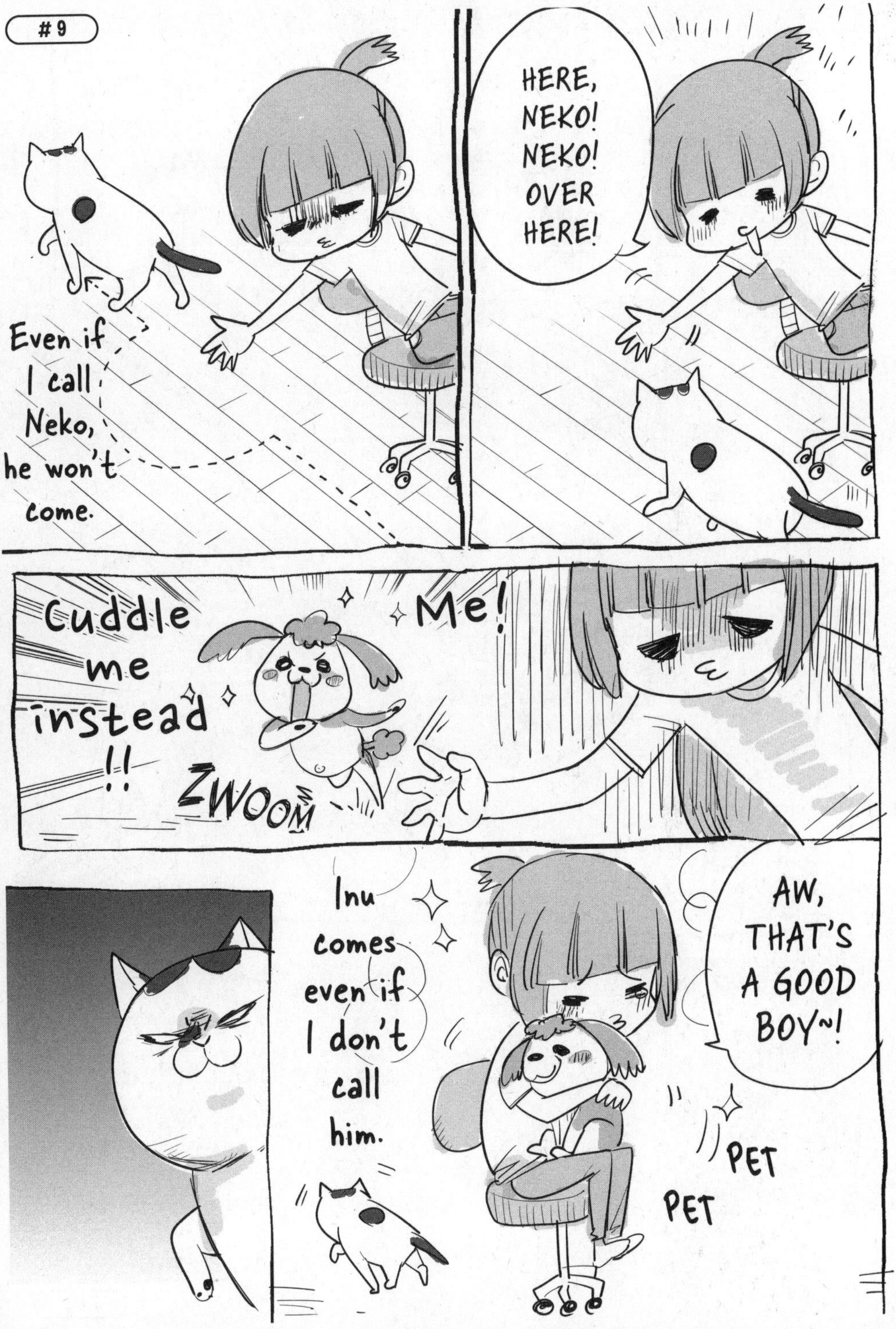
#9
HERE, NEKO! NEKO! OVER HERE!
Even if I call Neko, he won't come.
Me!
Cuddle me instead!!
ZWOOM
AW, THAT'S A GOOD BOY~!
PET
PET
Inu comes even if I don't call him.

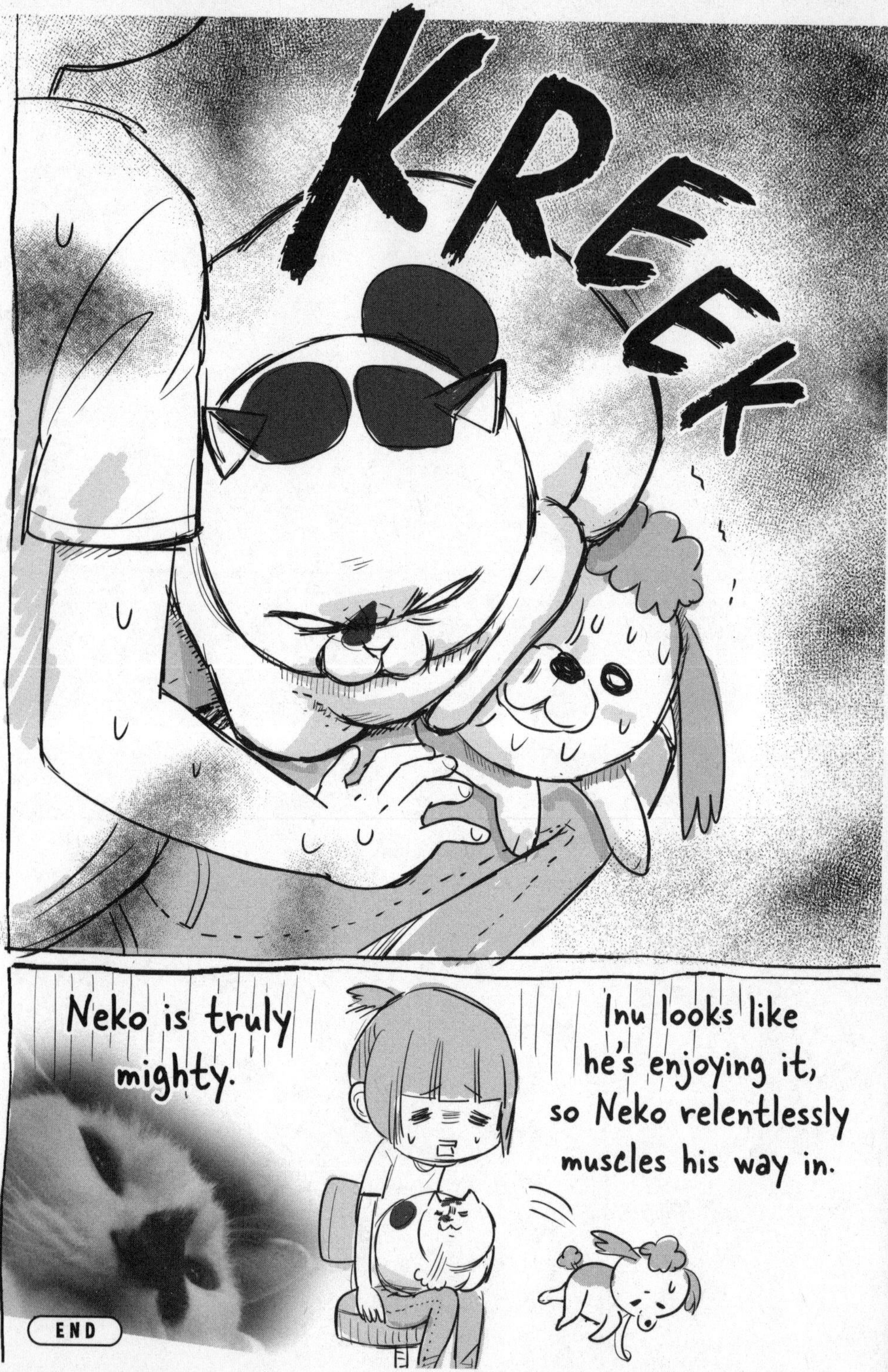
KREEK
Inu looks like he's enjoying it, so Neko relentlessly muscles his way in.
Neko is truly mighty.
END

A rare occasion of being surprised by something.

Newly-Drawn 4-Panel Strip

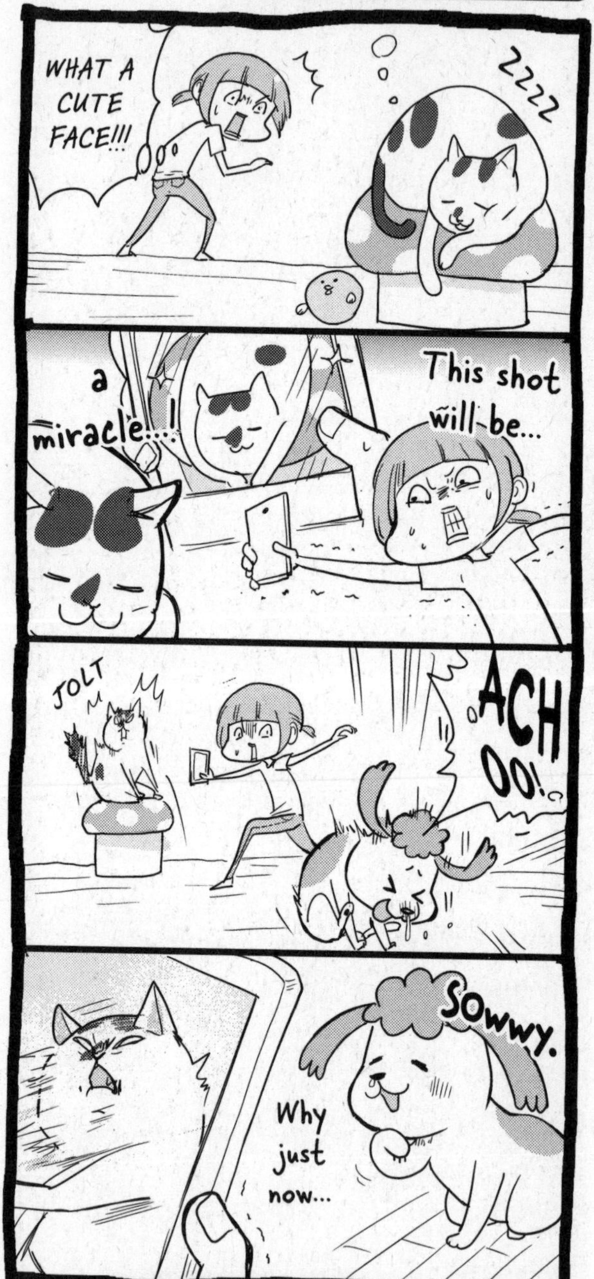
WHAT A CUTE FACE!!!
ZZZZ
This shot will be...
a miracle...!
JOLT
ACH OO!
Sowwy.
Why just now...

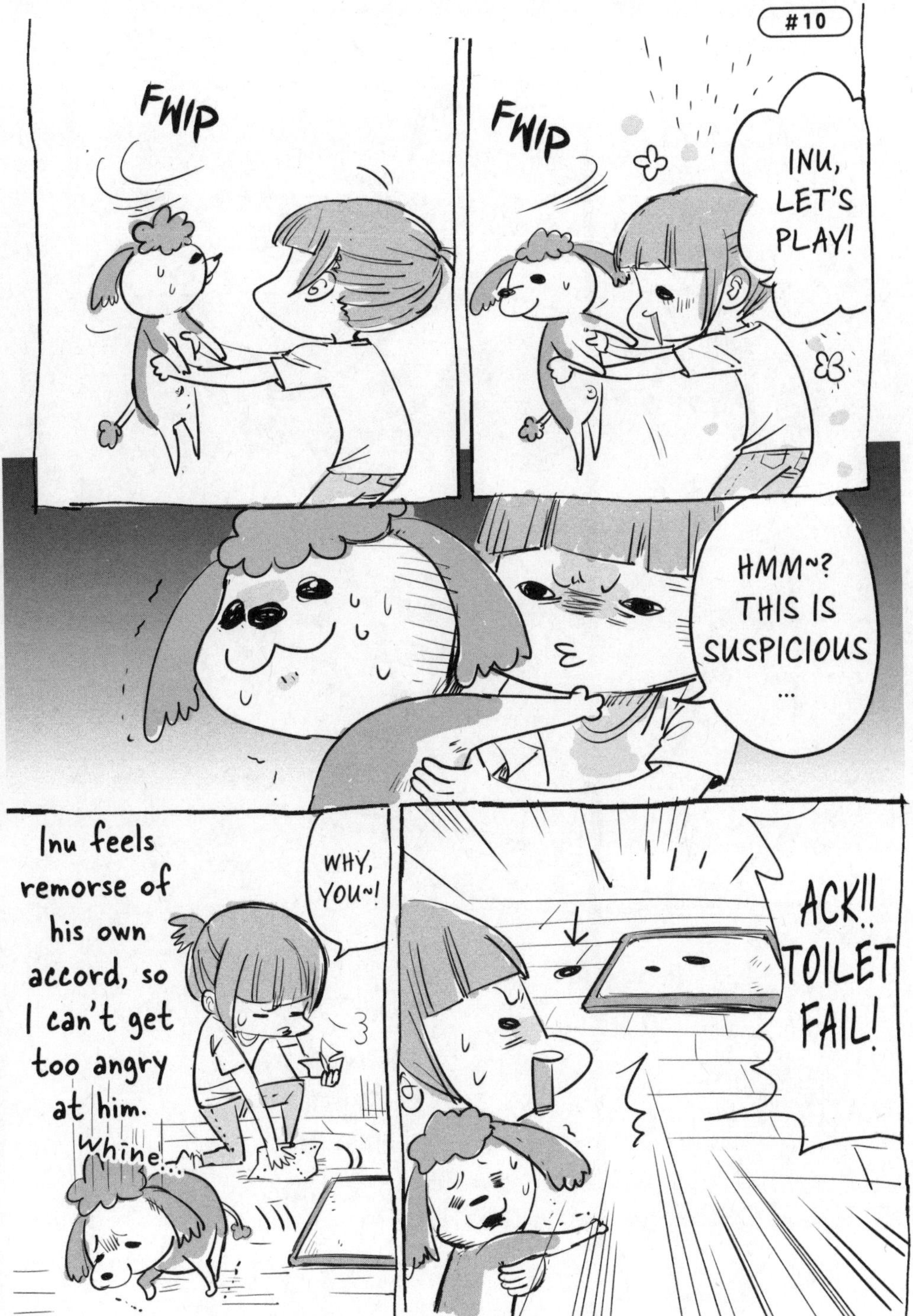
#10
FWIP
INU, LET'S PLAY!
FWIP
HMM~? THIS IS SUSPICIOUS ...
ACK!! TOILET FAIL!
WHY, YOU~!
Inu feels remorse of his own accord, so I can't get too angry at him.
Whine...

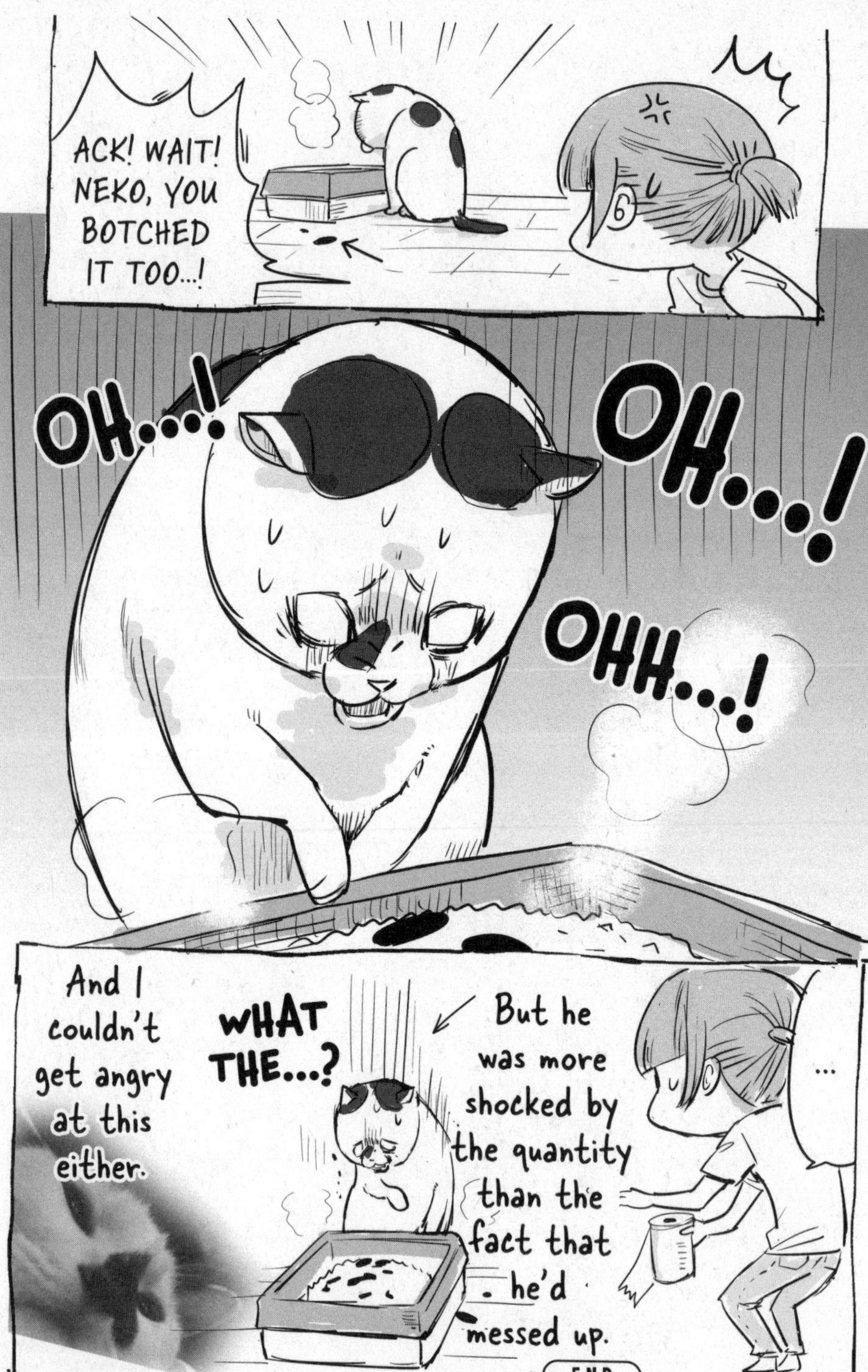
ACK! WAIT! NEKO, YOU BOTCHED IT TOO...!
OH...!
OH...!
OHH...!
...
But he was more shocked by the quantity than the fact that he'd messed up.
WHAT THE...?
And I couldn't get angry at this either.
END

#11

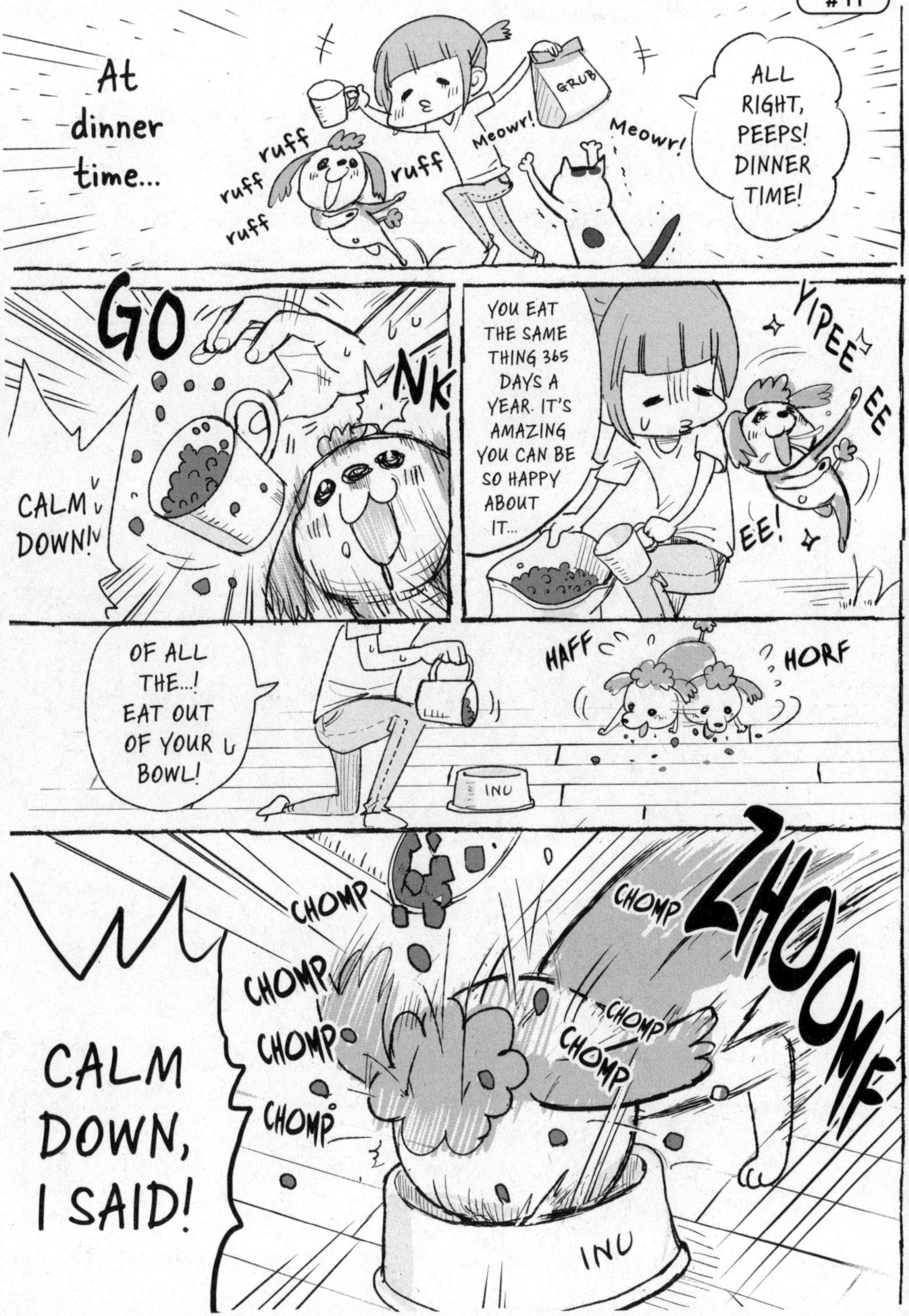

ALL RIGHT, PEEPS! DINNER TIME!
Meowr!
Meowr!
GRUB
ruff
ruff
ruff
ruff
At dinner time...
YIPEE EE EE!
YOU EAT THE SAME THING 365 DAYS A YEAR. IT'S AMAZING YOU CAN BE SO HAPPY ABOUT IT...
GONK
CALM DOWN!
HORF
HAFF
OF ALL THE...! EAT OUT OF YOUR BOWL!
INU
ZHOOMF
CHOMP
CHOMP
CHOMP
CHOMP
CHOMP
CHOMP
CHOMP
CALM DOWN, I SAID!
INU

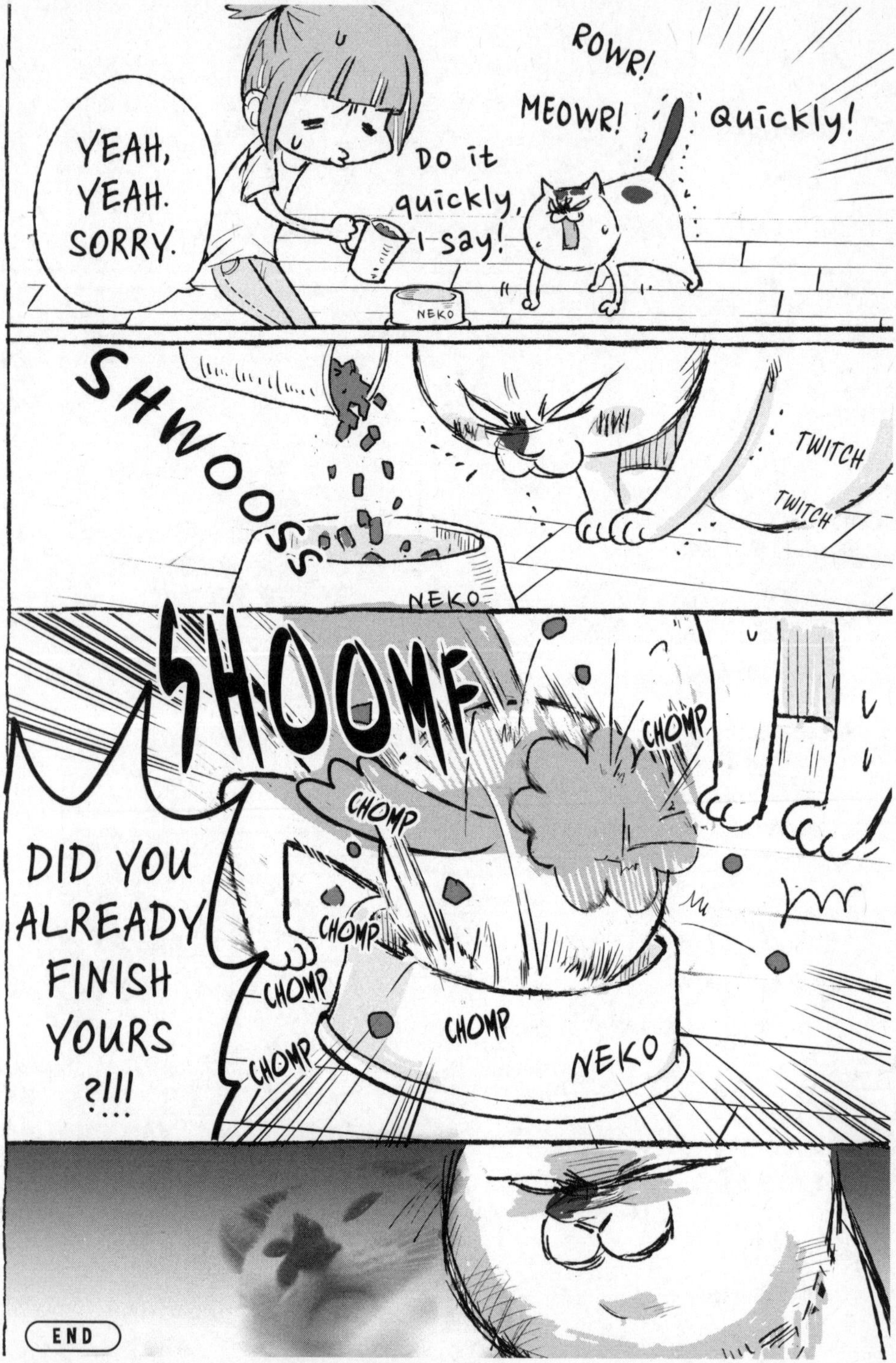

ROWR!
Quickly!
MEOWR!
Do it quickly, I say!
YEAH, YEAH. SORRY.
NEKO
TWITCH
TWITCH
SHWOOSS
NEKO
SHOOMF
CHOMP
CHOMP
CHOMP
CHOMP
CHOMP
CHOMP
DID YOU ALREADY FINISH YOURS?!!!...
NEKO
END

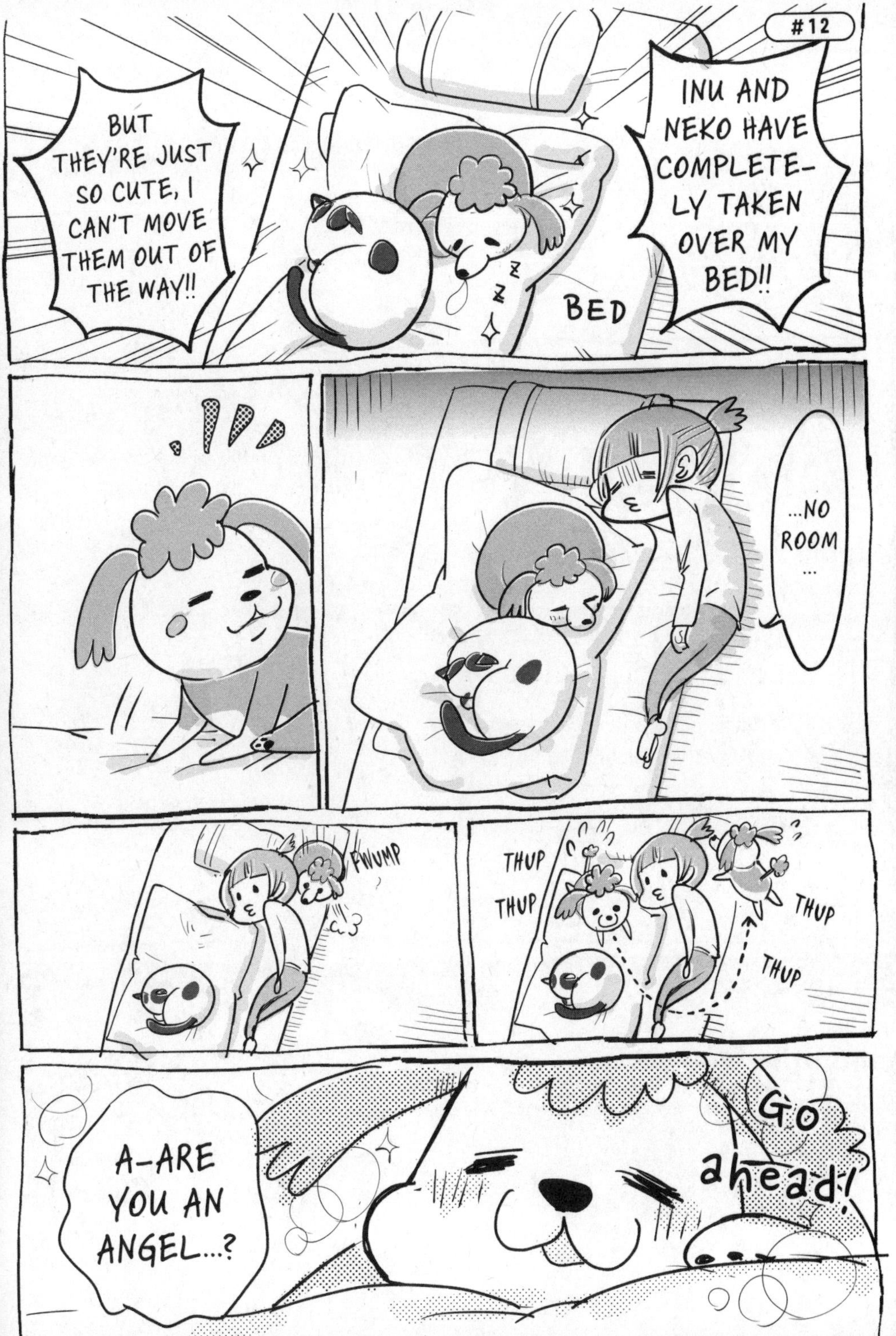
#12
INU AND NEKO HAVE COMPLETE-LY TAKEN OVER MY BED!!
BED
Z Z
BUT THEY'RE JUST SO CUTE, I CAN'T MOVE THEM OUT OF THE WAY!!
...NO ROOM ...
!!
THUP THUP
THUP THUP
FWUMP
Go ahead!
A-ARE YOU AN ANGEL...?

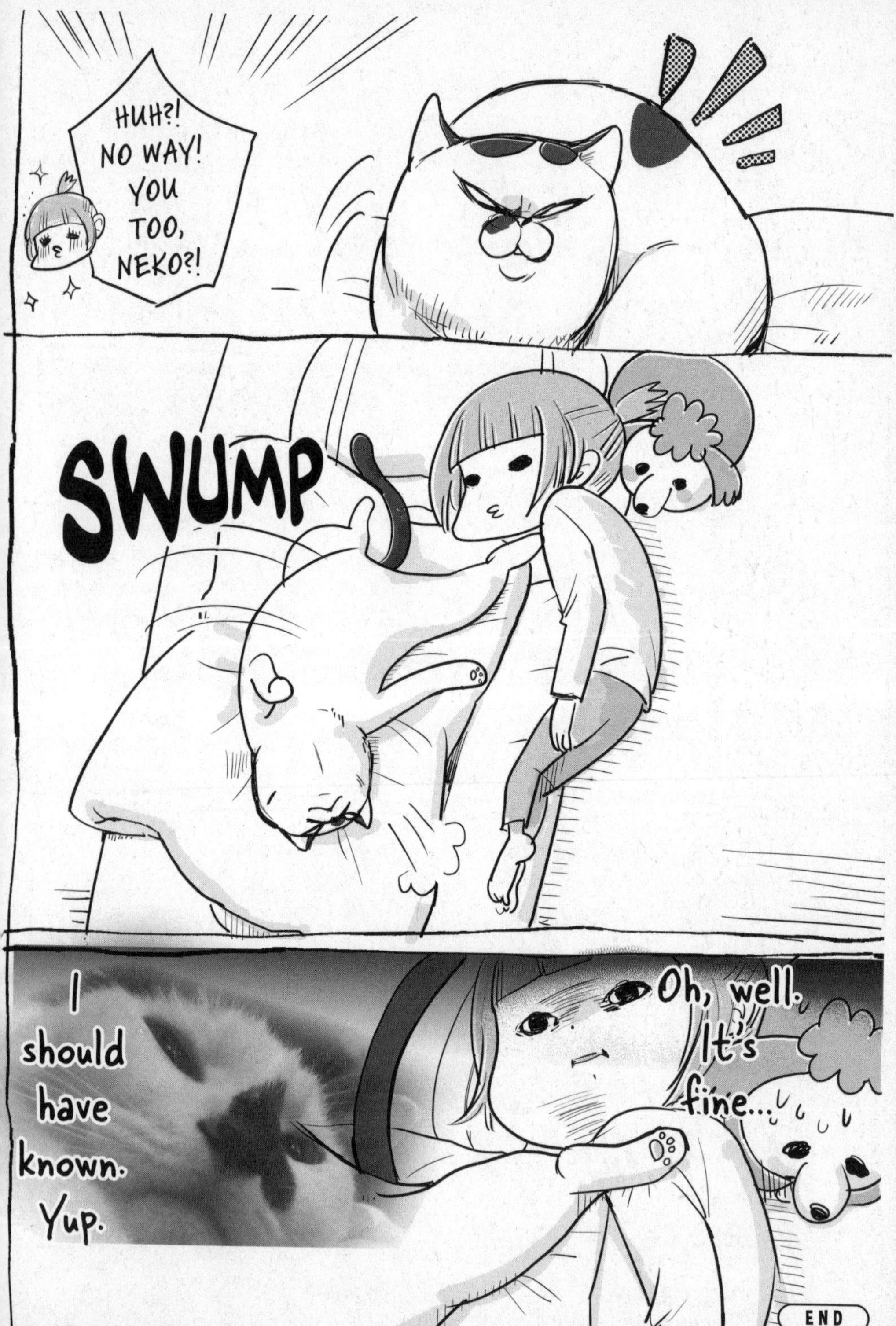

HUH?! NO WAY! YOU TOO, NEKO?!
SWUMP
Oh, well. It's fine...
I should have known. Yup.
END

He's looking my way, but he's just resting his chin.

Newly-Drawn 4-Panel Strip

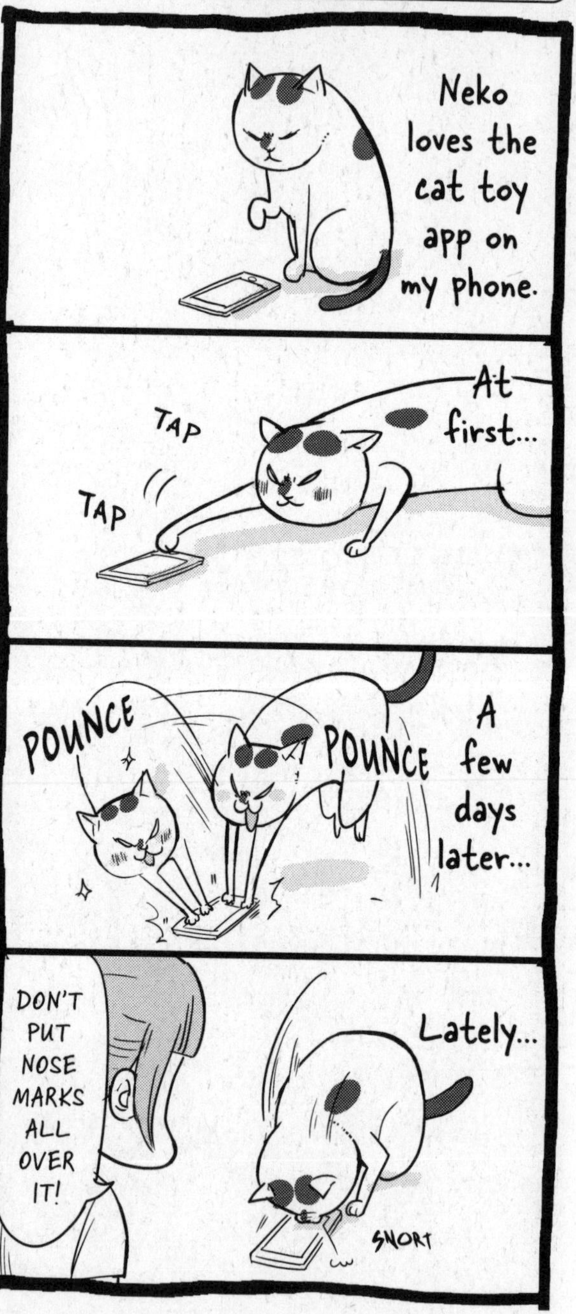

Neko loves the cat toy app on my phone.
At first...
TAP
TAP
A few days later...
POUNCE
POUNCE
Lately...
SNORT
DON'T PUT NOSE MARKS ALL OVER IT!

#13

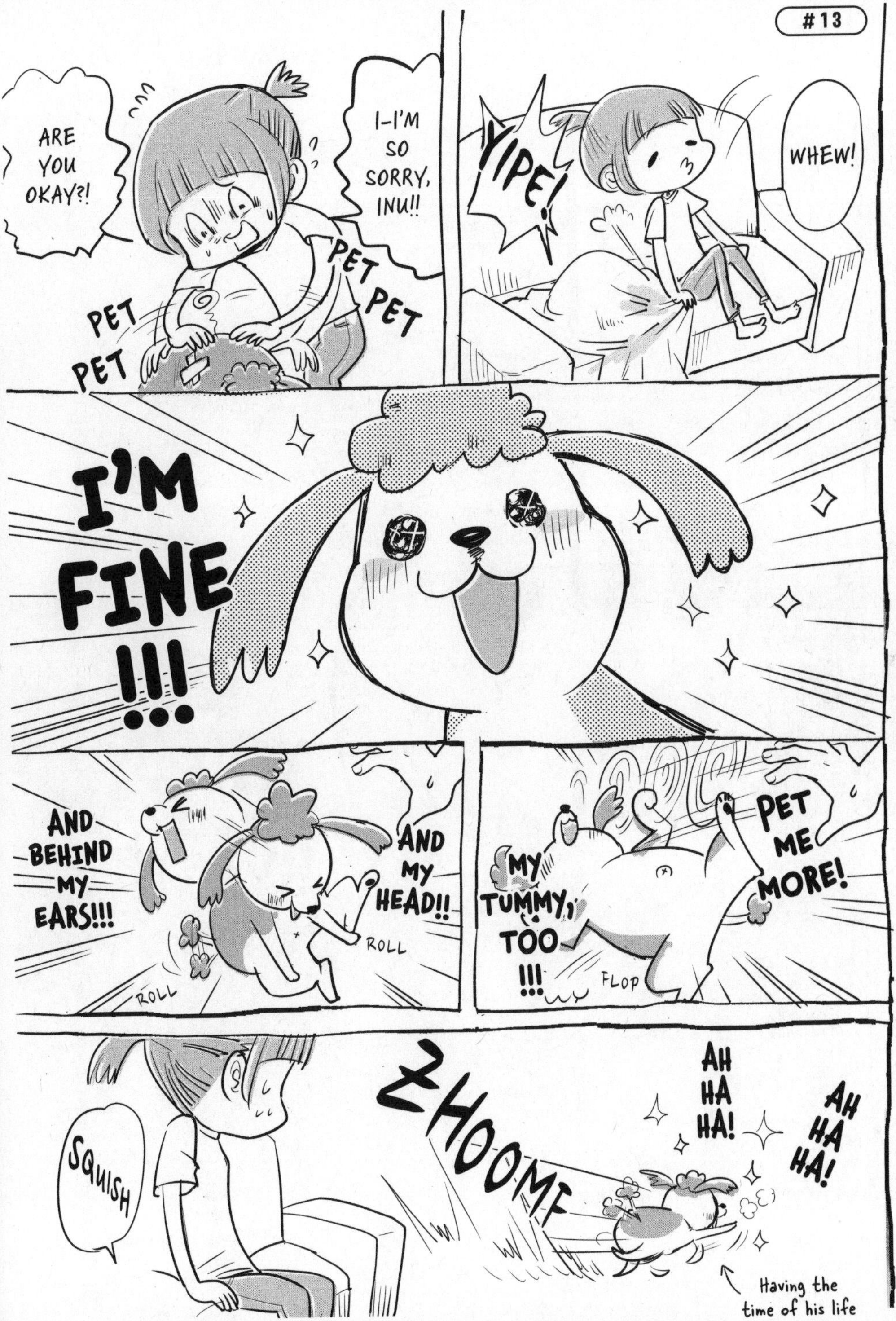
WHEW!
YIPE!
I-I'M SO SORRY, INU!!
ARE YOU OKAY?!
PET PET
PET PET
I'M FINE!!!
PET ME MORE!
MY TUMMY, TOO!!!
FLOP
AND MY HEAD!!
AND BEHIND MY EARS!!!!
ROLL
ROLL
AH HA HA!
AH HA HA!
ZHOOM
SQUISH
Having the time of his life

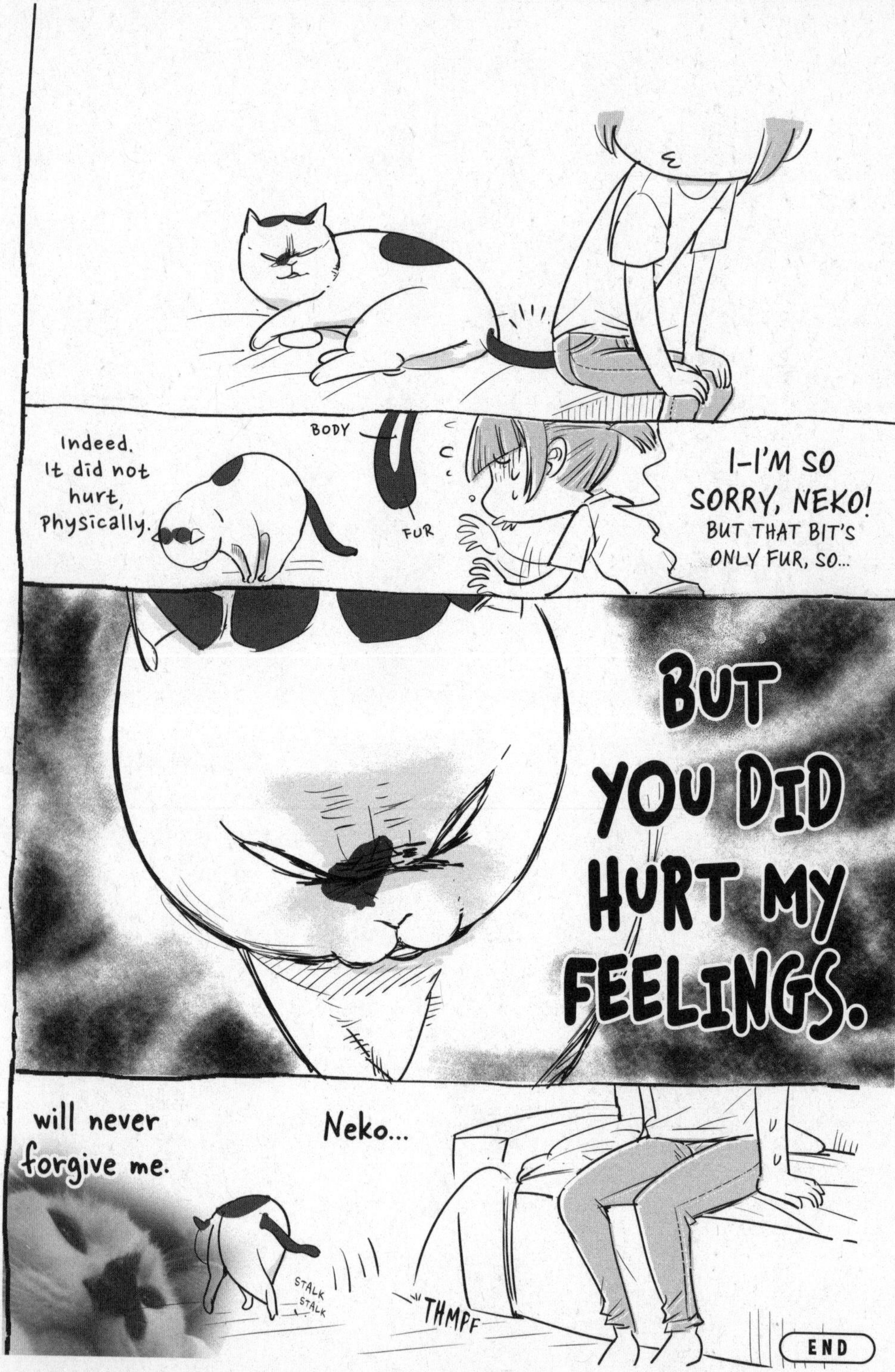
I-I'M SO SORRY, NEKO!
BUT THAT BIT'S ONLY FUR, SO...
BODY
FUR
Indeed. It did not hurt, physically.
BUT YOU DID HURT MY FEELINGS.
Neko...
THMPF
STALK STALK
will never forgive me.
END

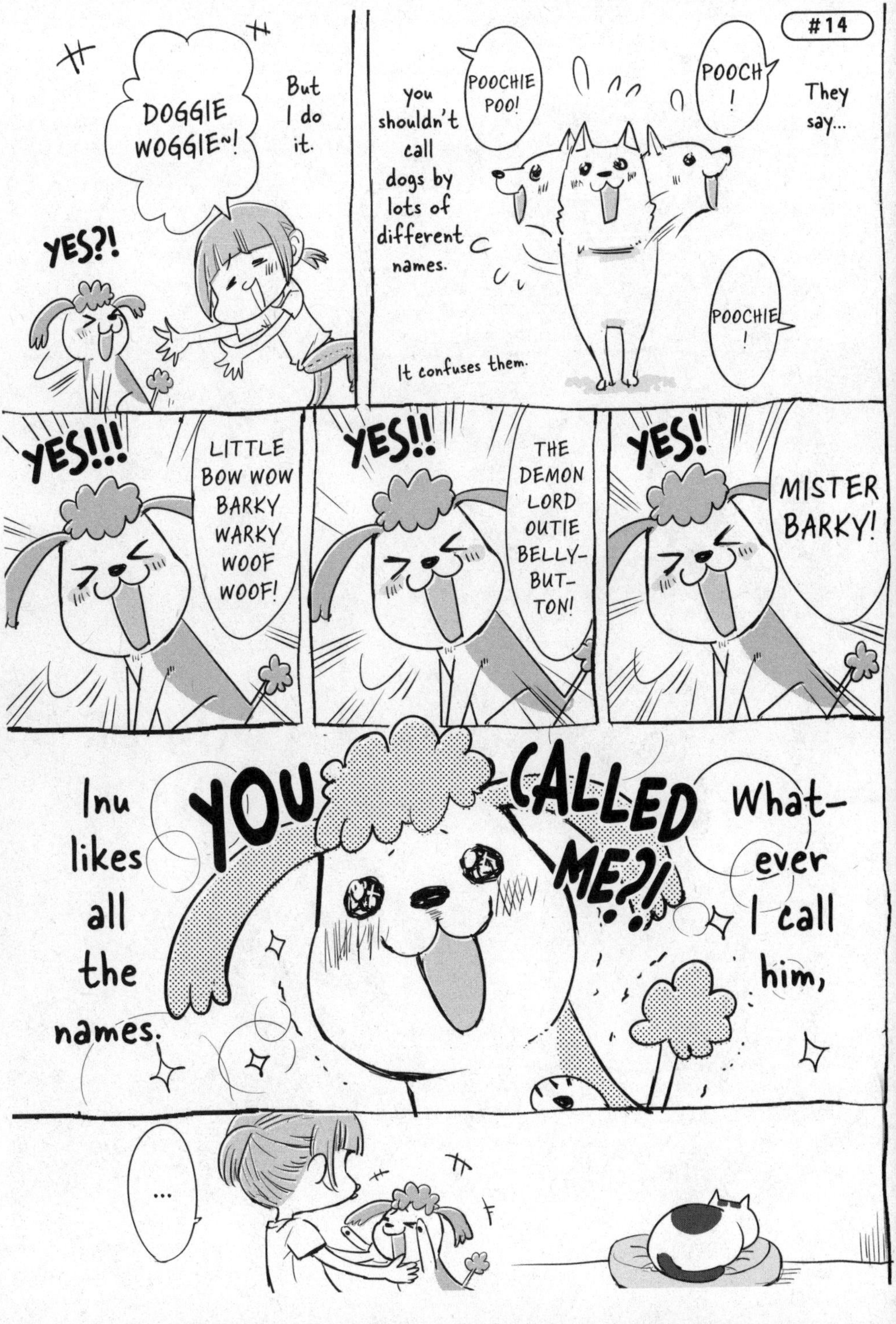
#14
They say...
POOCH!
POOCHIE POO!
you shouldn't call dogs by lots of different names.
POOCHIE!
It confuses them.
But I do it.
DOGGIE WOGGIE~!
YES?!
MISTER BARKY!
YES!
THE DEMON LORD OUTIE BELLY-BUTTON!
YES!!
LITTLE BOW WOW BARKY WARKY WOOF WOOF!
YES!!!
Whatever I call him,
YOU CALLED ME?!
Inu likes all the names.
...

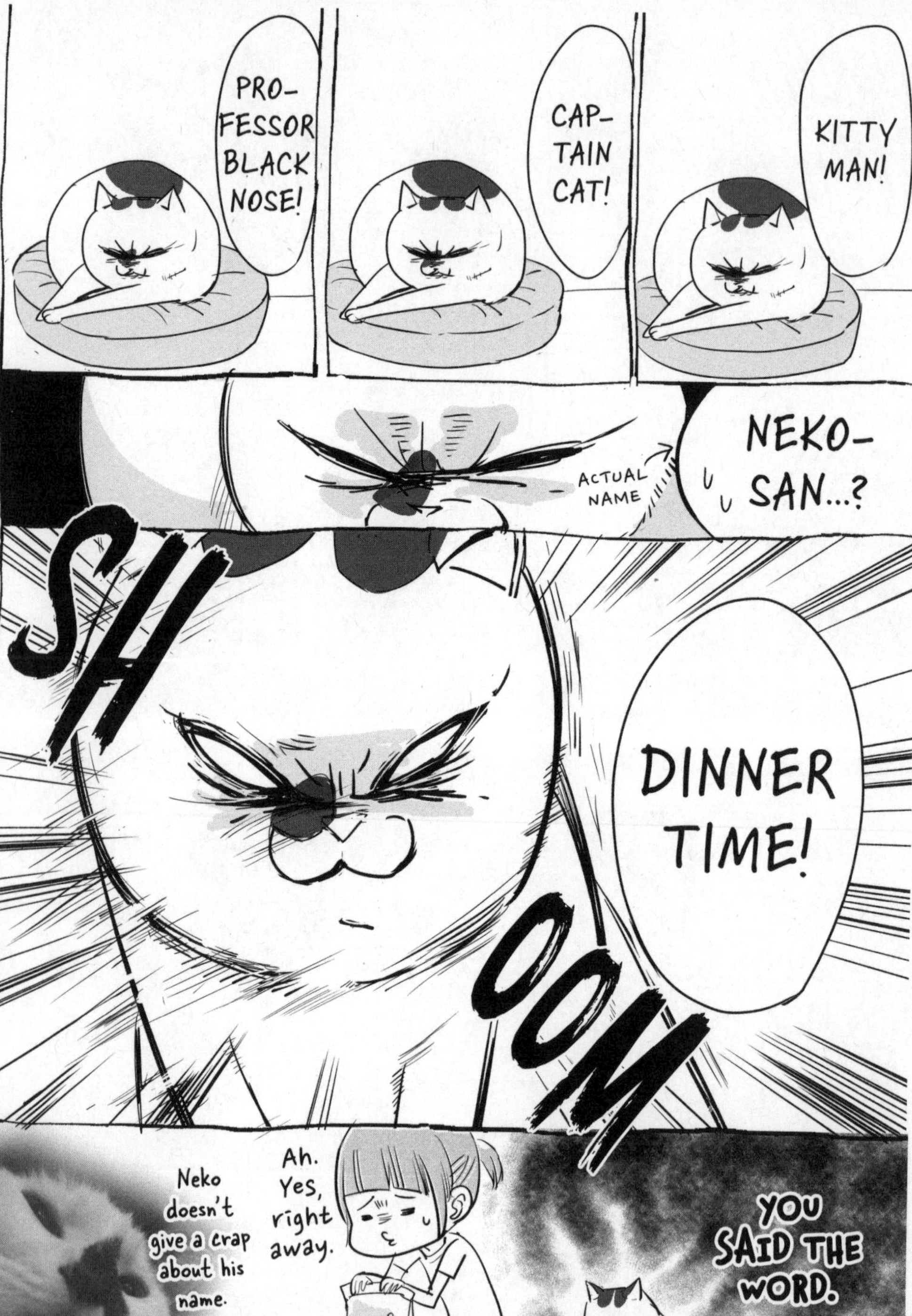
KITTY MAN!
CAP-TAIN CAT!
PRO-FESSOR BLACK NOSE!
NEKO-SAN...?
ACTUAL NAME
SHOOM
DINNER TIME!
YOU SAID THE WORD.
Ah. Yes, right away.
FEED
Neko doesn't give a crap about his name.
END

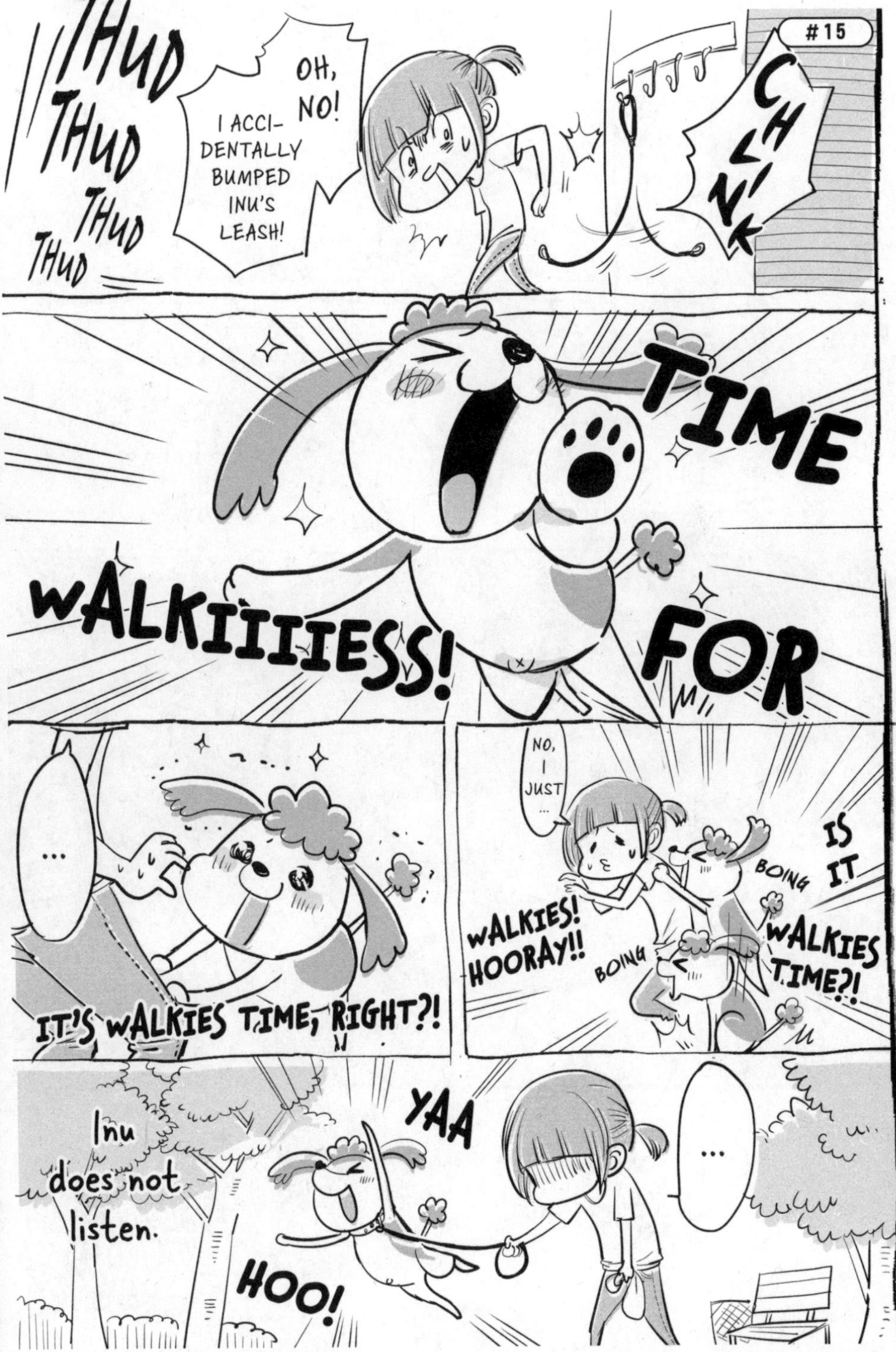

#15
CHINK
OH, NO!
I ACCIDENTALLY BUMPED INU'S LEASH!
THUD THUD THUD THUD
TIME FOR WALKIIIIESS!
NO, I JUST ...
IS IT WALKIES TIME?!
BOING
WALKIES! HOORAY!!
BOING
...
IT'S WALKIES TIME, RIGHT?!
...
YAA
HOO!
Inu does not listen.

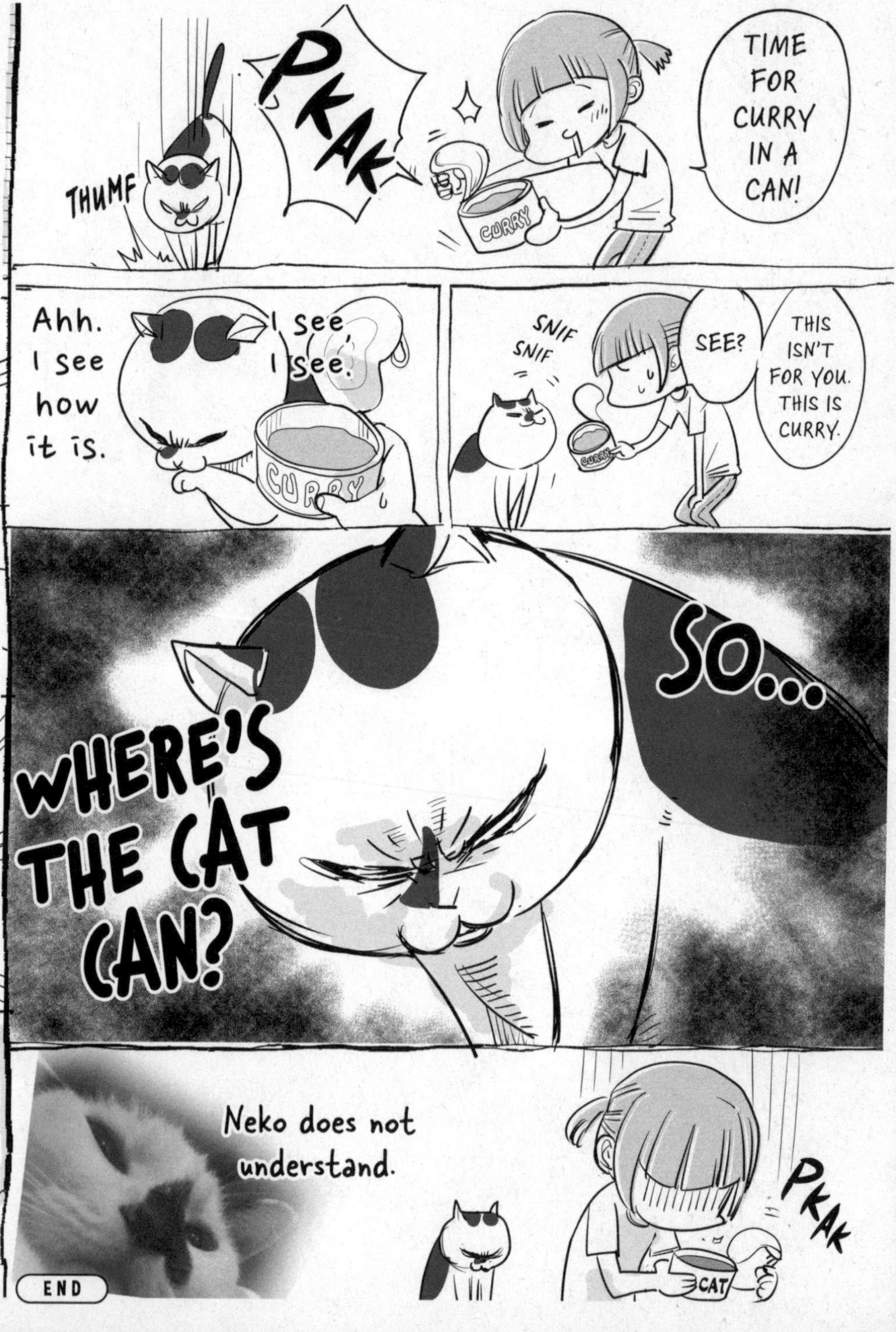
TIME FOR CURRY IN A CAN!
PKAK
CURRY
THUMF
THIS ISN'T FOR YOU. THIS IS CURRY.
SEE?
SNIF SNIF
CURRY
I see, I see.
Ahh. I see how it is.
CURRY
SO...
WHERE'S THE CAT CAN?
PKAK
CAT
Neko does not understand.
END

The moment Neko pulled off a Judo body
throw. Inu has no hope of victory.

Newly-Drawn 4-Panel Strip

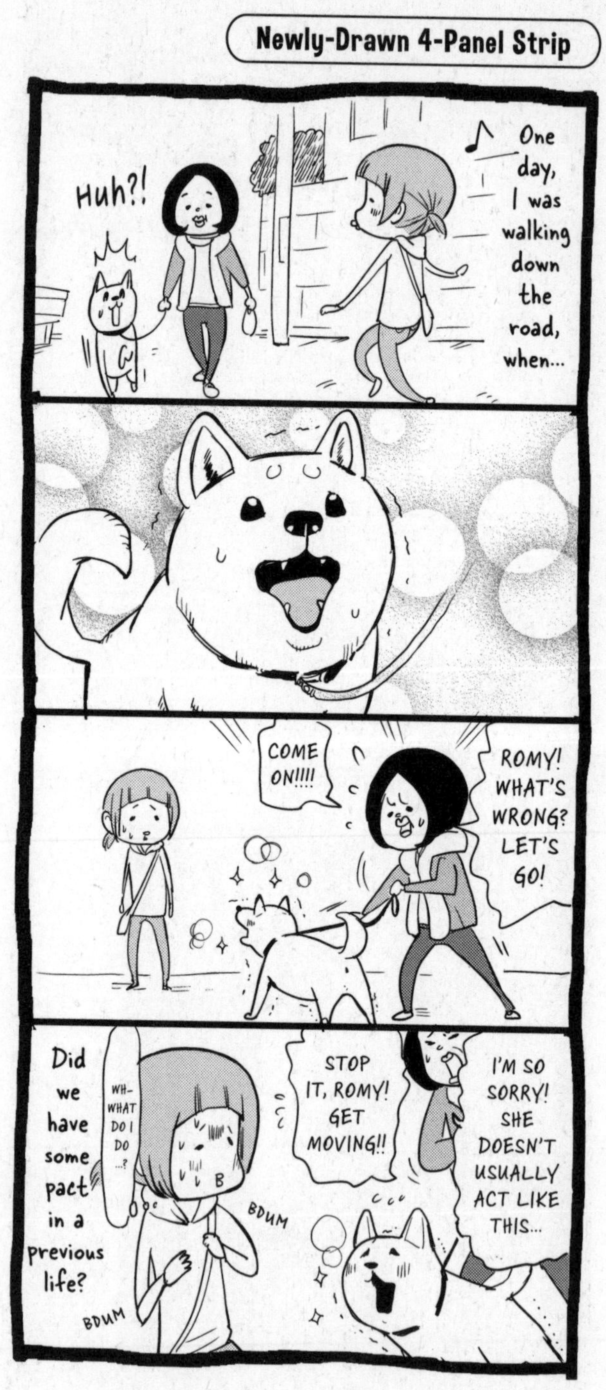
One day, I was walking down the road, when...
Huh?!
ROMY! WHAT'S WRONG? LET'S GO!
COME ON!!!!
I'M SO SORRY! SHE DOESN'T USUALLY ACT LIKE THIS...
STOP IT, ROMY! GET MOVING!!
BDUM
WH-WHAT DO I DO ...?
Did we have some pact in a previous life?
BDUM

#16

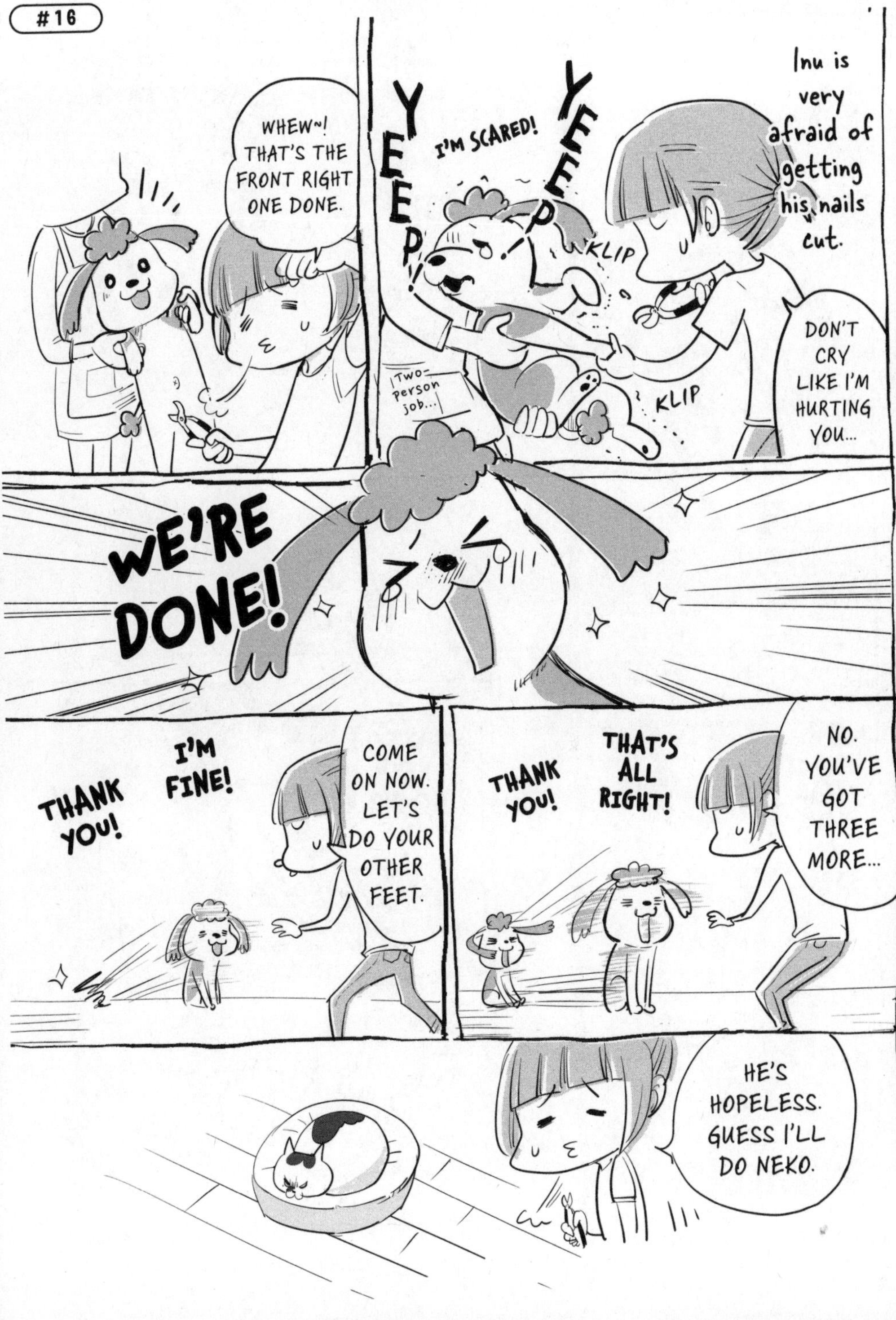
Inu is very afraid of getting his nails cut.
YEEP
YEEP!
I'M SCARED!
KLIP
DON'T CRY LIKE I'M HURTING YOU...
KLIP
Two-person job...
WHEW~! THAT'S THE FRONT RIGHT ONE DONE.
WE'RE DONE!
NO. YOU'VE GOT THREE MORE...
THAT'S ALL RIGHT!
THANK YOU!
COME ON NOW. LET'S DO YOUR OTHER FEET.
I'M FINE!
THANK YOU!
HE'S HOPELESS. GUESS I'LL DO NEKO.

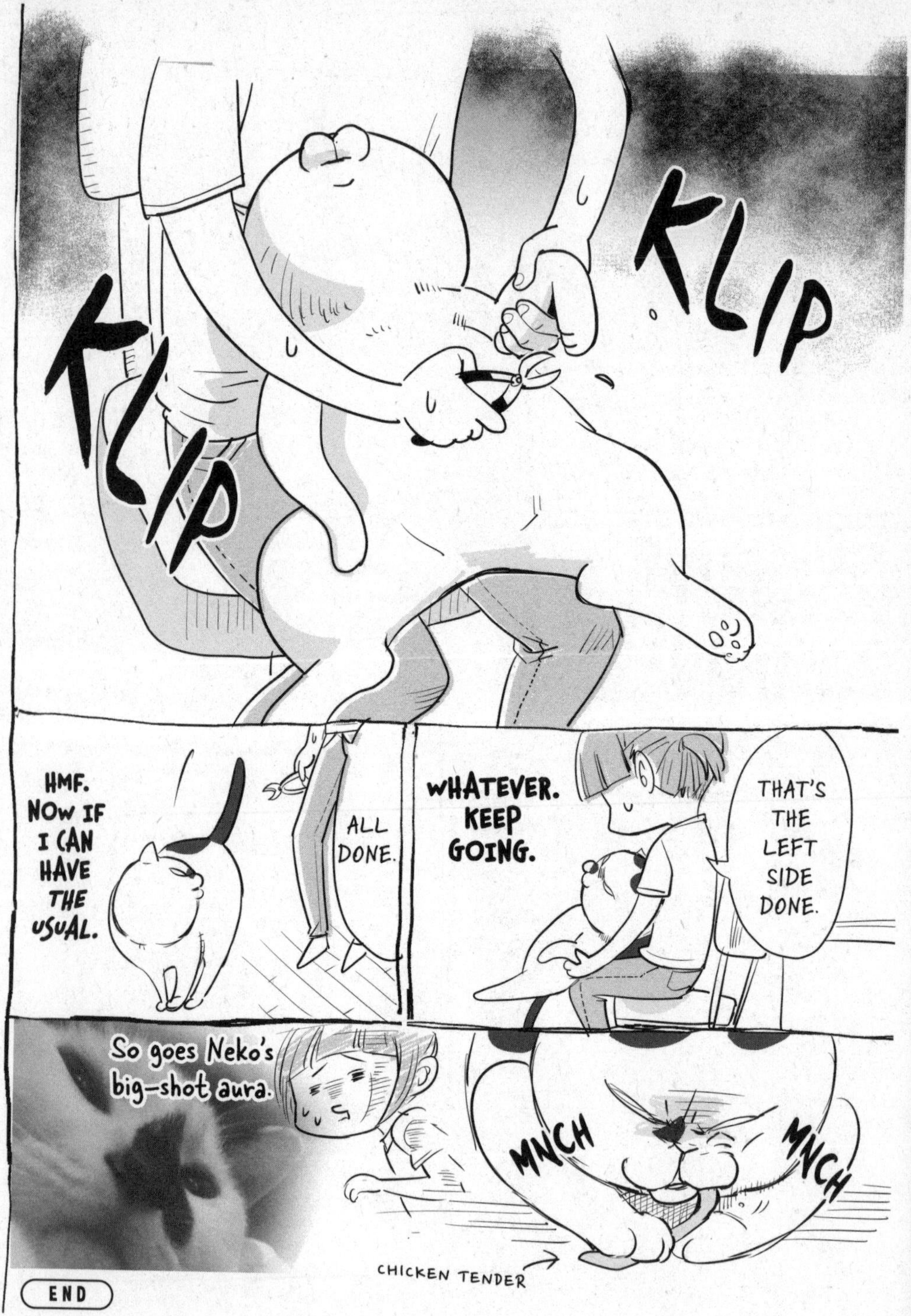
KLIP
KLIP
THAT'S THE LEFT SIDE DONE.
WHATEVER. KEEP GOING.
ALL DONE.
HMF. NOW IF I CAN HAVE THE USUAL.
MNCH
MNCH
CHICKEN TENDER
So goes Neko's big-shot aura.
END

#17

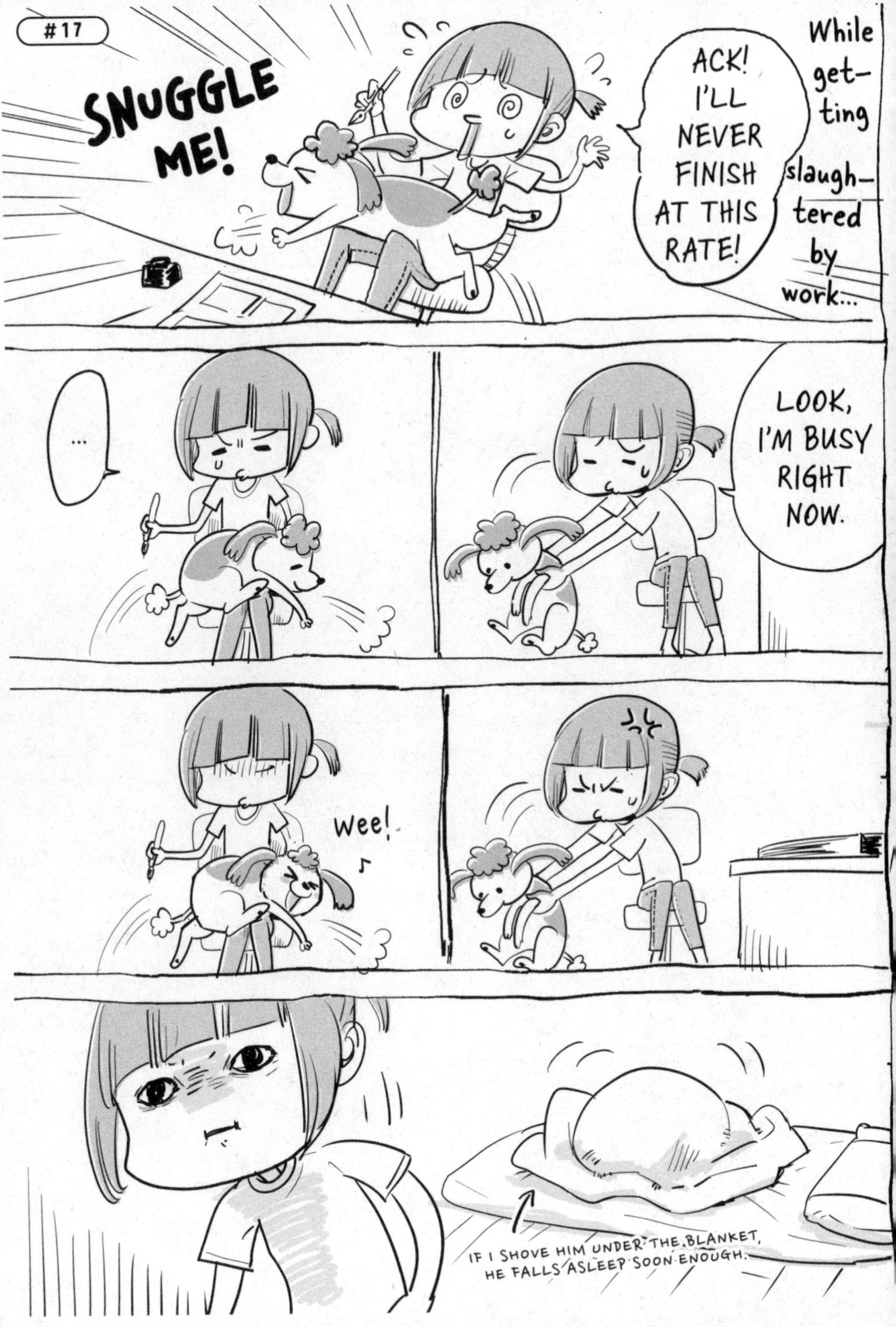
While getting slaughtered by work...
ACK! I'LL NEVER FINISH AT THIS RATE!
SNUGGLE ME!
LOOK, I'M BUSY RIGHT NOW.
...
Wee! ♪
IF I SHOVE HIM UNDER THE BLANKET, HE FALLS ASLEEP SOON ENOUGH.

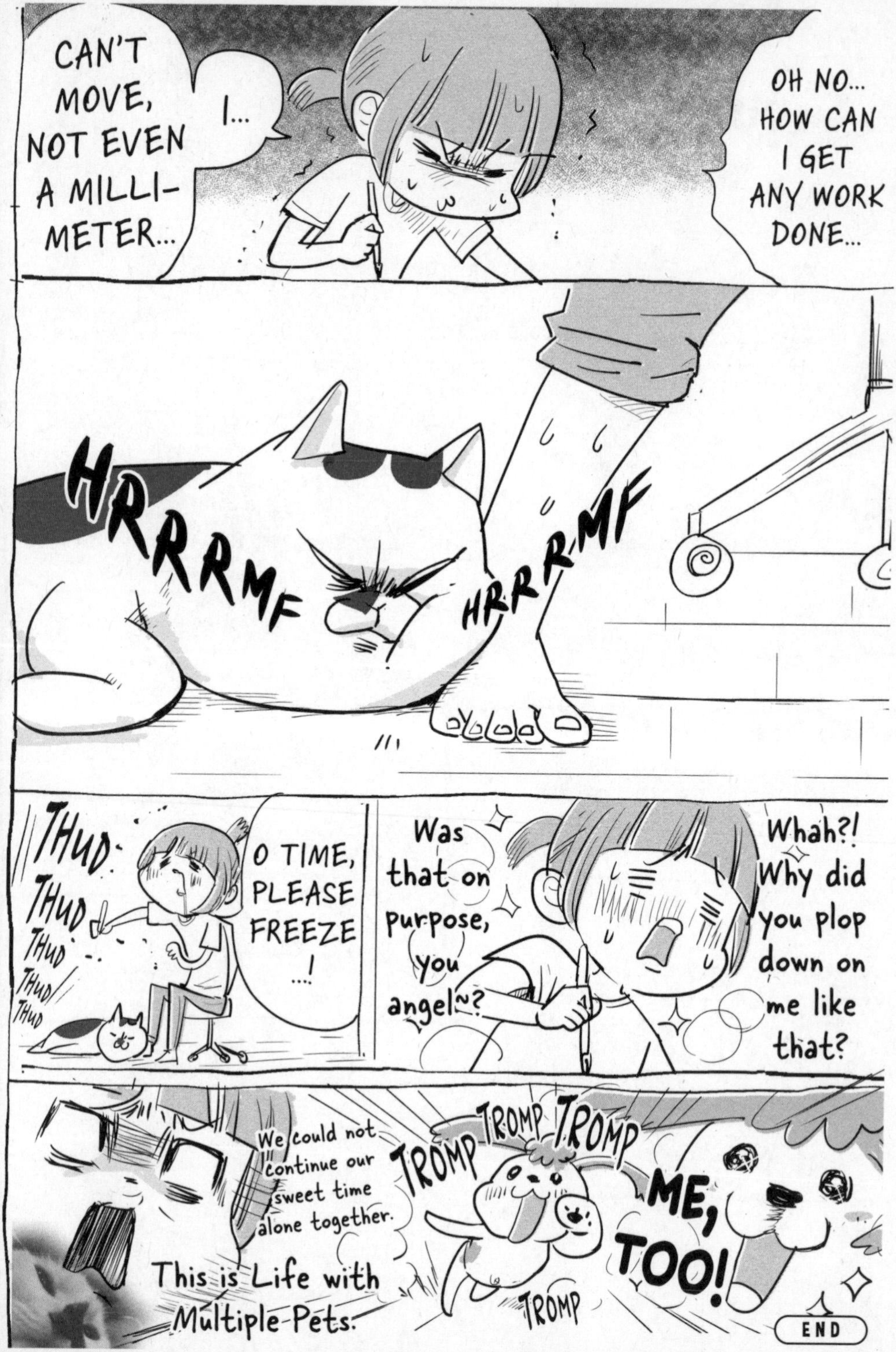
OH NO... HOW CAN I GET ANY WORK DONE...
I...
CAN'T MOVE, NOT EVEN A MILLI-METER...
HRRRMF
HRRRMF
Whah?! Why did you plop down on me like that?
Was that on purpose, you angel~?
O TIME, PLEASE FREEZE ...!
THUD THUD THUD THUD THUD
END
ME, TOO!
TROMP TROMP TROMP TROMP
TROMP
We could not continue our sweet time alone together.
This is Life with Multiple Pets.

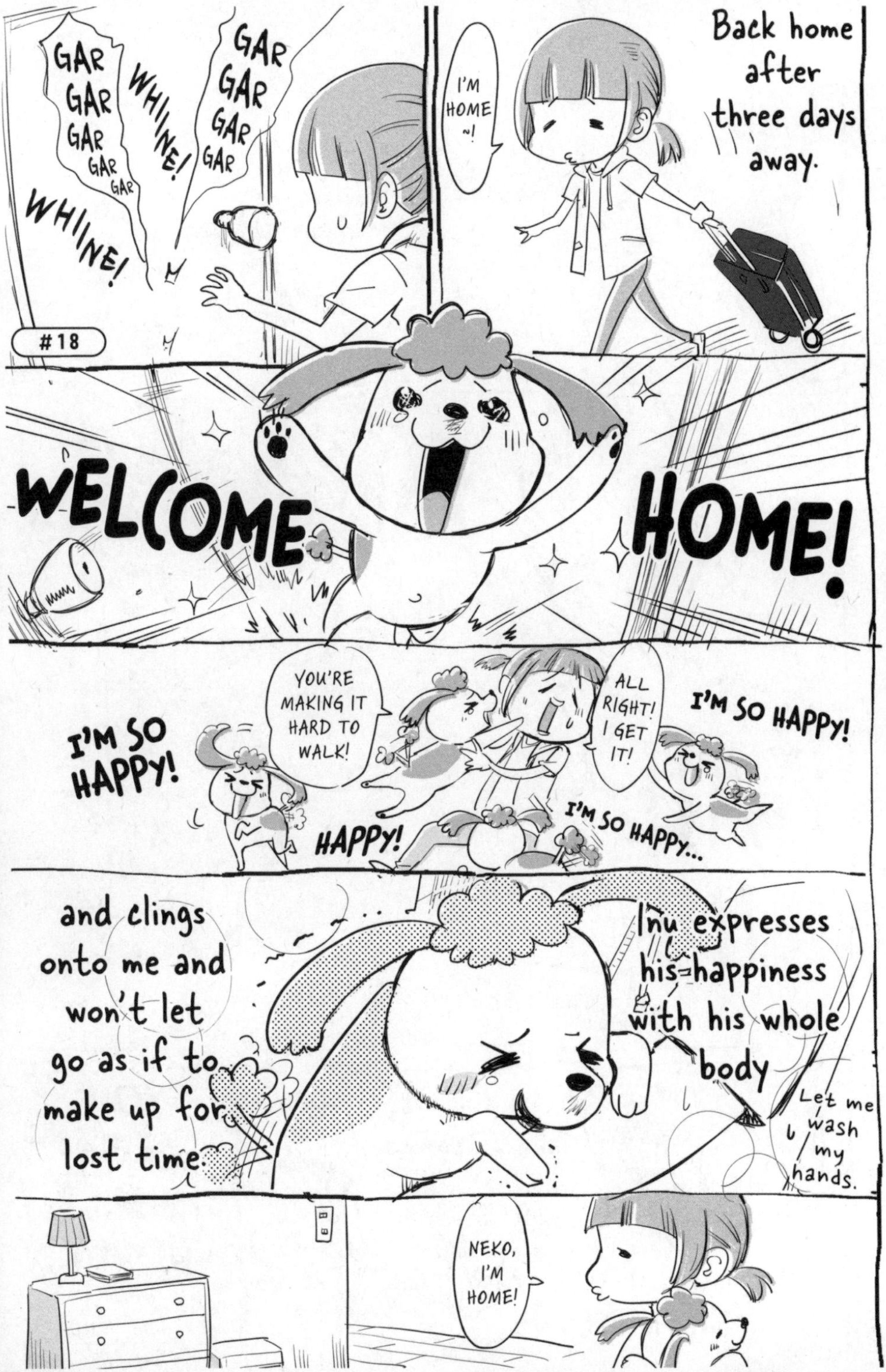
Back home after three days away.
I'M HOME ~!
GAR GAR GAR GAR
WHIINE!
GAR GAR GAR GAR GAR
WHIINE!
#18
WELCOME HOME!
I'M SO HAPPY!
ALL RIGHT! I GET IT!
YOU'RE MAKING IT HARD TO WALK!
I'M SO HAPPY!
I'M SO HAPPY...
HAPPY!
Inu expresses his happiness with his whole body
Let me wash my hands.
and clings onto me and won't let go as if to make up for lost time.
NEKO, I'M HOME!

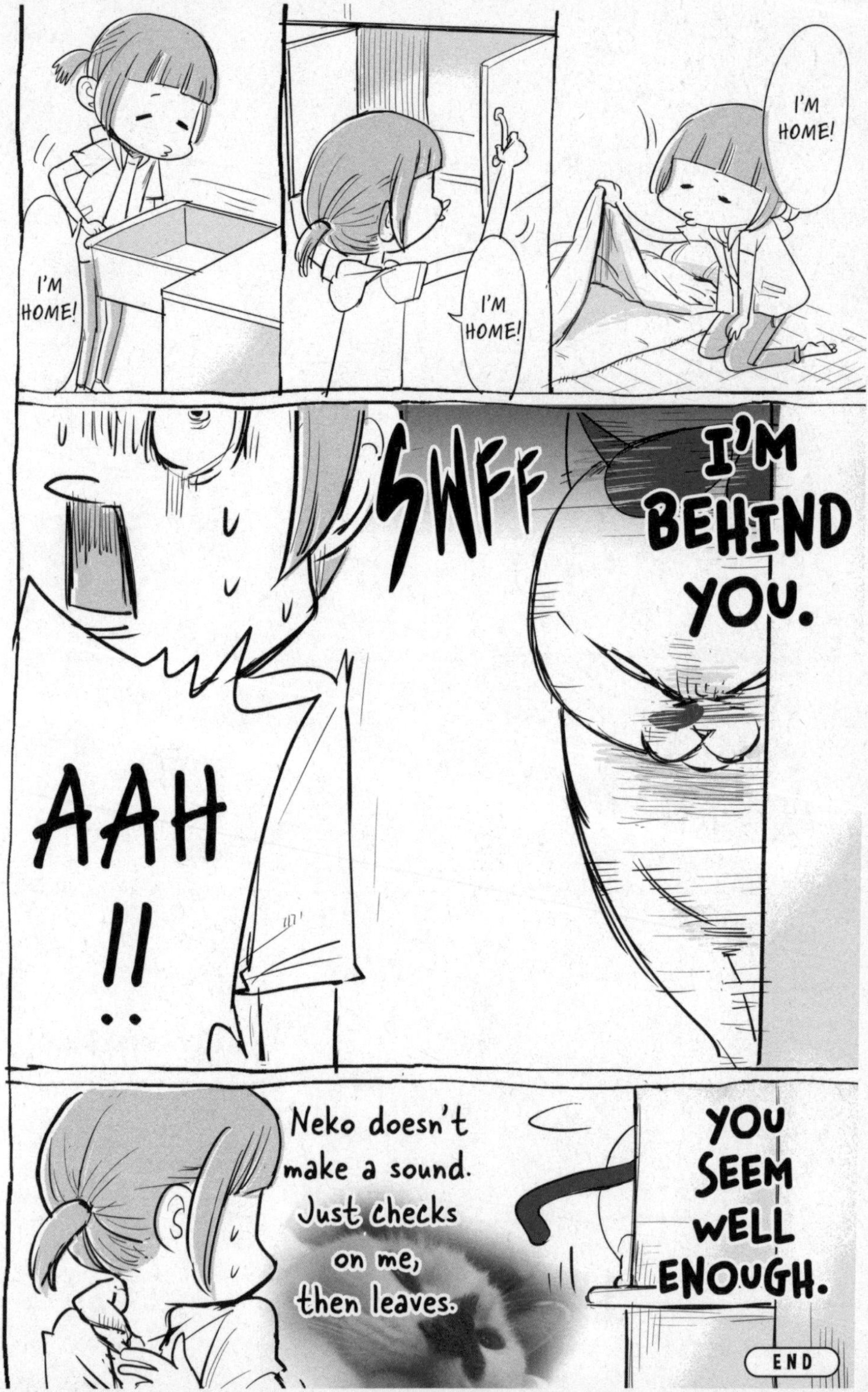
I'M HOME!
I'M HOME!
I'M HOME!
I'M BEHIND YOU.
SNFF
AAH !!
YOU SEEM WELL ENOUGH.
Neko doesn't make a sound. Just checks on me, then leaves.
END

Neko, in the back, watches in silence as Inu frolics.

Newly-Drawn 4-Panel Strip

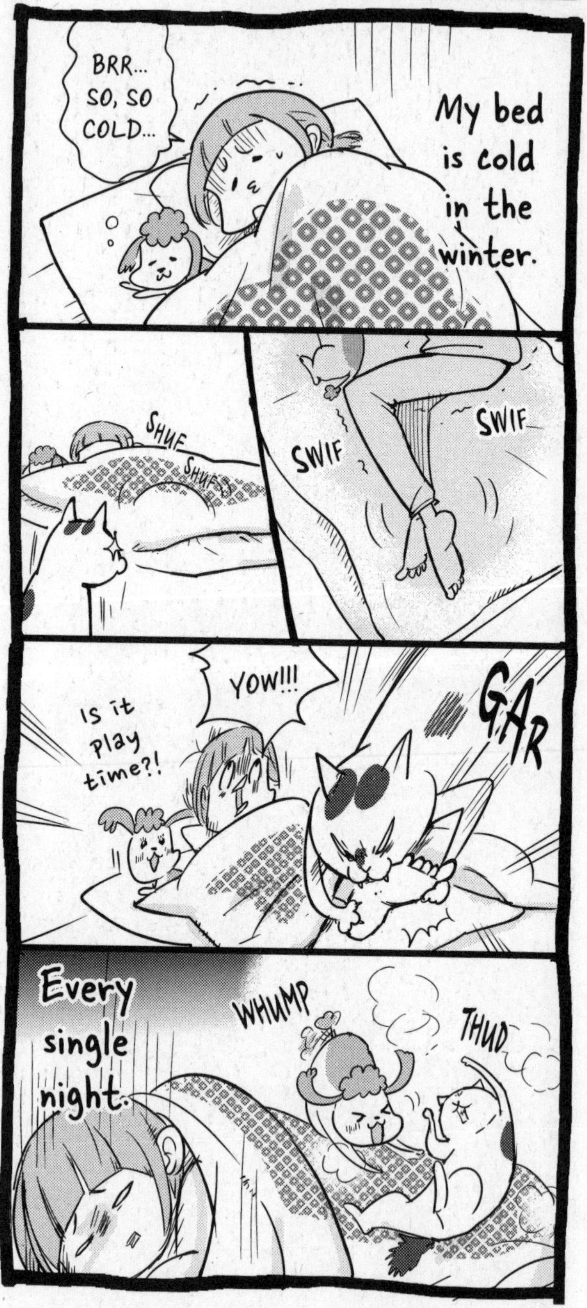
My bed is cold in the winter.
BRR... SO, SO COLD...
SWIF
SWIF
SHUF
SHUF
GAR
YOW!!!
Is it play time?!
THUD
WHUMP
Every single night.

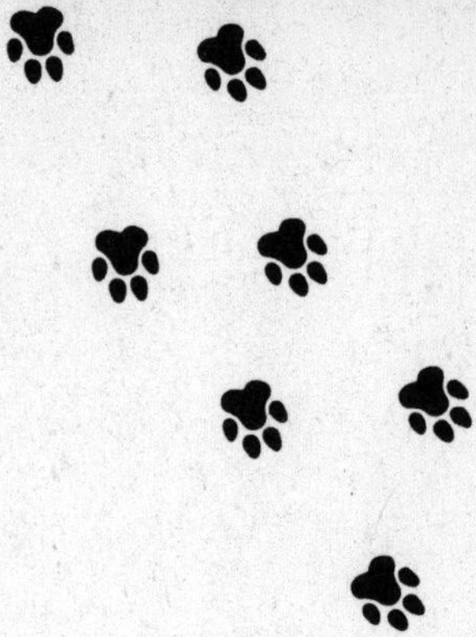

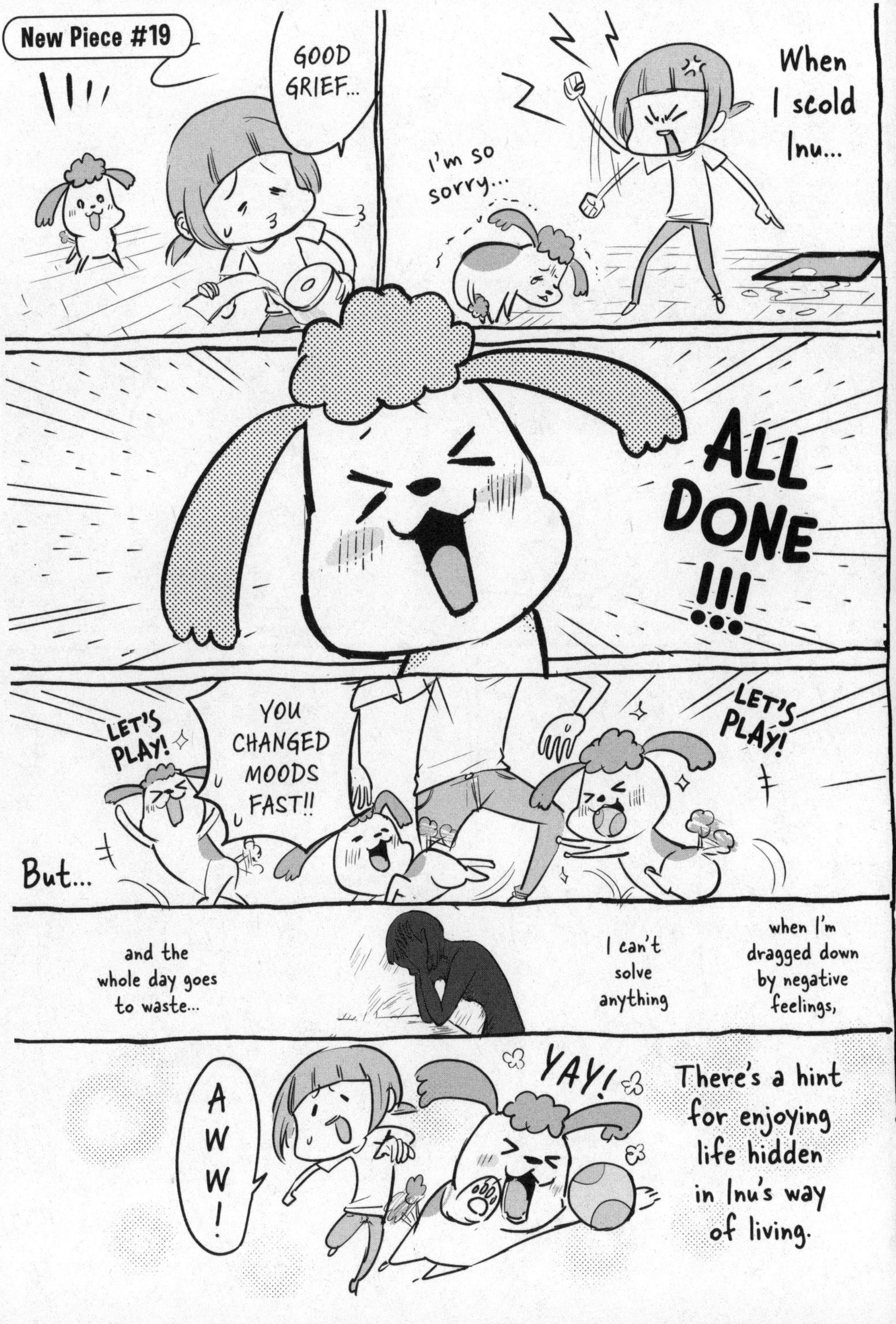
New Piece #19
When I scold Inu...
I'm so sorry...
GOOD GRIEF...
ALL DONE!!!
LET'S PLAY!
YOU CHANGED MOODS FAST!!
LET'S PLAY!
But...
when I'm dragged down by negative feelings,
I can't solve anything
and the whole day goes to waste...
There's a hint for enjoying life hidden in Inu's way of living.
YAY!
AWW!

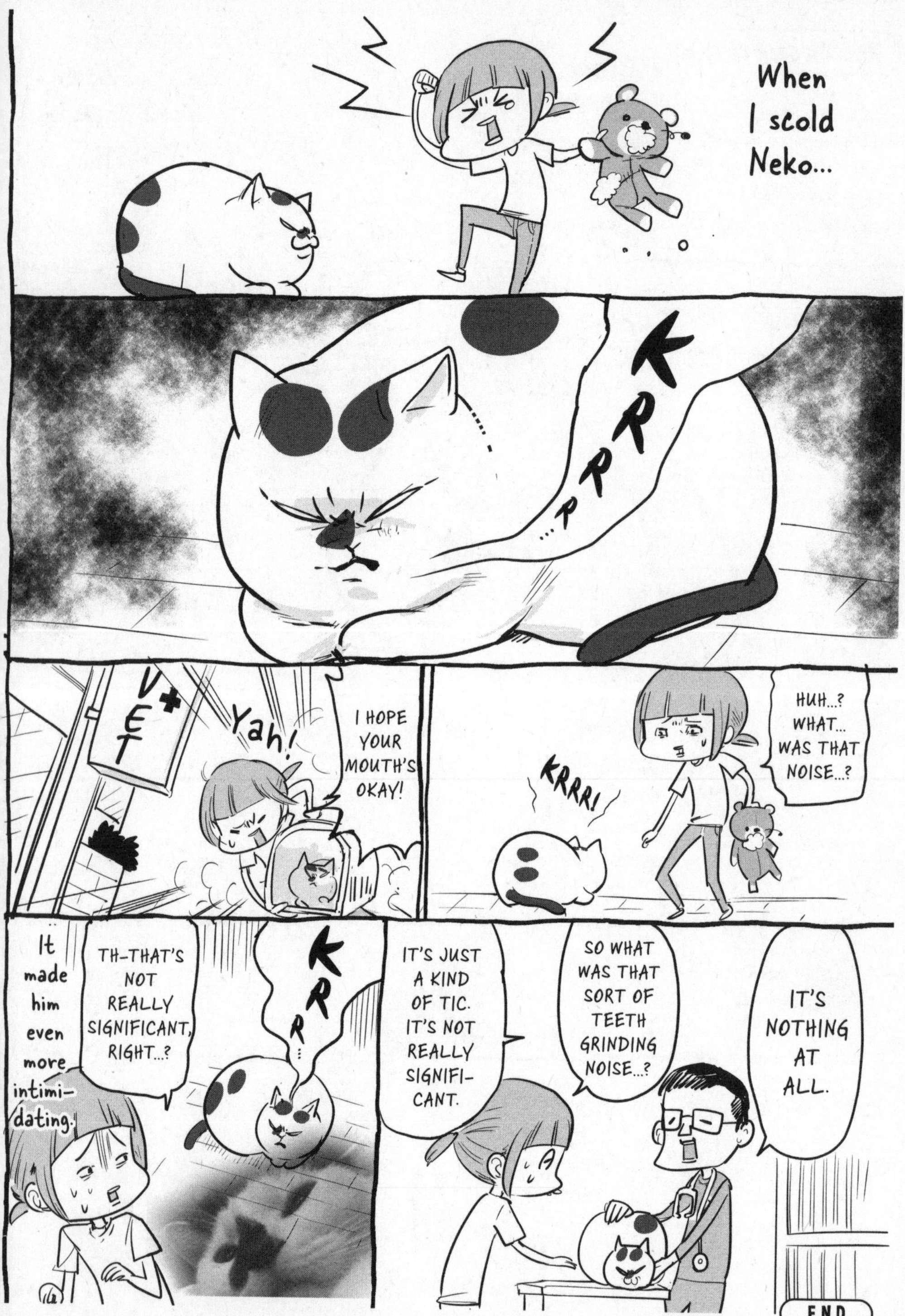
When I scold Neko...
...RRRRK
HUH...? WHAT... WAS THAT NOISE...?
KRRR!
I HOPE YOUR MOUTH'S OKAY!
Yah!
VET
SO WHAT WAS THAT SORT OF TEETH GRINDING NOISE...?
IT'S NOTHING AT ALL.
IT'S JUST A KIND OF TIC. IT'S NOT REALLY SIGNIFICANT.
KRR...
TH-THAT'S NOT REALLY SIGNIFICANT, RIGHT...?
It made him even more intimi-dating.
END

New Piece #20

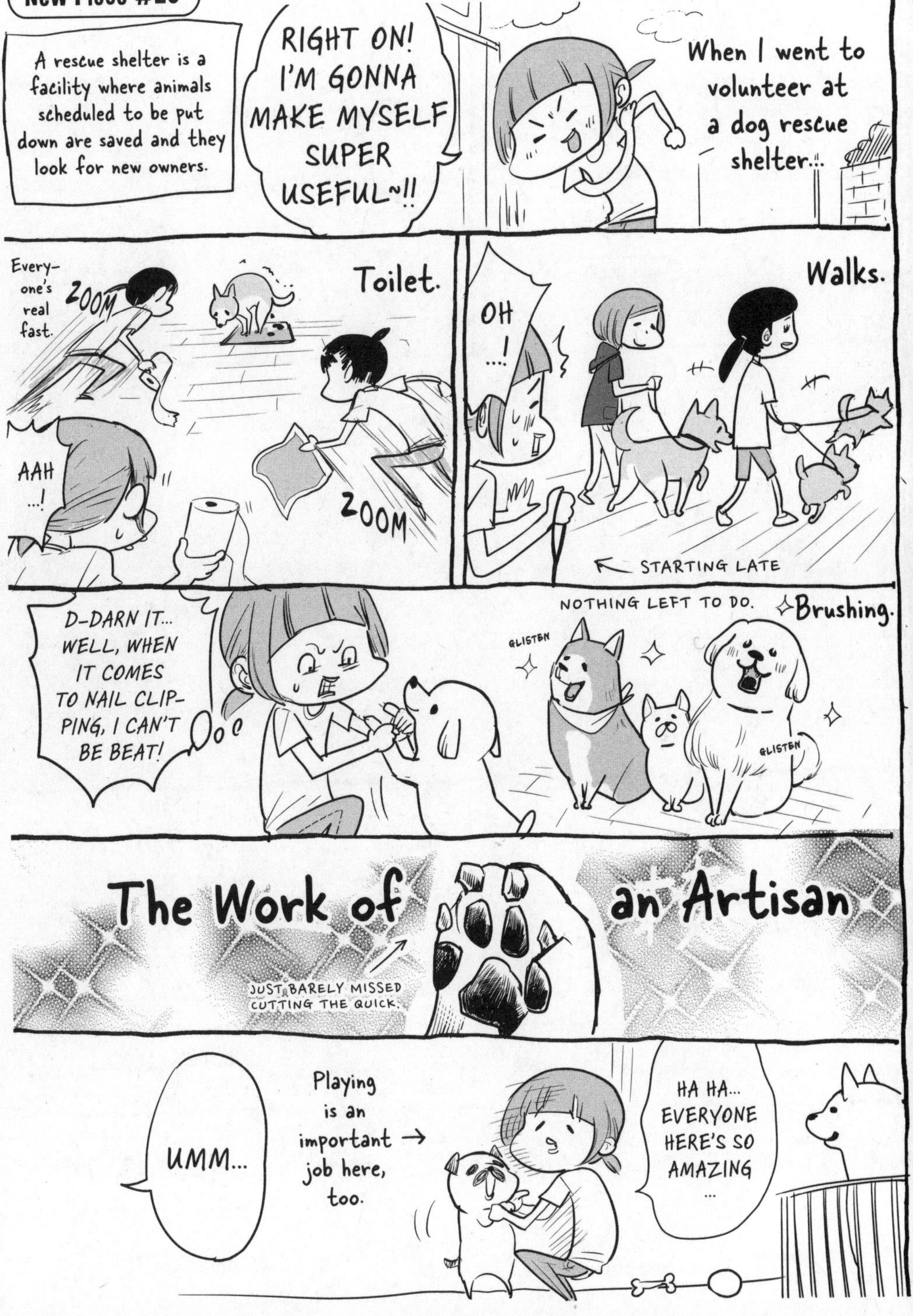
When I went to volunteer at a dog rescue shelter...
RIGHT ON! I'M GONNA MAKE MYSELF SUPER USEFUL~!!
A rescue shelter is a facility where animals scheduled to be put down are saved and they look for new owners.
Walks.
OH ...!
STARTING LATE
Toilet.
Every-one's real fast.
ZOOM
ZOOM
AAH ...!
Brushing.
NOTHING LEFT TO DO.
GLISTEN
GLISTEN
D-DARN IT... WELL, WHEN IT COMES TO NAIL CLIP-PING, I CAN'T BE BEAT!
The Work of an Artisan
JUST BARELY MISSED CUTTING THE QUICK.
HA HA... EVERYONE HERE'S SO AMAZING ...
Playing is an important job here, too.
UMM...

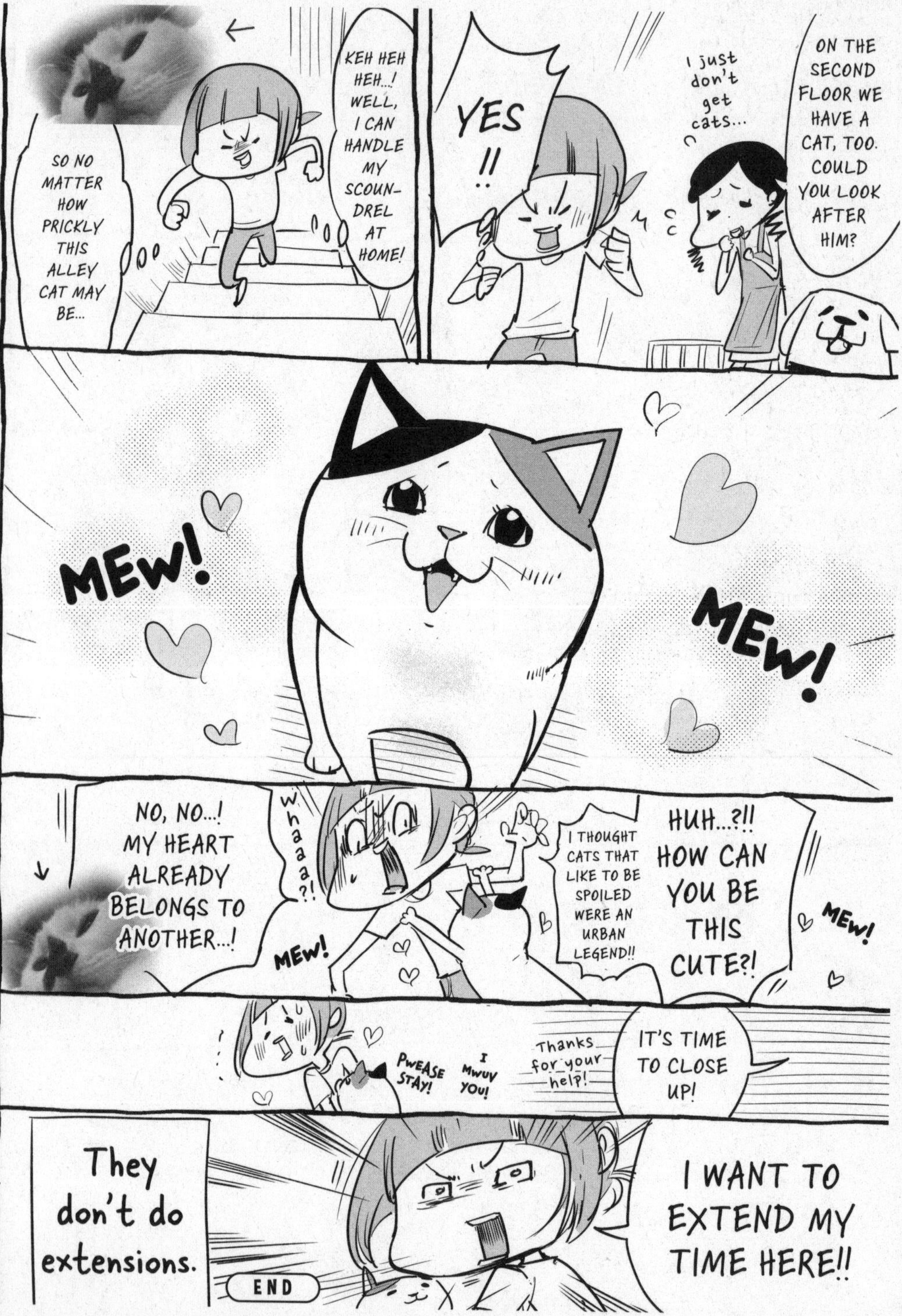
ON THE SECOND FLOOR WE HAVE A CAT, TOO. COULD YOU LOOK AFTER HIM?
I just don't get cats...
YES!!
KEH HEH HEH...! WELL, I CAN HANDLE MY SCOUNDREL AT HOME!
SO NO MATTER HOW PRICKLY THIS ALLEY CAT MAY BE...
MEW!
MEW!
MEW!
HUH...?!! HOW CAN YOU BE THIS CUTE?!
I THOUGHT CATS THAT LIKE TO BE SPOILED WERE AN URBAN LEGEND!!
MEW!
Whaaaa?!
NO, NO...! MY HEART ALREADY BELONGS TO ANOTHER...!
IT'S TIME TO CLOSE UP!
Thanks for your help!
I MWUV YOU!
PWEASE STAY!
I WANT TO EXTEND MY TIME HERE!!
They don't do extensions.
END

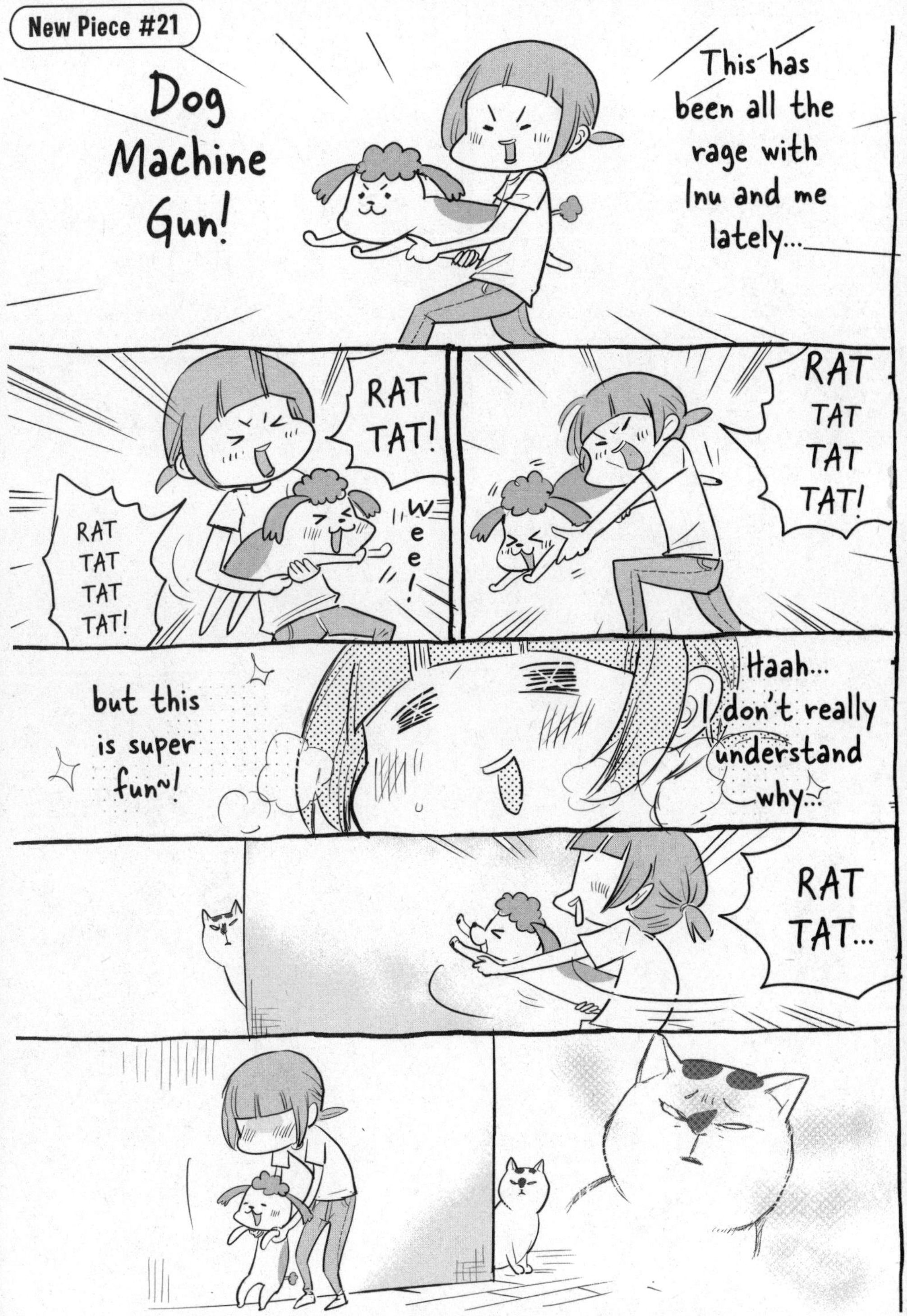
New Piece #21
This has been all the rage with Inu and me lately...
Dog Machine Gun!
RAT TAT TAT TAT!
RAT TAT!
Wee!
RAT TAT TAT TAT!
Haaah... I don't really understand why...
but this is super fun~!
RAT TAT...

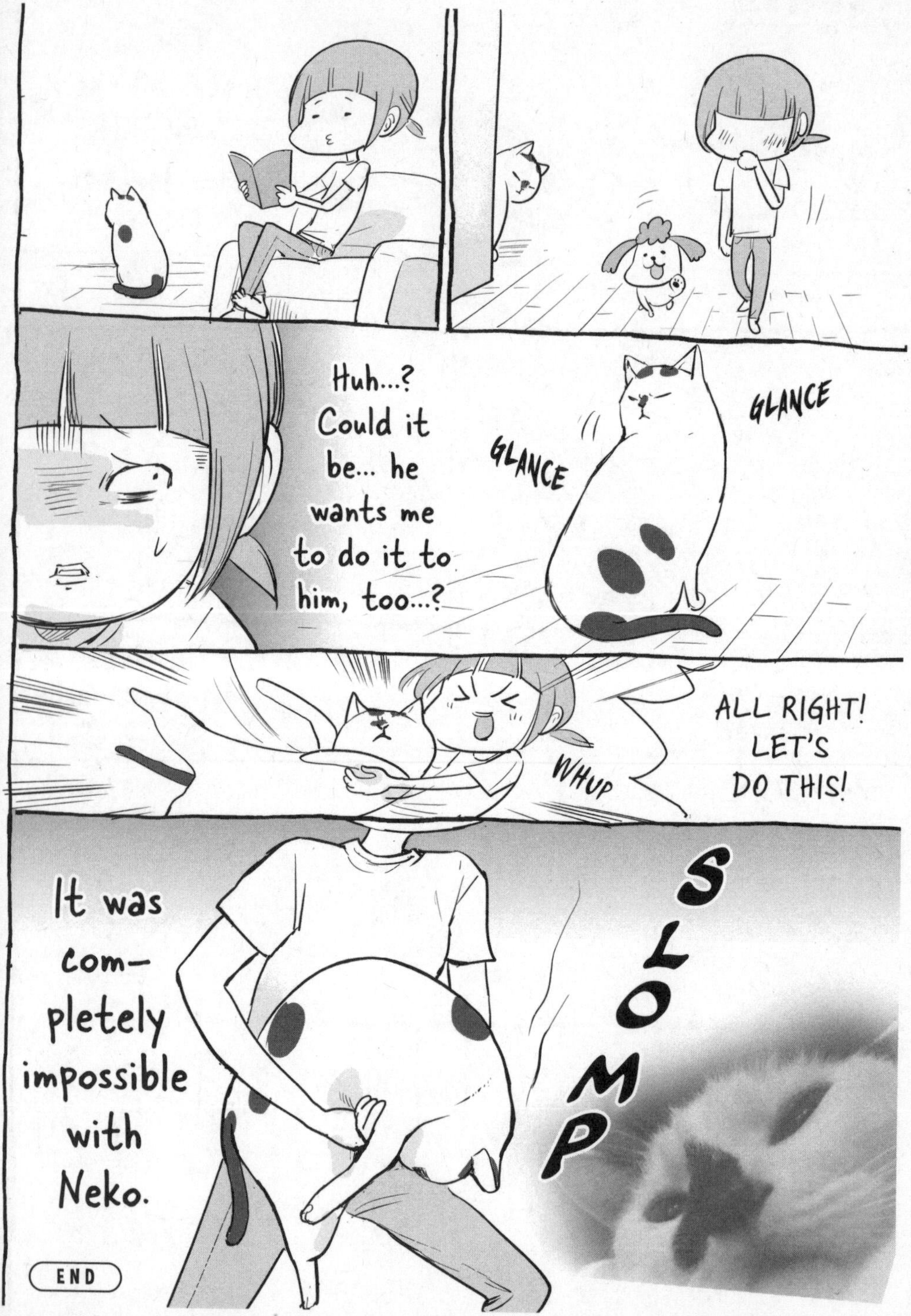
GLANCE
GLANCE
Huh...? Could it be... he wants me to do it to him, too...?
ALL RIGHT! LET'S DO THIS!
WHUP
SLOMP
It was com-pletely impossible with Neko.
END

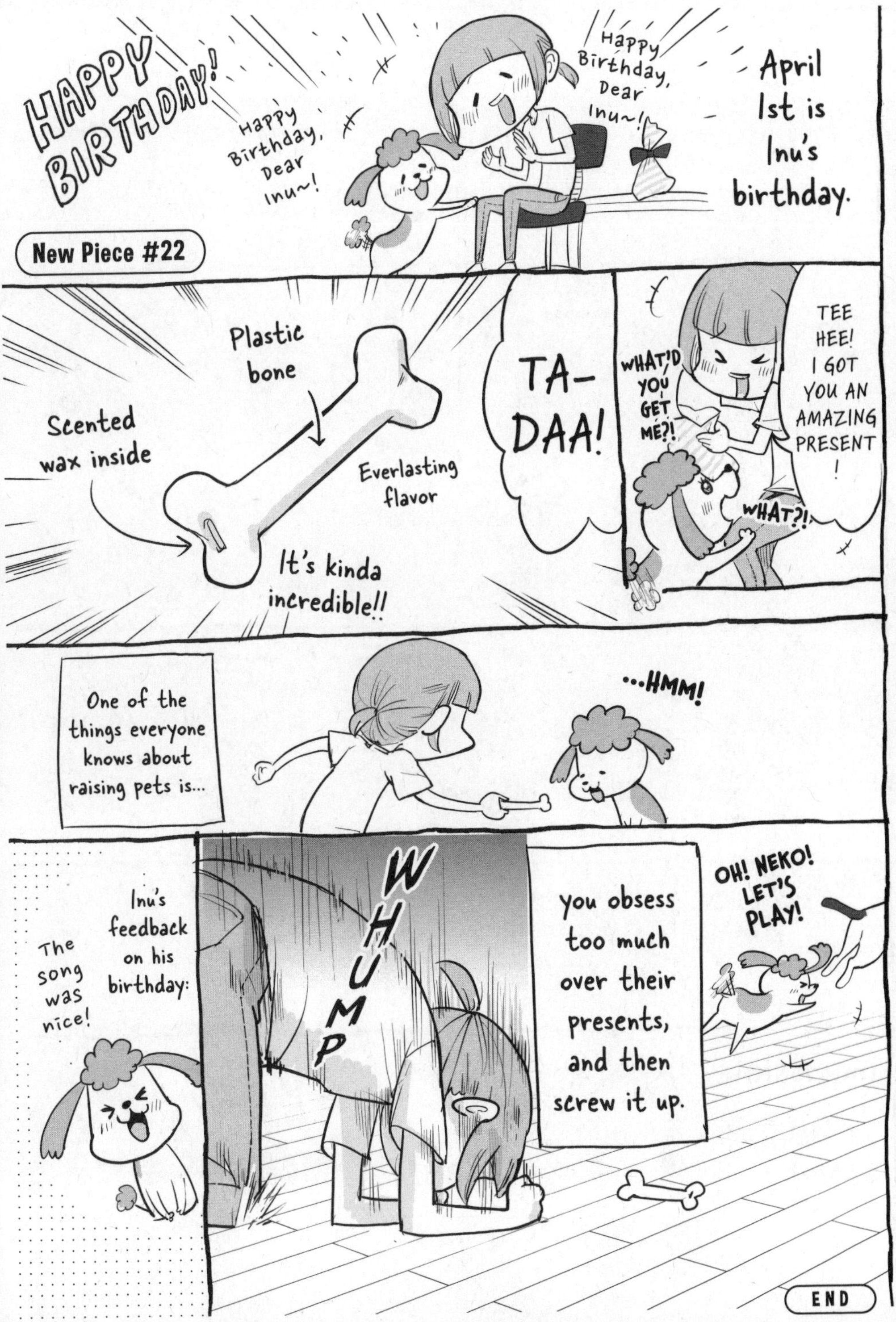
April 1st is Inu's birthday.
Happy Birthday, Dear Inu~!
Happy Birthday, Dear Inu~!
HAPPY BIRTHDAY!
New Piece #22
TEE HEE! I GOT YOU AN AMAZING PRESENT!
WHAT'D YOU GET ME?!
WHAT?!
TA-DAA!
Plastic bone
Everlasting flavor
Scented wax inside
It's kinda incredible!!
...HMM!
One of the things everyone knows about raising pets is...
OH! NEKO! LET'S PLAY!
you obsess too much over their presents, and then screw it up.
WHUMP
Inu's feedback on his birthday:
The song was nice!
END

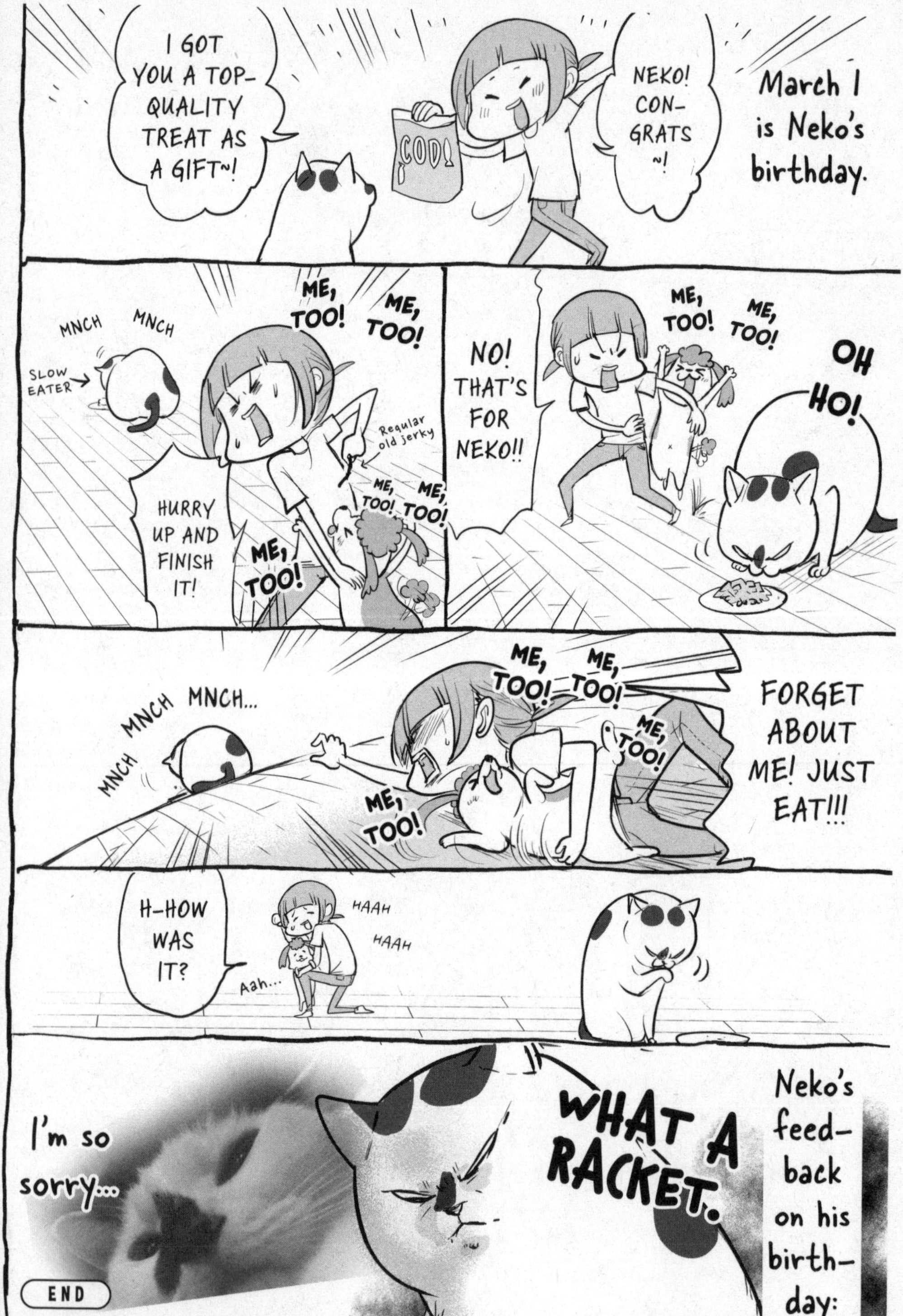
March 1 is Neko's birthday.
NEKO! CON-GRATS ~!
I GOT YOU A TOP-QUALITY TREAT AS A GIFT~!
OH HO!
ME, TOO!
ME, TOO!
NO! THAT'S FOR NEKO!!
ME, TOO!
ME, TOO!
Regular old jerky
ME, TOO!
ME, TOO!
MNCH
MNCH
SLOW EATER
HURRY UP AND FINISH IT!
ME, TOO!
FORGET ABOUT ME! JUST EAT!!!
ME, TOO!
ME, TOO!
ME, TOO!
ME, TOO!
MNCH MNCH... MNCH
HAAH
HAAH
Aah...
H-HOW WAS IT?
Neko's feed-back on his birth-day:
WHAT A RACKET.
I'm so sorry...
END

Melted.

Newly-Drawn 4-Panel Strip

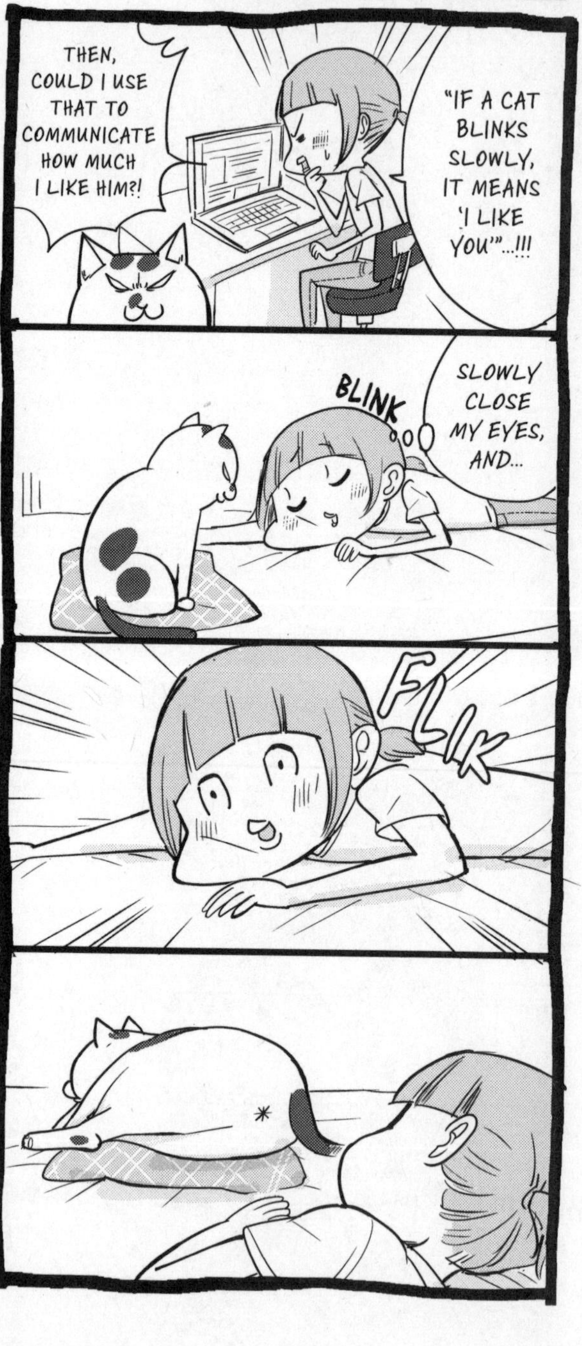
"IF A CAT BLINKS SLOWLY, IT MEANS 'I LIKE YOU'"...!!!
THEN, COULD I USE THAT TO COMMUNICATE HOW MUCH I LIKE HIM?!
SLOWLY CLOSE MY EYES, AND...
BLINK
FLIK

#23

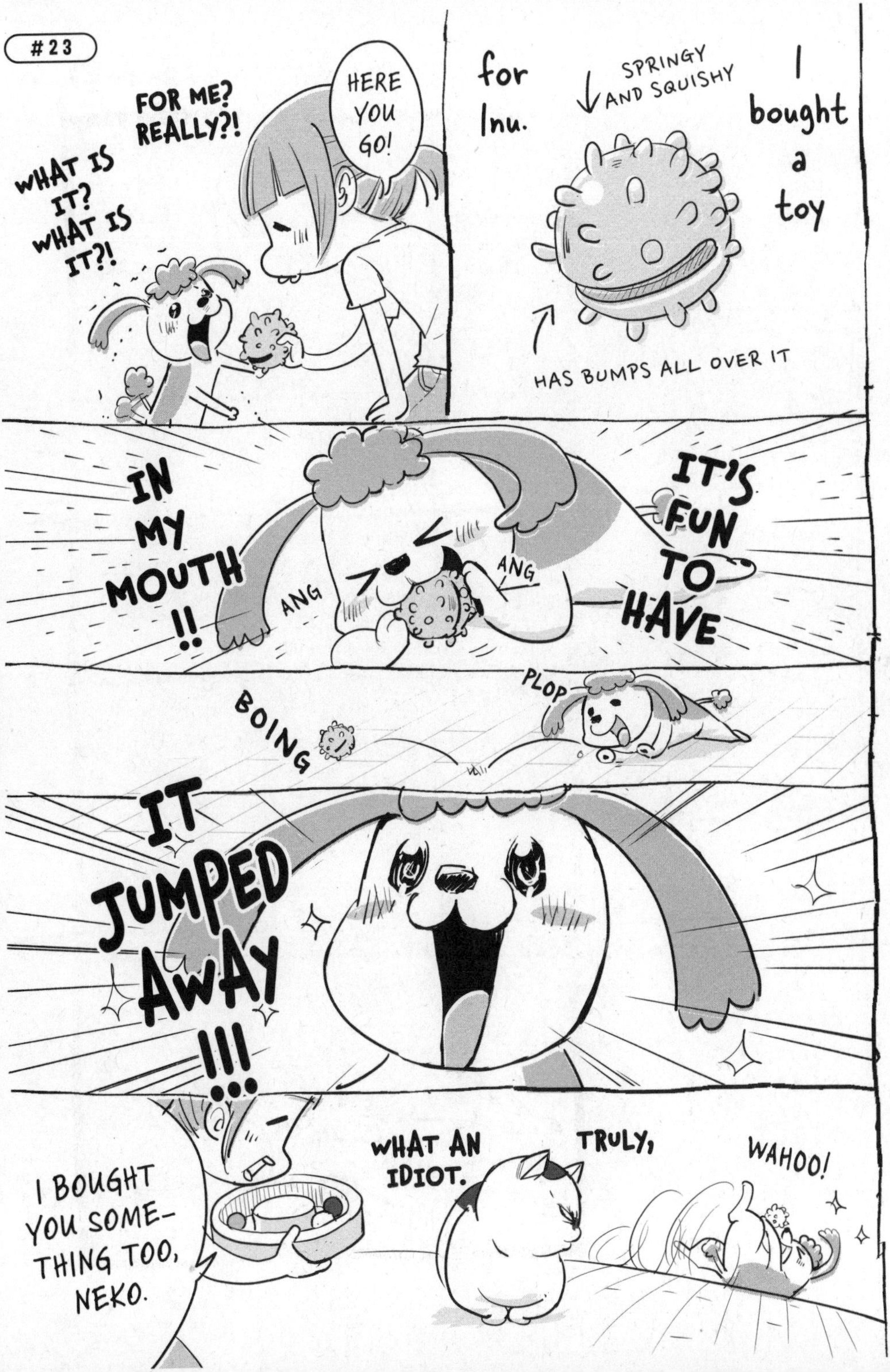
I bought a toy for Inu.
SPRINGY AND SQUISHY
HAS BUMPS ALL OVER IT
HERE YOU GO!
FOR ME? REALLY?!
WHAT IS IT? WHAT IS IT?!
IT'S FUN TO HAVE
IN MY MOUTH!!
ANG
ANG
PLOP
BOING
IT JUMPED AWAY!!!
...
WAHOO!
TRULY, WHAT AN IDIOT.
I BOUGHT YOU SOME-THING TOO, NEKO.

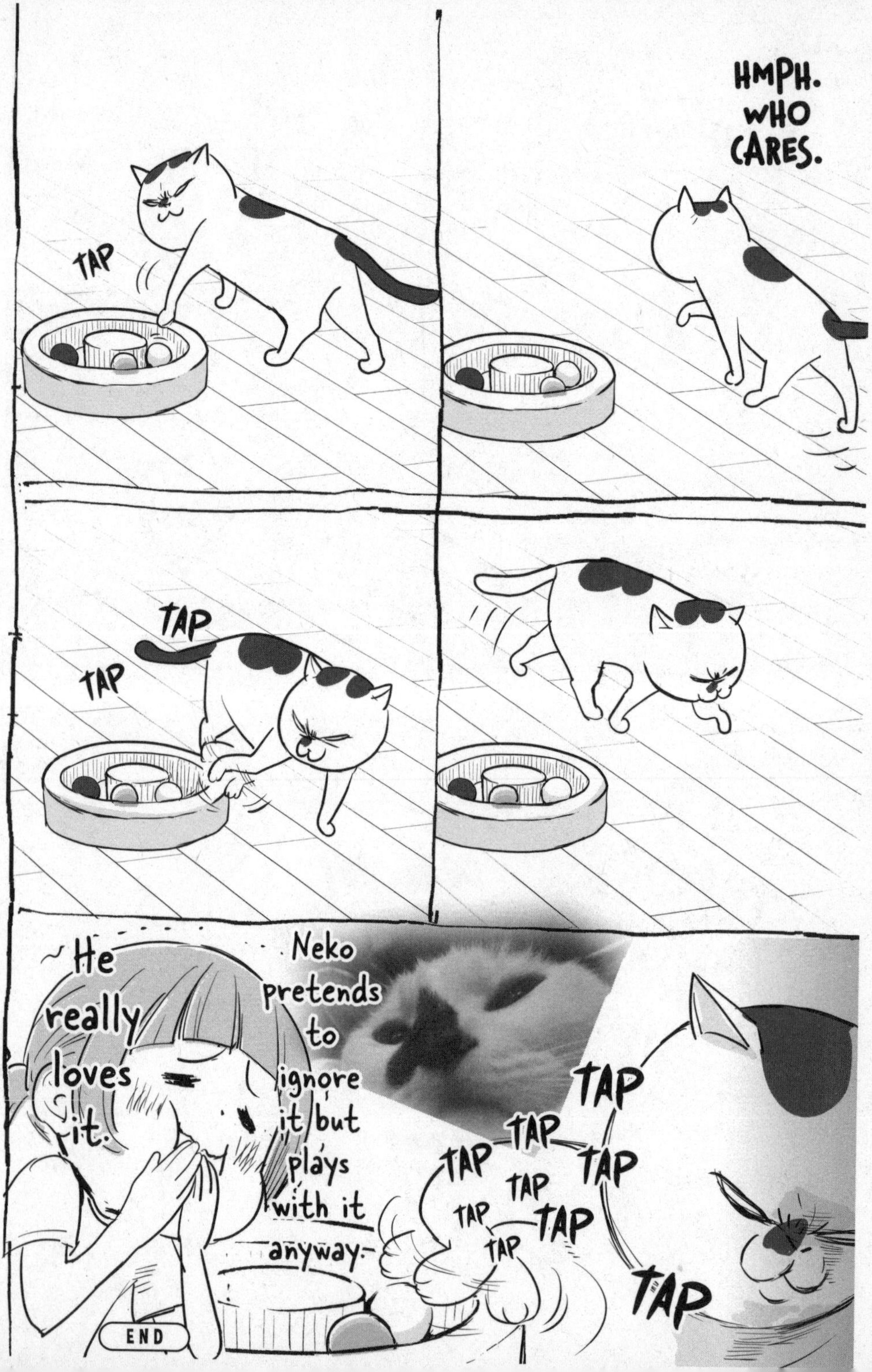
HMPH. WHO CARES.
TAP
TAP
TAP
TAP TAP TAP TAP TAP TAP TAP TAP TAP
Neko pretends to ignore it but plays with it anyway.
He really loves it.
END

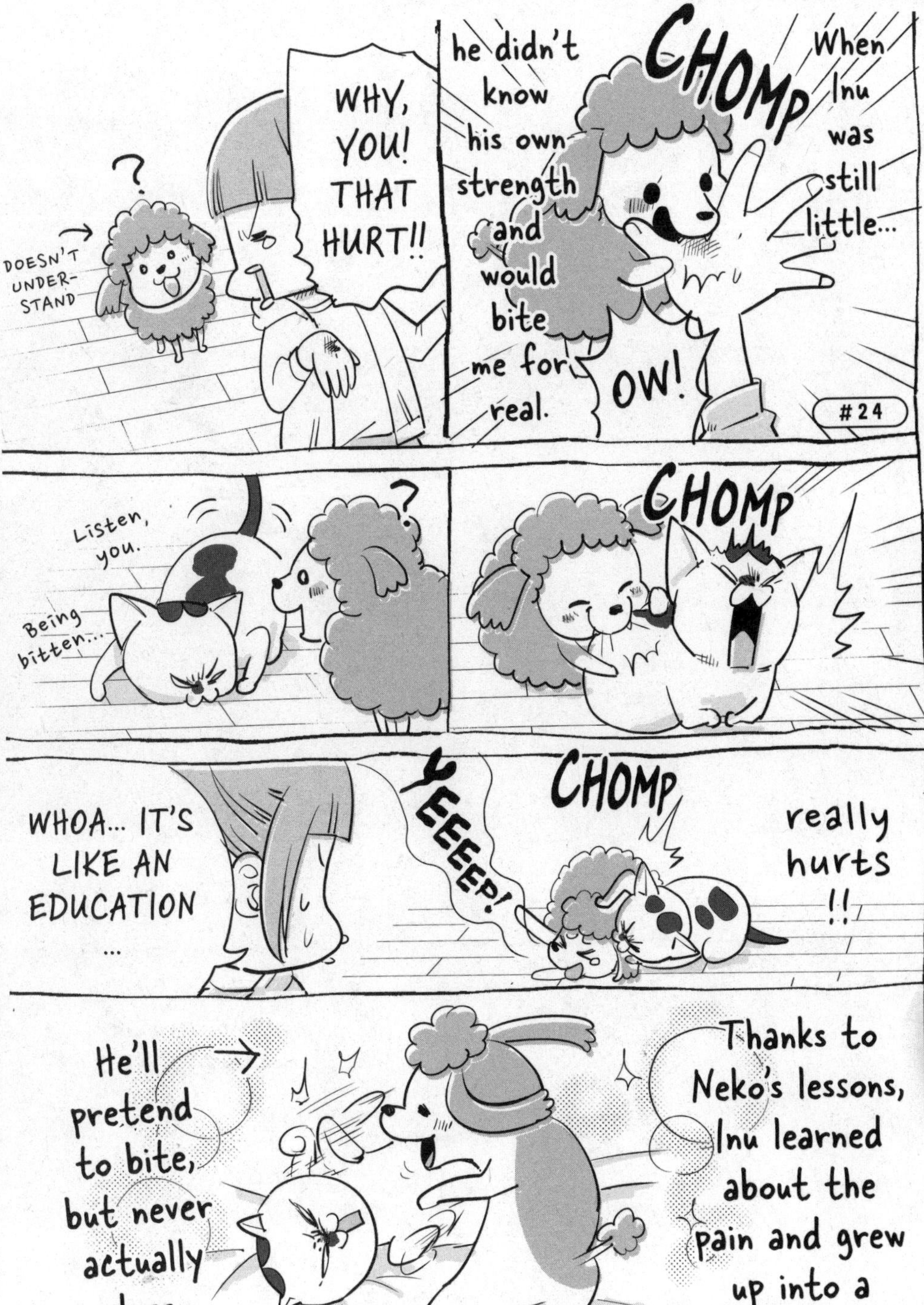
When Inu was still little...
CHOMP
he didn't know his own strength and would bite me for real.
OW!
#24
WHY, YOU! THAT HURT!!
?
DOESN'T UNDERSTAND
CHOMP
?
Listen, you.
Being bitten...
really hurts!!
CHOMP
YEEEEP!
WHOA... IT'S LIKE AN EDUCATION ...
Thanks to Neko's lessons, Inu learned about the pain and grew up into a fine adult.
He'll pretend to bite, but never actually does.

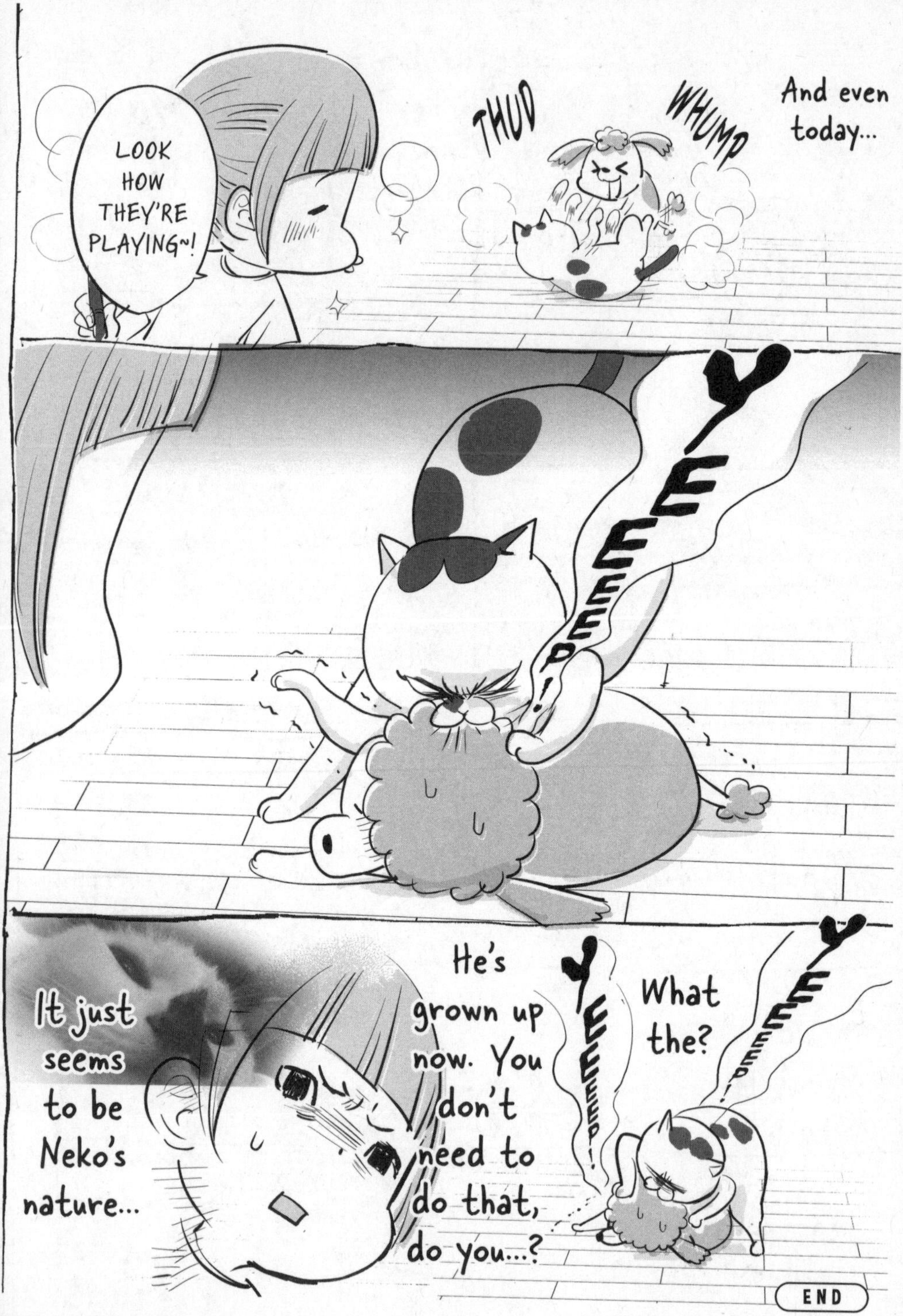
And even today...
WHUMP
THUD
LOOK HOW THEY'RE PLAYING~!
YEEEEEEP!
YEEEEP!
What the?
YEEEEEP!
He's grown up now. You don't need to do that, do you...?
It just seems to be Neko's nature...
END

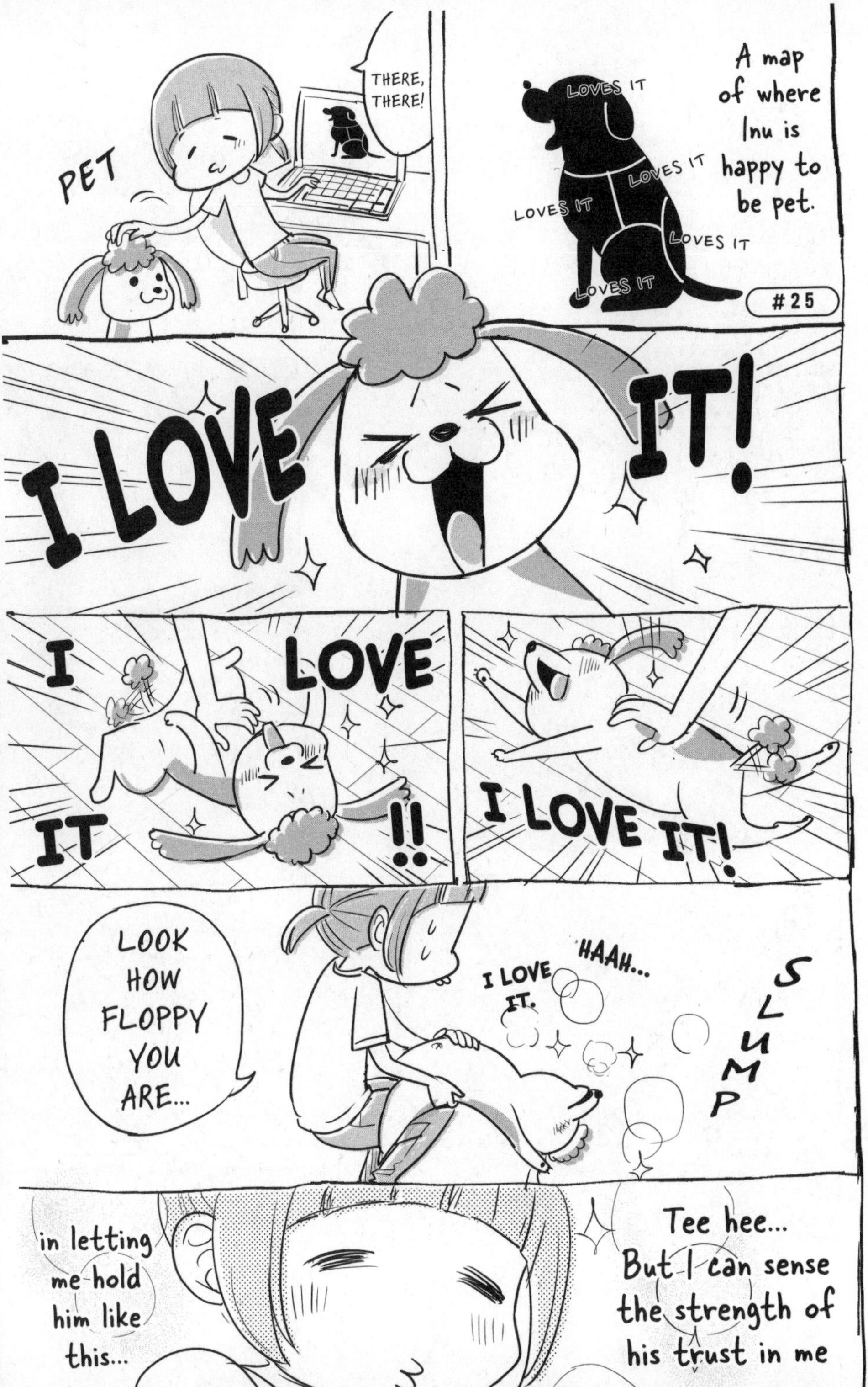
A map of where Inu is happy to be pet.
LOVES IT
LOVES IT
LOVES IT
LOVES IT
LOVES IT
#25
THERE, THERE!
PET
I LOVE IT!
I LOVE IT!
I LOVE IT!!
SLUMP
HAAH...
I LOVE IT.
LOOK HOW FLOPPY YOU ARE...
Tee hee... But I can sense the strength of his trust in me
in letting me hold him like this...

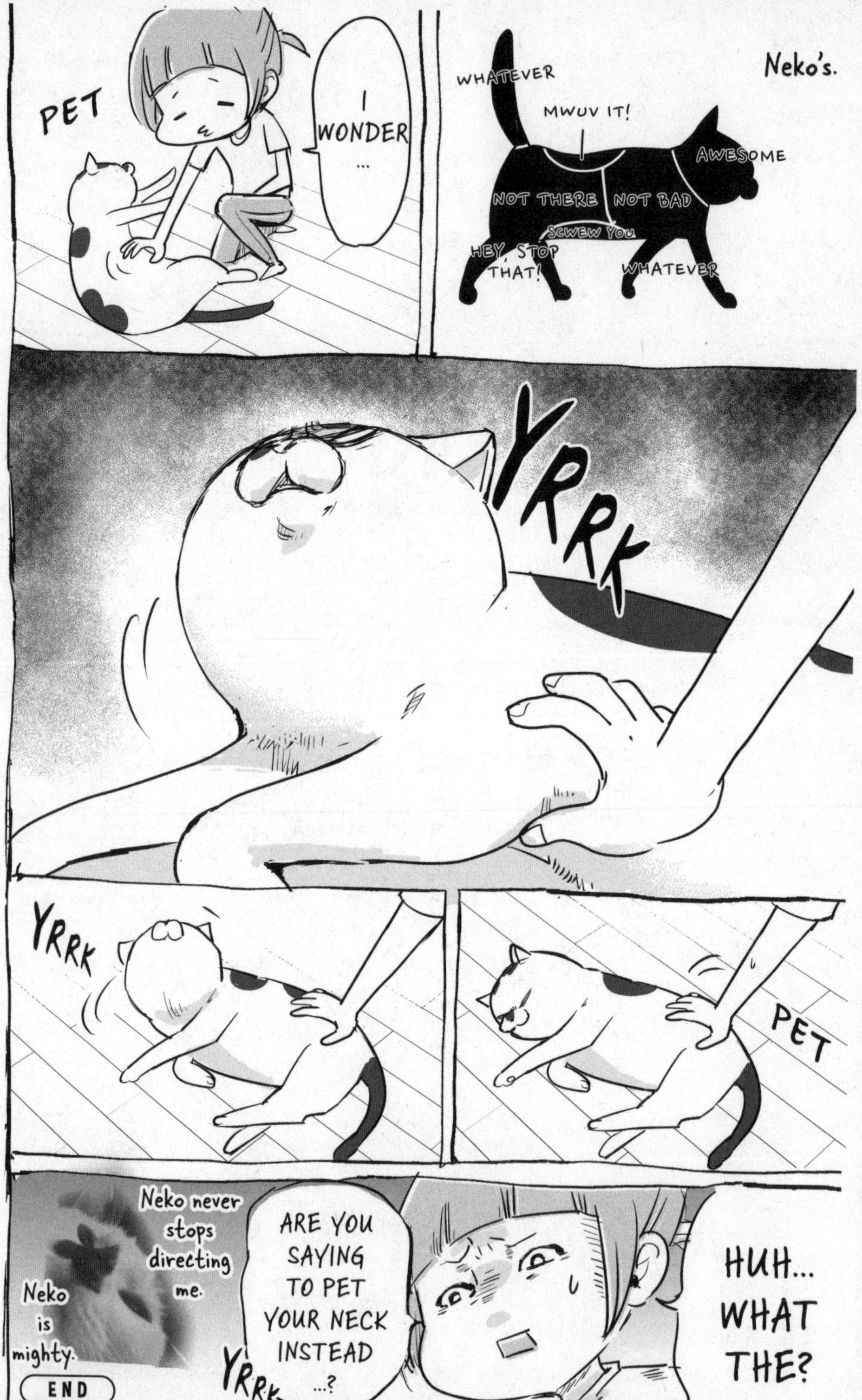
Neko's.
WHATEVER
MWUV IT!
AWESOME
NOT THERE
NOT BAD
SCWEW YOU
HEY, STOP THAT!
WHATEVER
I WONDER ...
PET
YRRK
PET
YRRK
HUH... WHAT THE?
ARE YOU SAYING TO PET YOUR NECK INSTEAD ...?
YRRK
Neko never stops directing me.
Neko is mighty.
END

I'm kinda sleepy, but... what? You're still taking a pic?

Newly-Drawn 4-Panel Strip

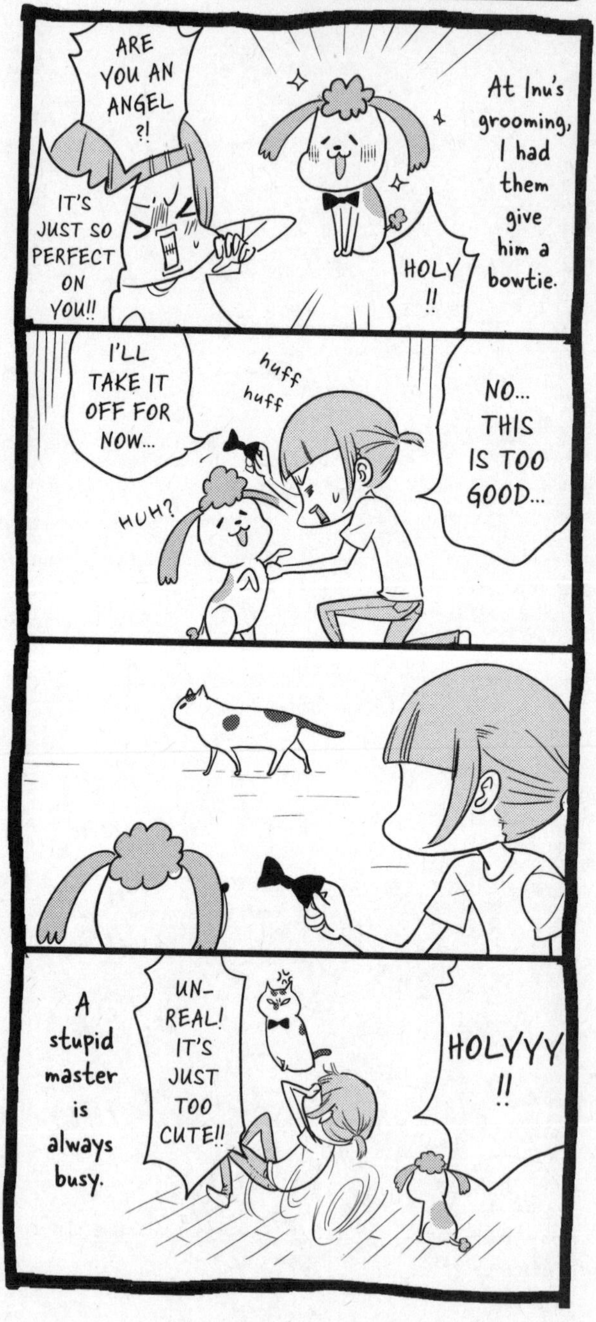

#26

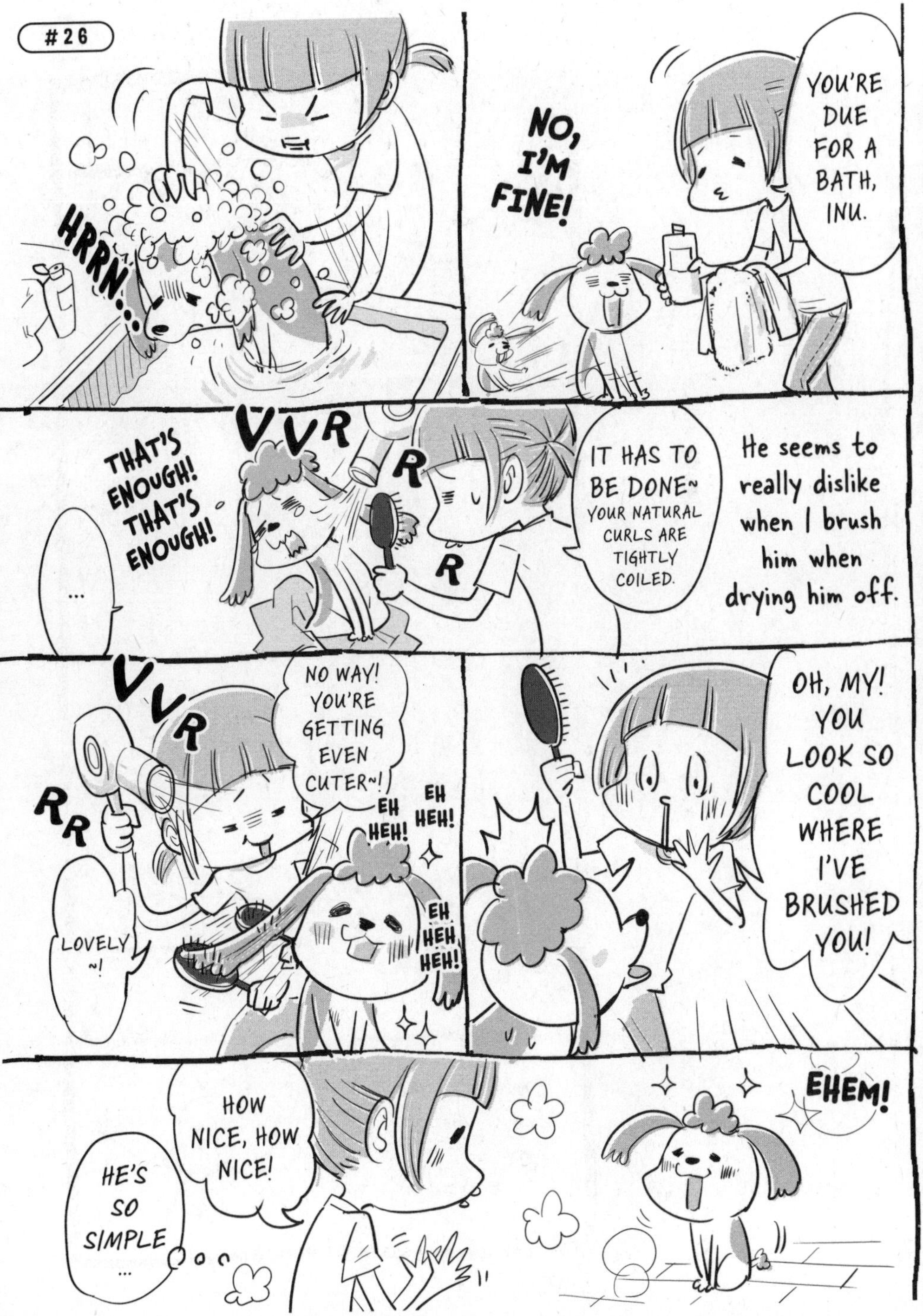

YOU'RE DUE FOR A BATH, INU.
NO, I'M FINE!
HRRN...
He seems to really dislike when I brush him when drying him off.
IT HAS TO BE DONE~ YOUR NATURAL CURLS ARE TIGHTLY COILED.
VVR
R
R
THAT'S ENOUGH! THAT'S ENOUGH!
...
OH, MY! YOU LOOK SO COOL WHERE I'VE BRUSHED YOU!
NO WAY! YOU'RE GETTING EVEN CUTER~!
VVR
EH HEH!
EH HEH!
EH HEH HEH!
RR
LOVELY ~!
EHEM!
HOW NICE, HOW NICE!
HE'S SO SIMPLE ...

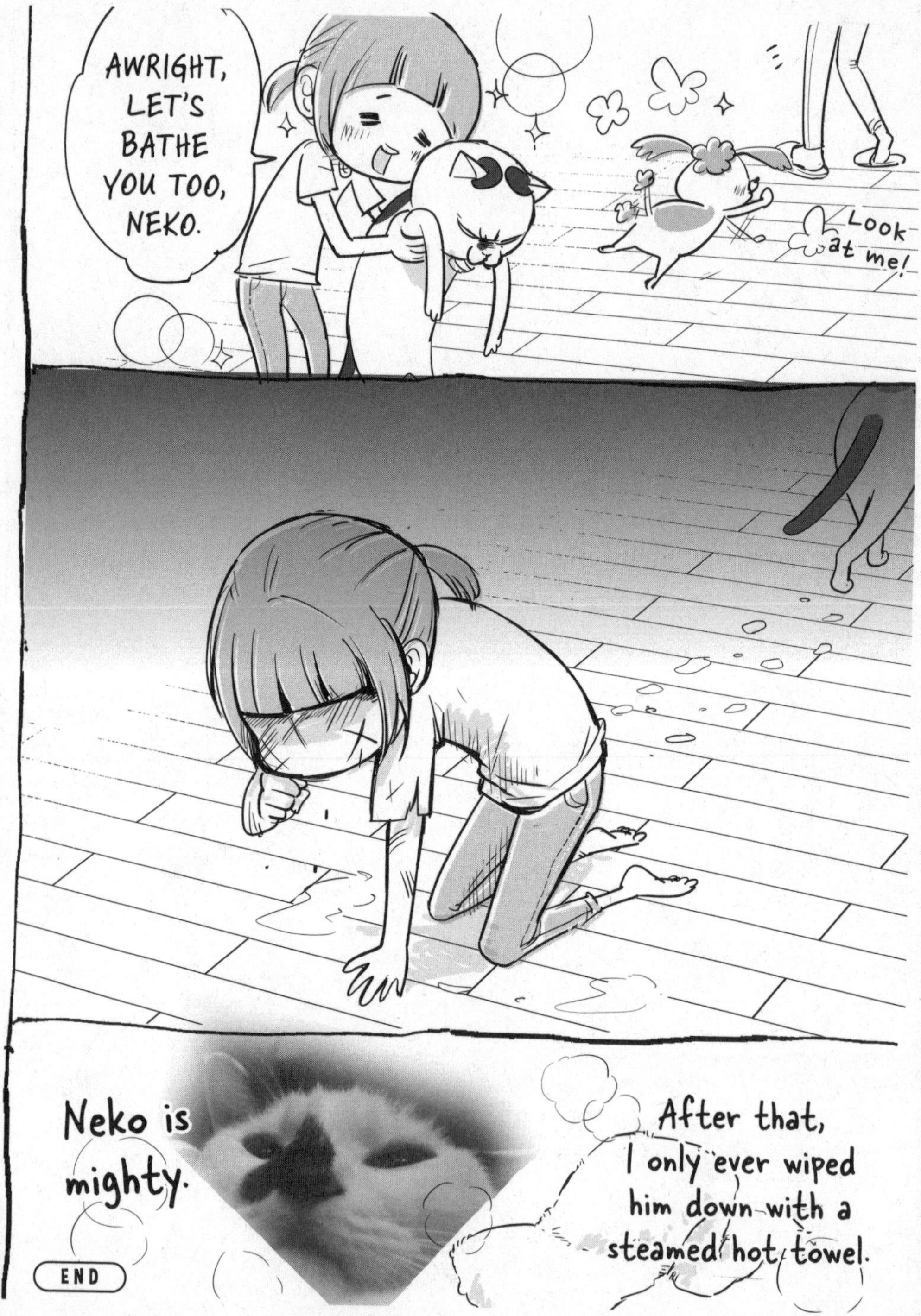
AWRIGHT, LET'S BATHE YOU TOO, NEKO.
Look at me!
After that, I only ever wiped him down with a steamed hot towel.
Neko is mighty.
END

#27

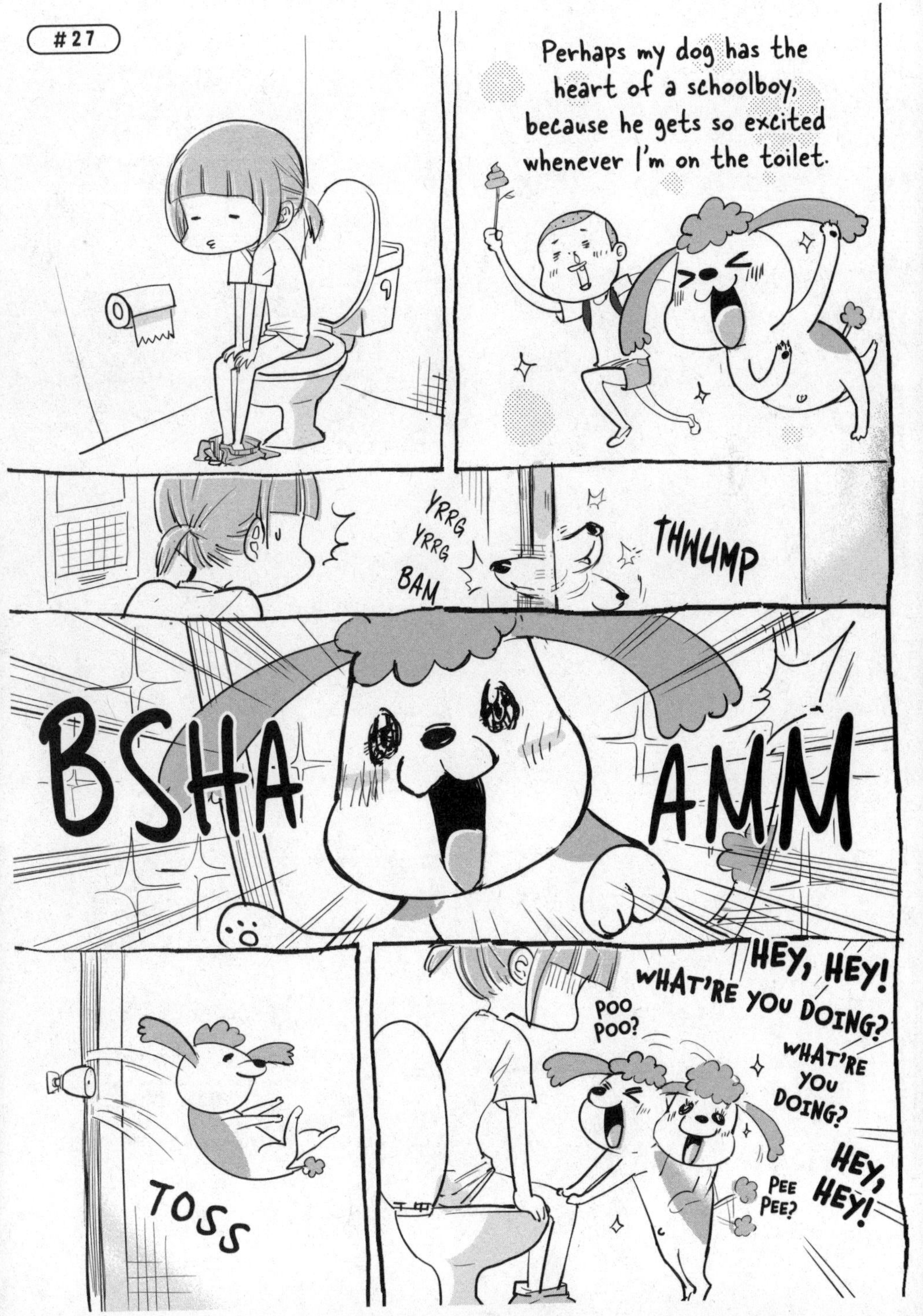

Perhaps my dog has the heart of a schoolboy, because he gets so excited whenever I'm on the toilet.
YRRG
YRRG
BAM
THWUMP
BSHAAMM
HEY, HEY!
WHAT'RE YOU DOING?
POO POO?
WHAT'RE YOU DOING?
HEY, HEY!
PEE PEE?
TOSS

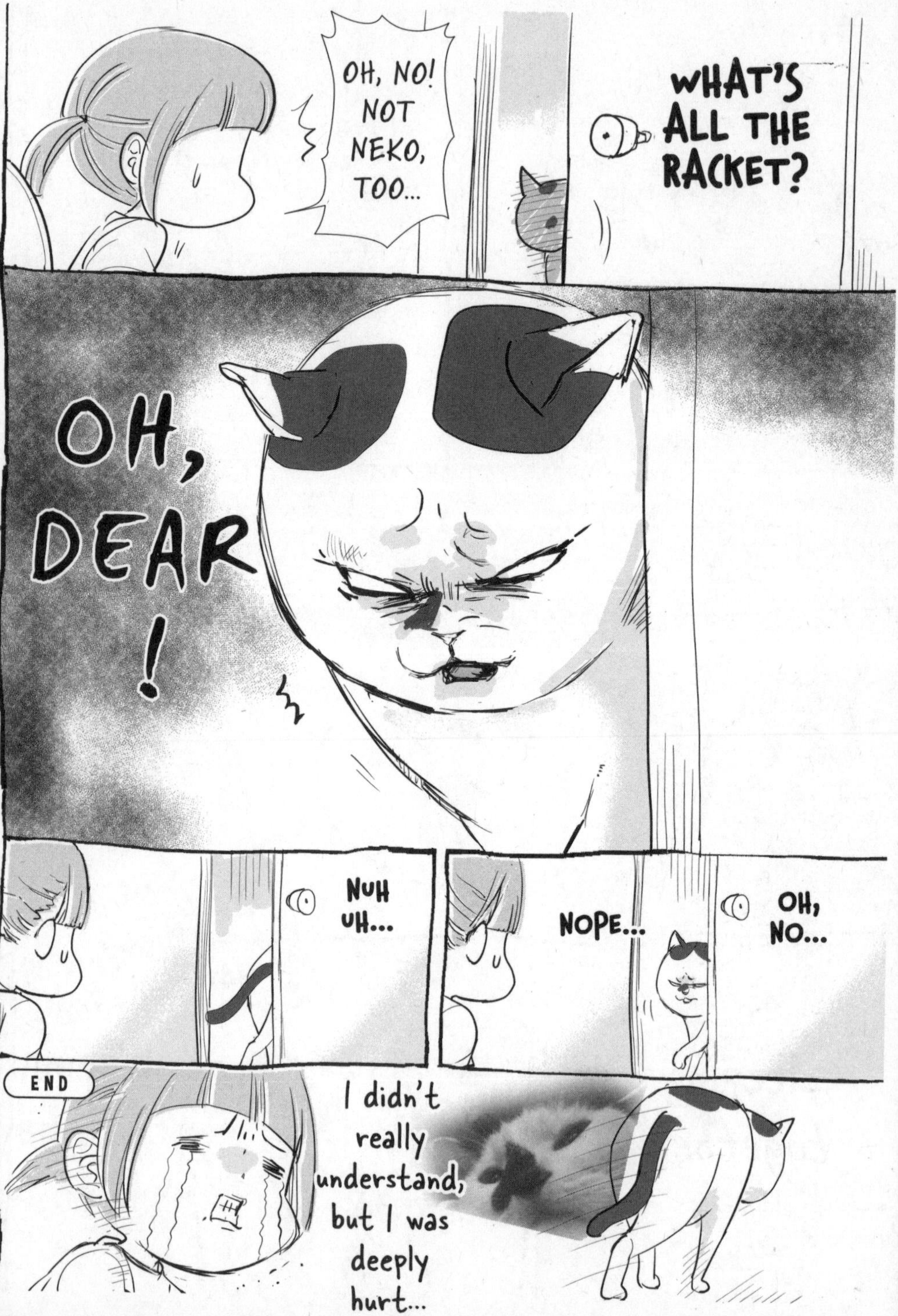
WHAT'S ALL THE RACKET?
OH, NO! NOT NEKO, TOO...
OH, DEAR!
OH, NO...
NOPE...
NUH UH...
I didn't really understand, but I was deeply hurt...
END

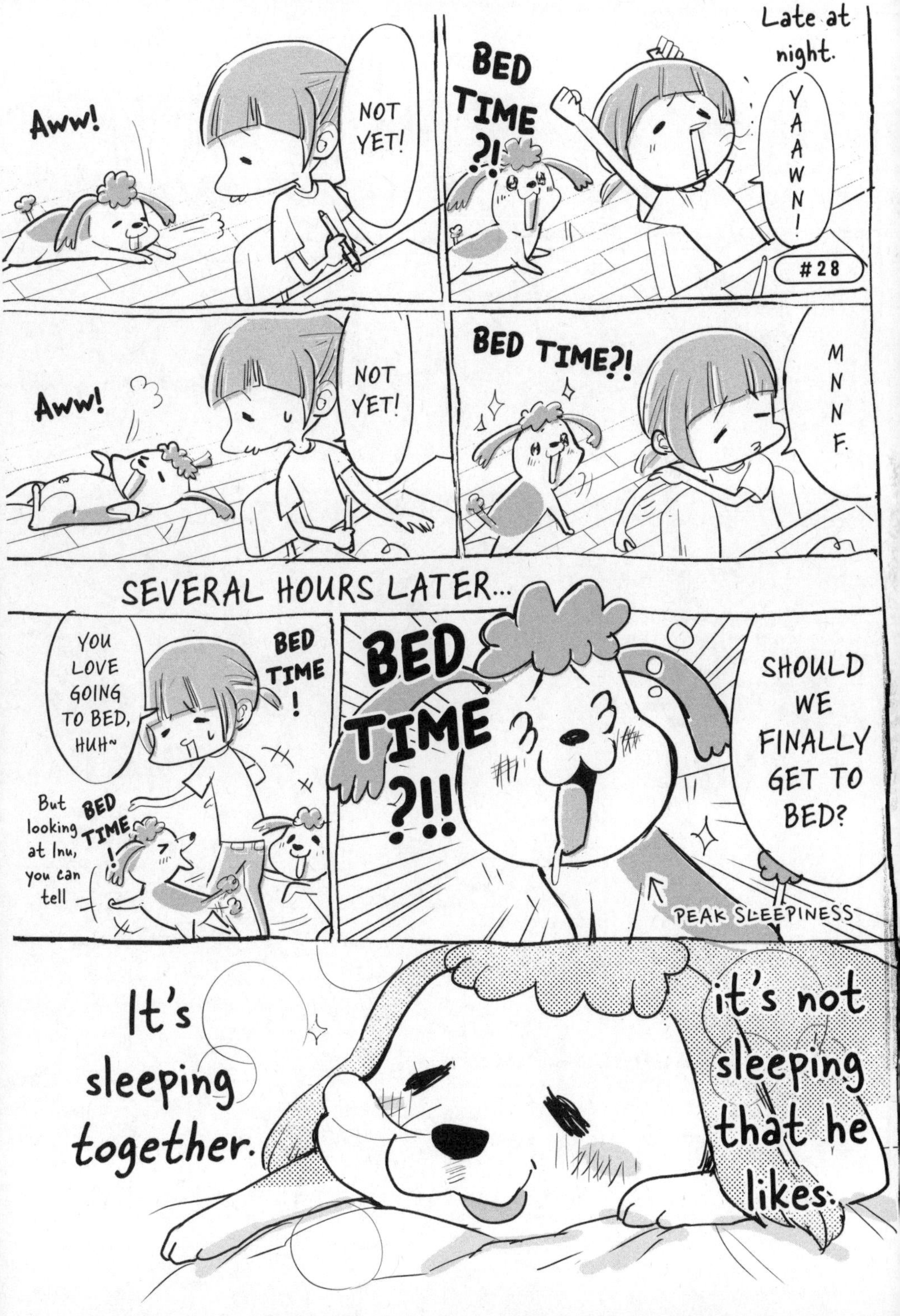
Late at night.
YAAWN!
#28
BED TIME?!
NOT YET!
Aww!
MNNF.
BED TIME?!
NOT YET!
Aww!
SEVERAL HOURS LATER...
SHOULD WE FINALLY GET TO BED?
BED TIME?!!
PEAK SLEEPINESS
BED TIME!
YOU LOVE GOING TO BED, HUH~
But looking at Inu, you can tell
BED TIME!
it's not sleeping that he likes.
It's sleeping together.

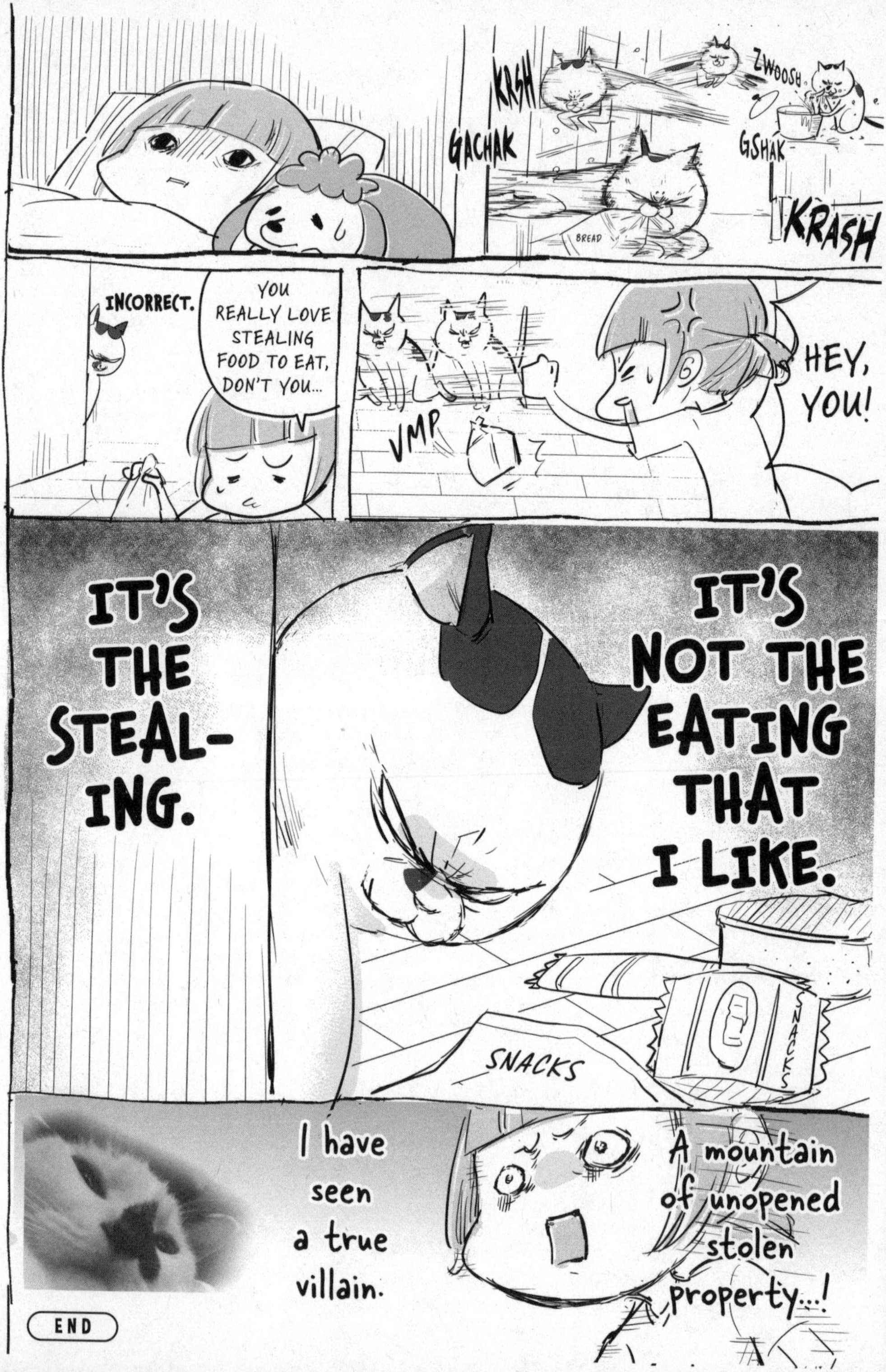
ZWOOSH
KRSH
GACHAK
GSHAK
KRASH
BREAD
HEY, YOU!
VMP
YOU REALLY LOVE STEALING FOOD TO EAT, DON'T YOU...
INCORRECT.
IT'S NOT THE EATING THAT I LIKE.
IT'S THE STEALING.
SNACKS
SNACKS
A mountain of unopened stolen property...!
I have seen a true villain.
END

I thought this photo was cute and showed it to
my assistant, and it scared the wits out of her.

Newly-Drawn 4-Panel Strip

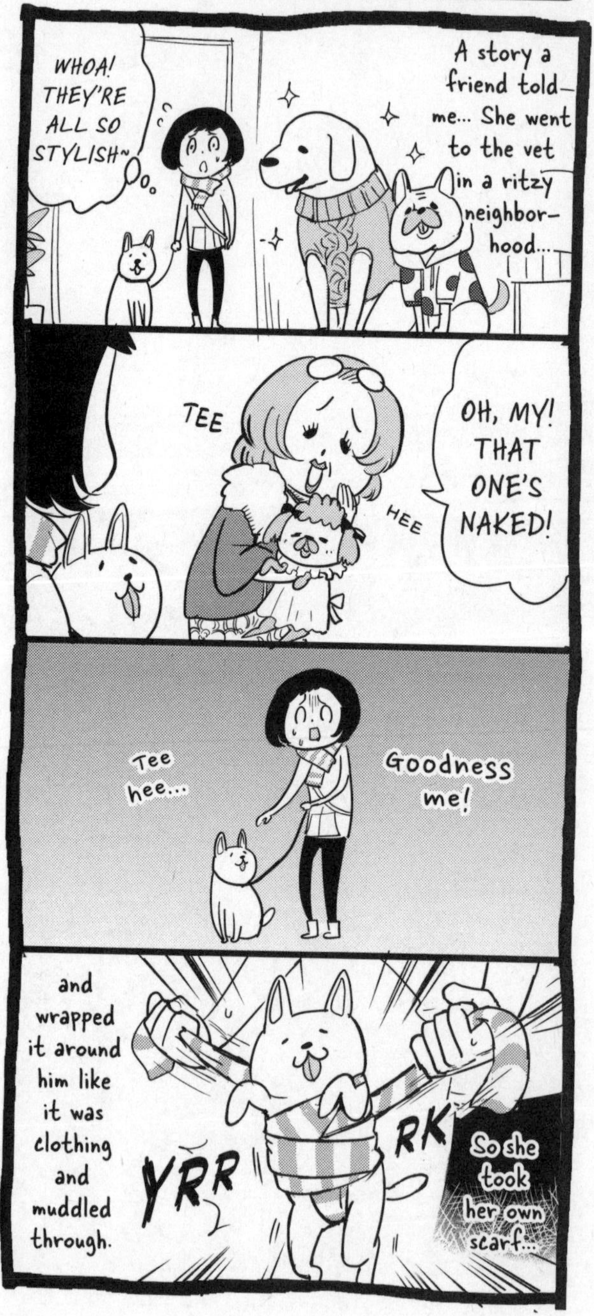
A story a friend told— me... She went to the vet in a ritzy neighbor-hood...
WHOA! THEY'RE ALL SO STYLISH~
OH, MY! THAT ONE'S NAKED!
TEE
HEE
Goodness me!
Tee hee...
So she took her own scarf...
RK
YRR
and wrapped it around him like it was clothing and muddled through.

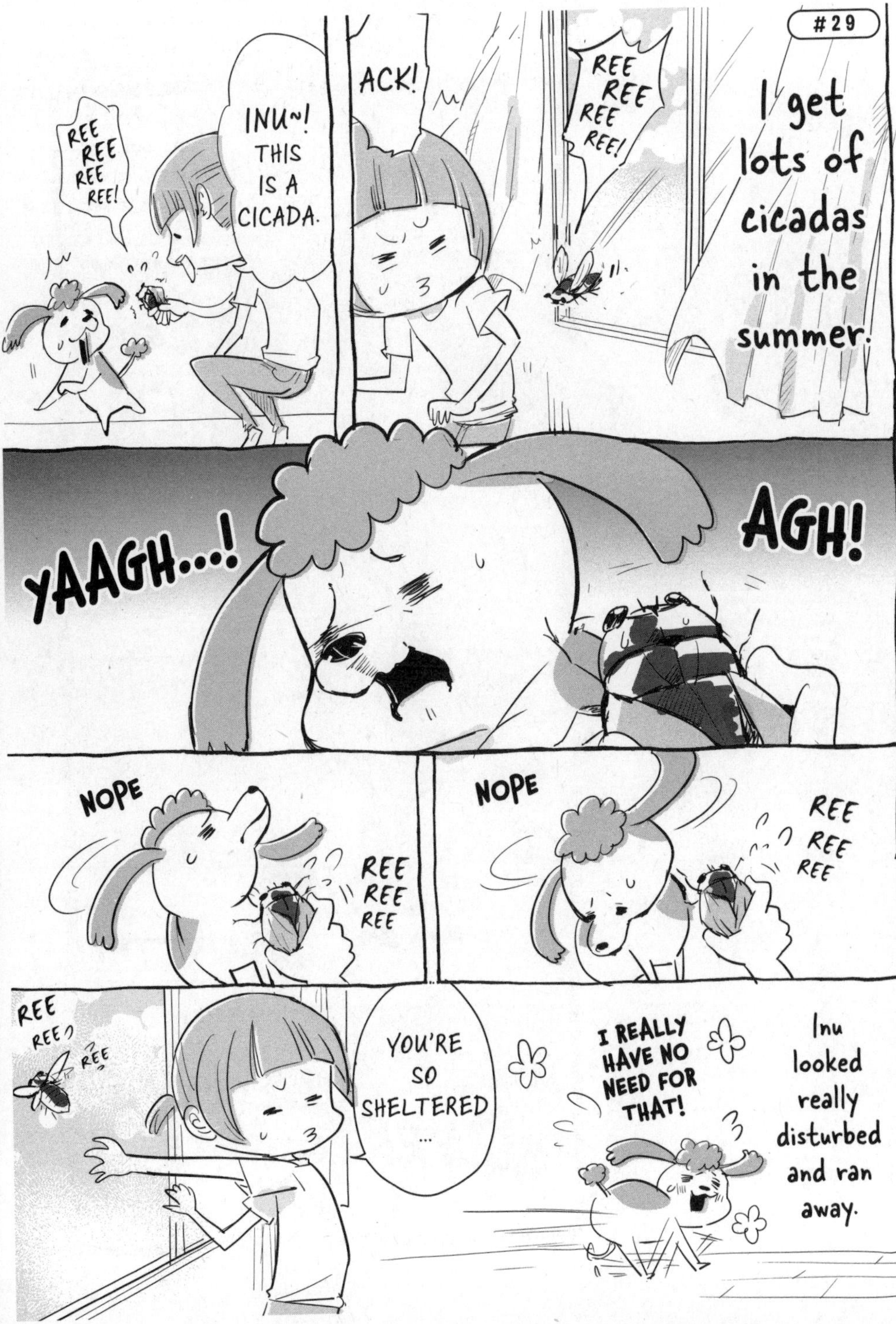
#29
I get lots of cicadas in the summer.
REE REE REE REE!
ACK!
INU~! THIS IS A CICADA.
REE REE REE REE!
AGH!
YAAGH...!
NOPE
REE REE REE
NOPE
REE REE REE
Inu looked really disturbed and ran away.
I REALLY HAVE NO NEED FOR THAT!
YOU'RE SO SHELTERED ...
REE REE REE

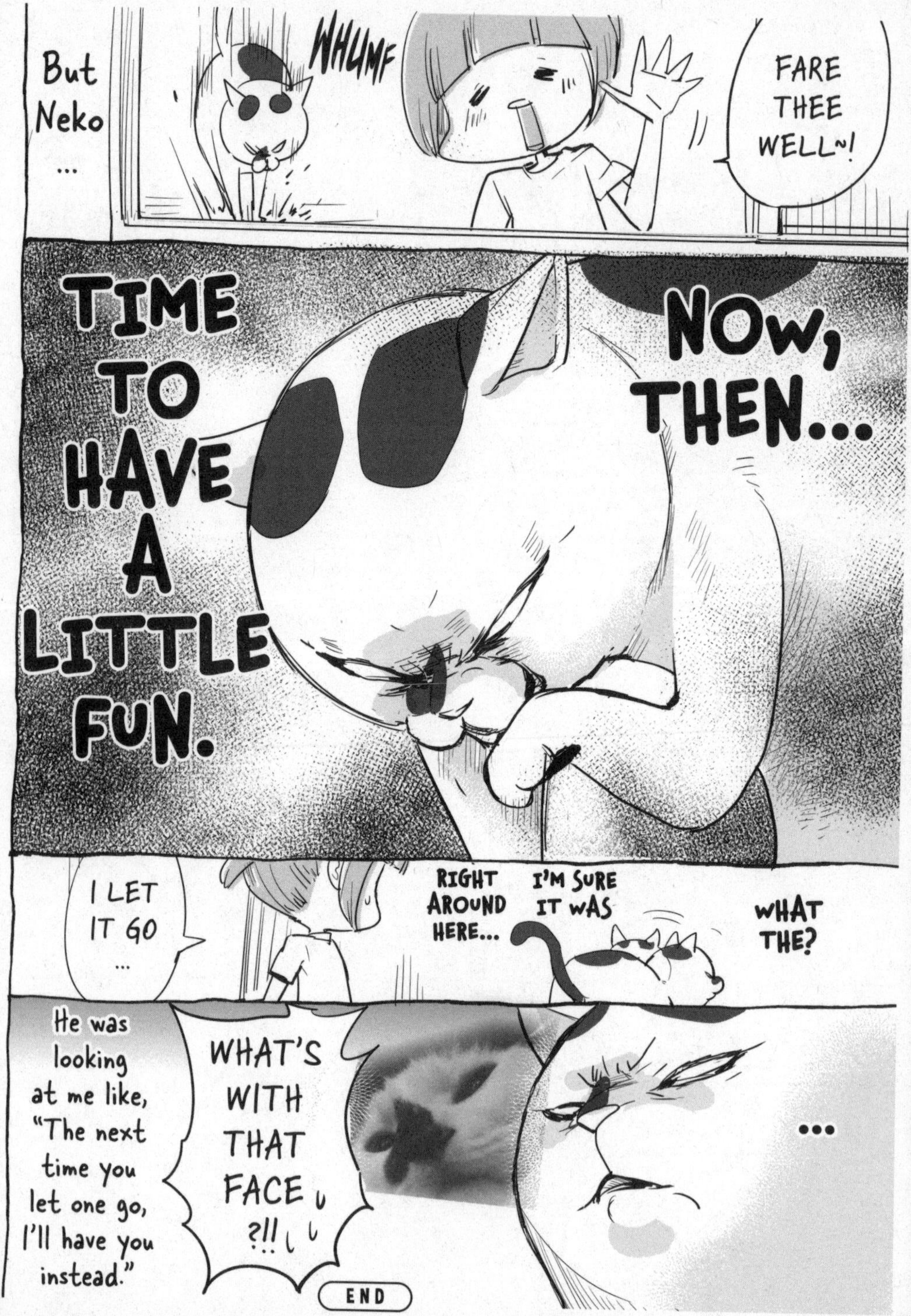
FARE THEE WELL~!
WHUMF
But Neko ...
NOW, THEN...
TIME TO HAVE A LITTLE FUN.
WHAT THE?
I'M SURE IT WAS
RIGHT AROUND HERE...
I LET IT GO ...
...
WHAT'S WITH THAT FACE ?!!
He was looking at me like, "The next time you let one go, I'll have you instead."
END

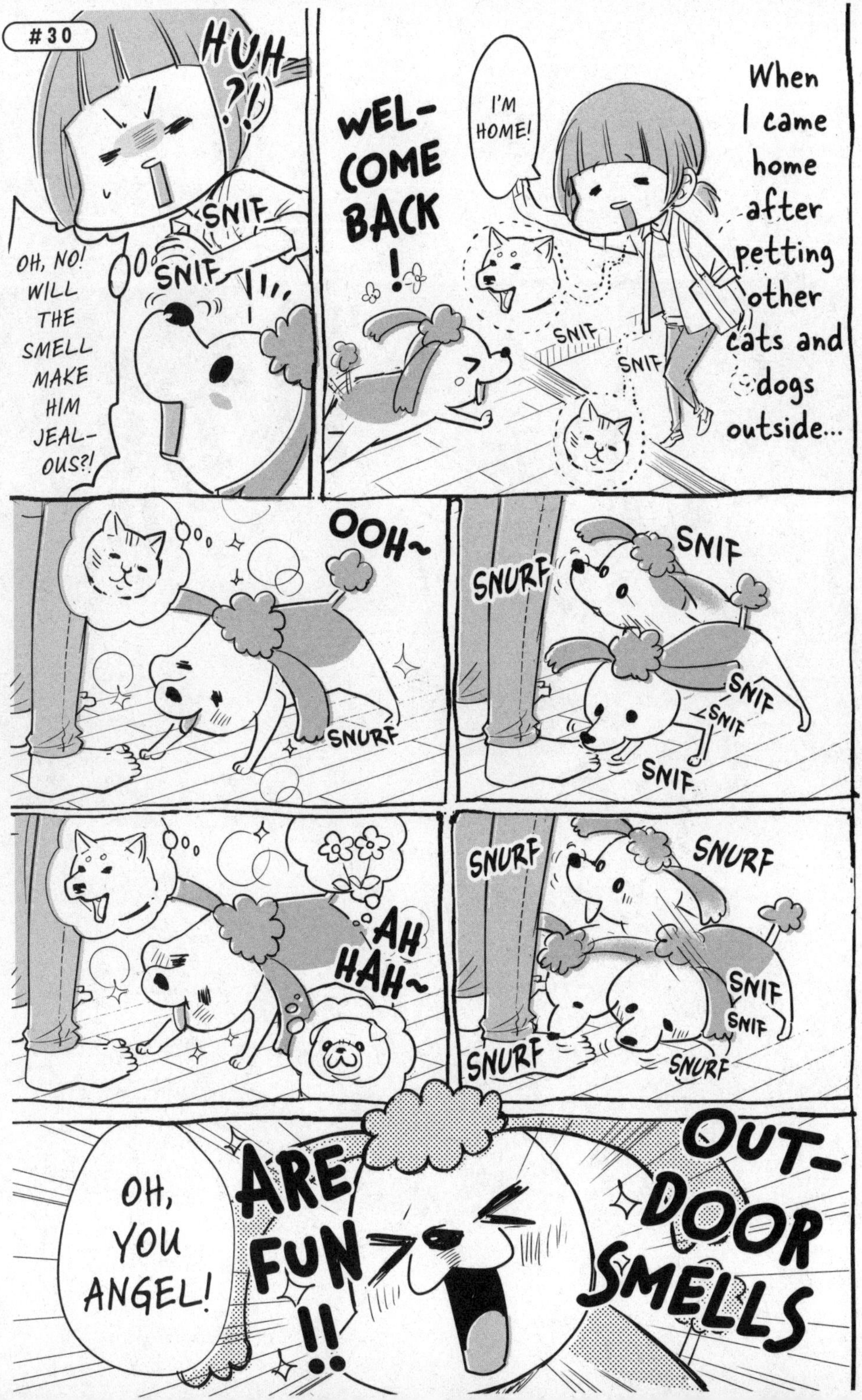

#30
When I came home after petting other cats and dogs outside...
I'M HOME!
WEL-COME BACK!
SNIF
SNIF
HUH?!
SNIF
SNIF
OH, NO! WILL THE SMELL MAKE HIM JEAL-OUS?!
SNIF
SNURF
SNIF
SNIF
SNIF
OOH~
SNURF
SNURF
SNURF
SNIF
SNIF
SNURF
SNURF
AH HAH~
OUT-DOOR SMELLS
ARE FUN!!
OH, YOU ANGEL!

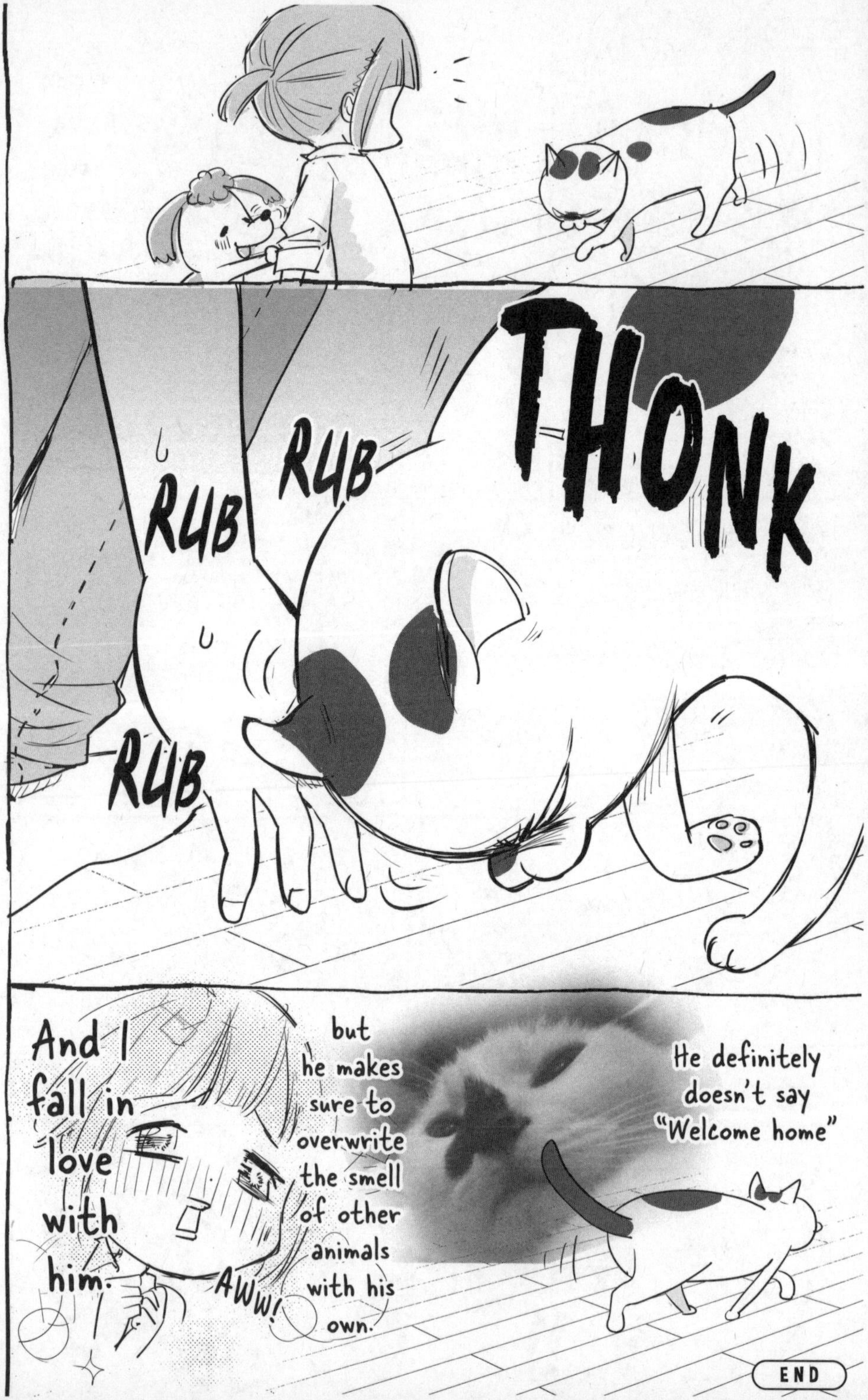
THONK
RUB
RUB
RUB
He definitely doesn't say "Welcome home"
but he makes sure to overwrite the smell of other animals with his own.
AWW!
And I fall in love with him.
END

#31

When it comes to ranking dog and cat masters
my mom is number one around here.
No. 1
Even if I'm playing with Inu...
Tra la la!
INU!
MOM
ZWOOM
It vexes me, so...
I-I'M IN AGONY ...!
WHEEZE
I CAN'T GO ON~! INU, SAVE ME!
WHEEZE
WHEEZE
Huh...?
Umm...
INU!
MOM

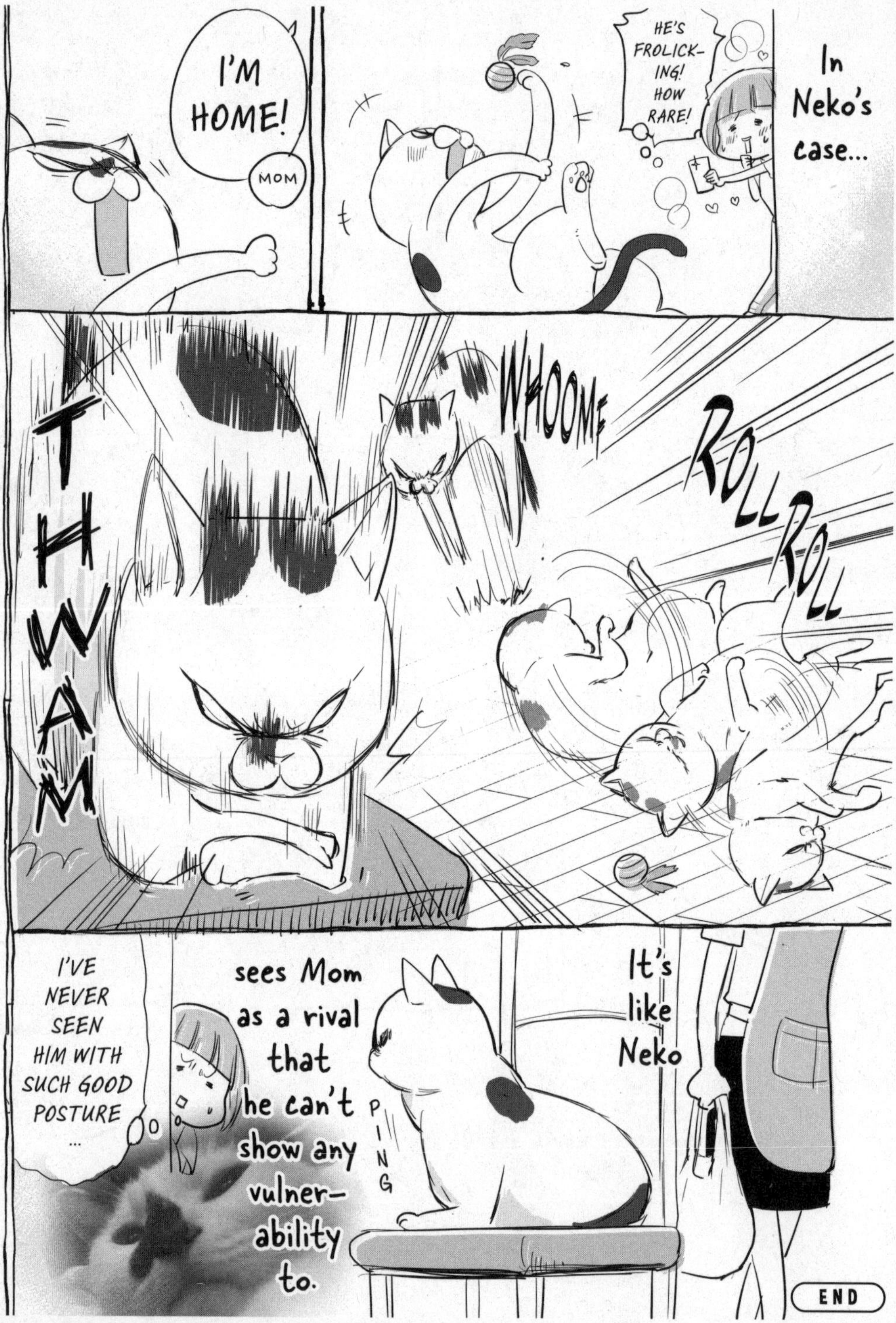
In Neko's case...
HE'S FROLICK-ING! HOW RARE!
I'M HOME!
MOM
WHOOMF
ROLLROLL
THWAM
It's like Neko
sees Mom as a rival that he can't show any vulner-ability to.
PING
I'VE NEVER SEEN HIM WITH SUCH GOOD POSTURE ...
END

The fiercely insistent Inu.

Newly-Drawn 4-Panel Strip

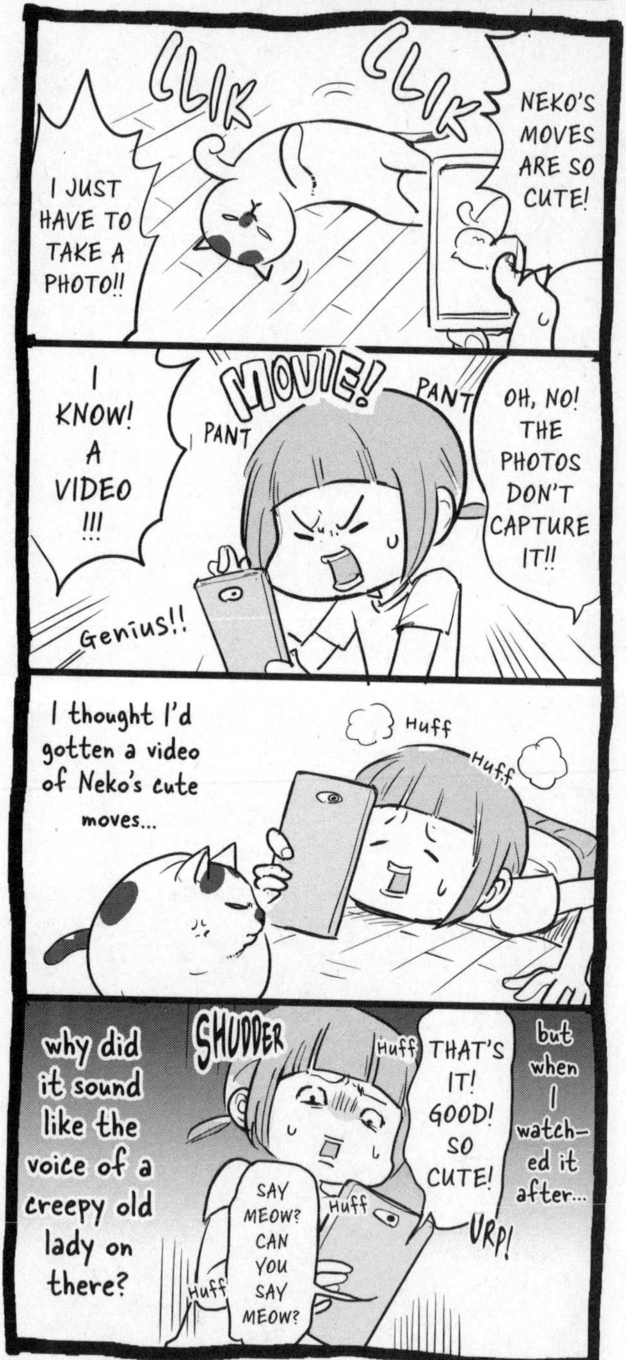

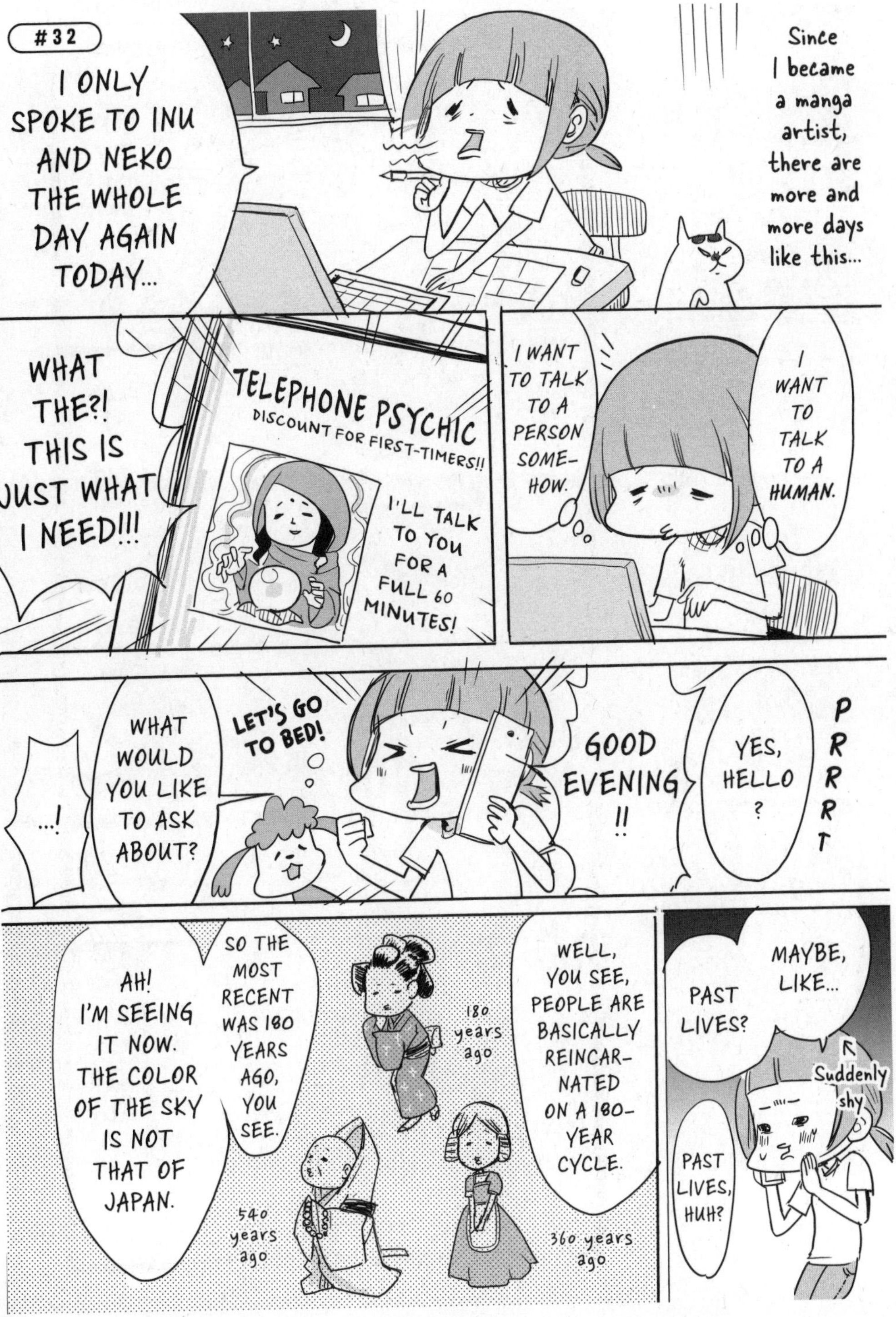
#32
Since I became a manga artist, there are more and more days like this...
I ONLY SPOKE TO INU AND NEKO THE WHOLE DAY AGAIN TODAY...
I WANT TO TALK TO A HUMAN.
I WANT TO TALK TO A PERSON SOMEHOW.
TELEPHONE PSYCHIC
DISCOUNT FOR FIRST-TIMERS!!
I'LL TALK TO YOU FOR A FULL 60 MINUTES!
WHAT THE?! THIS IS JUST WHAT I NEED!!!
PRRRT
YES, HELLO?
GOOD EVENING!!
LET'S GO TO BED!
WHAT WOULD YOU LIKE TO ASK ABOUT?
...!
MAYBE, LIKE...
PAST LIVES?
Suddenly shy
PAST LIVES, HUH?
WELL, YOU SEE, PEOPLE ARE BASICALLY REINCARNATED ON A 180-YEAR CYCLE.
180 years ago
SO THE MOST RECENT WAS 180 YEARS AGO, YOU SEE.
360 years ago
540 years ago
AH! I'M SEEING IT NOW. THE COLOR OF THE SKY IS NOT THAT OF JAPAN.

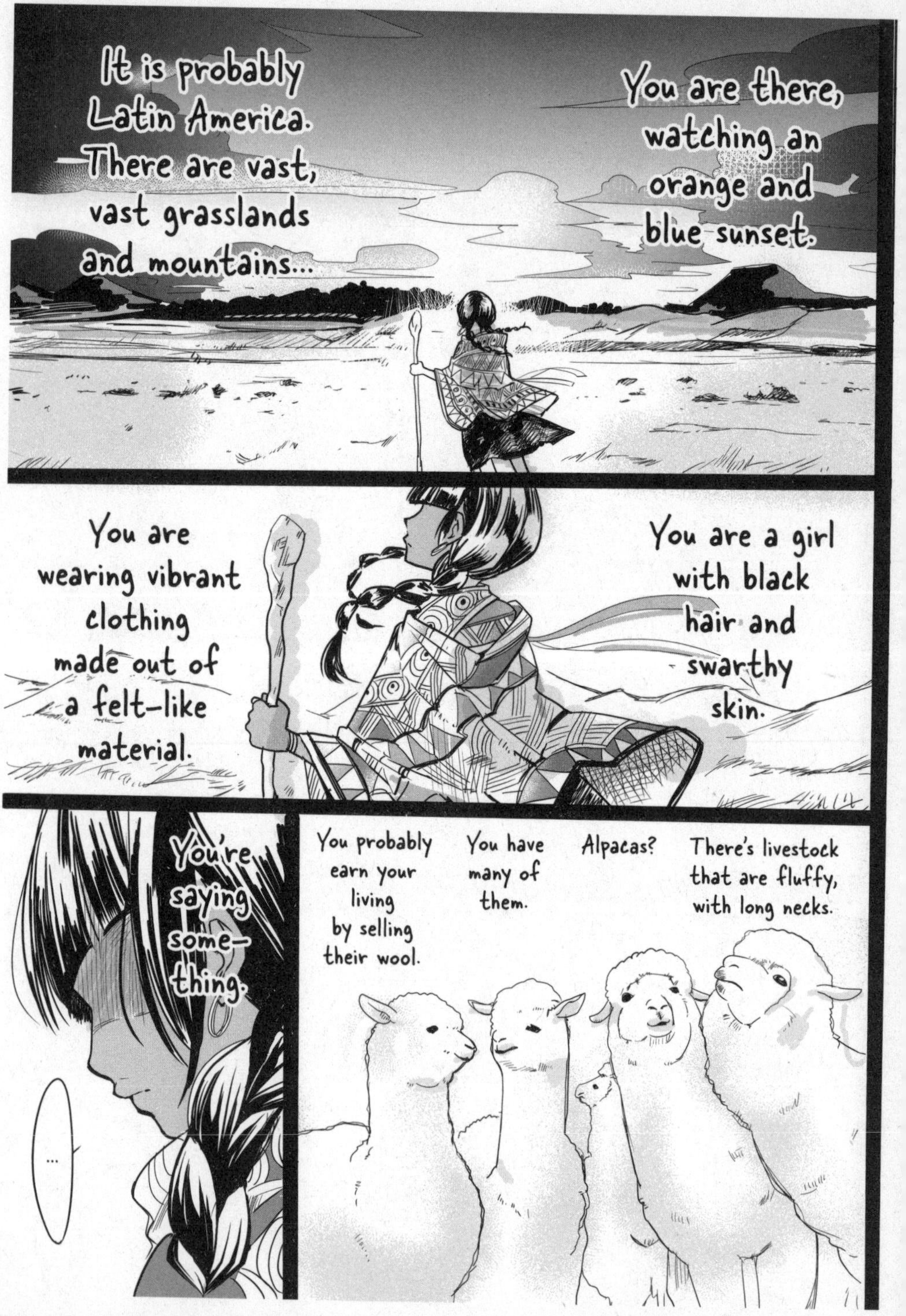
You are there, watching an orange and blue sunset.
It is probably Latin America. There are vast, vast grasslands and mountains...
You are a girl with black hair and swarthy skin.
You are wearing vibrant clothing made out of a felt-like material.
There's livestock that are fluffy, with long necks.
Alpacas?
You have many of them.
You probably earn your living by selling their wool.
You're saying some-thing.
...

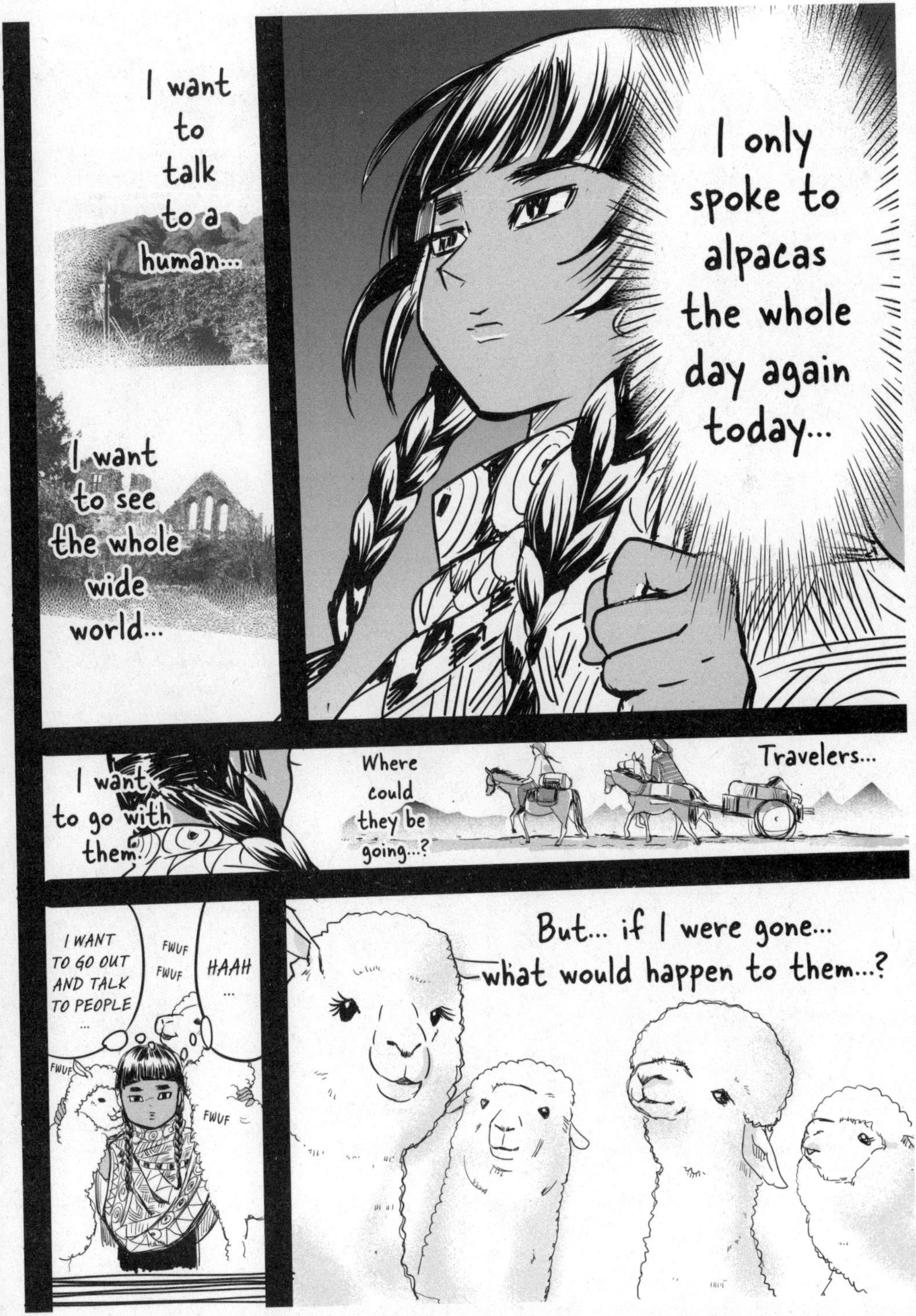
I only spoke to alpacas the whole day again today...
I want to talk to a human...
I want to see the whole wide world...
Travelers...
Where could they be going...?
I want to go with them.
But... if I were gone... what would happen to them...?
HAAH ...
FWUF FWUF
I WANT TO GO OUT AND TALK TO PEOPLE ...
FWUF
FWUF

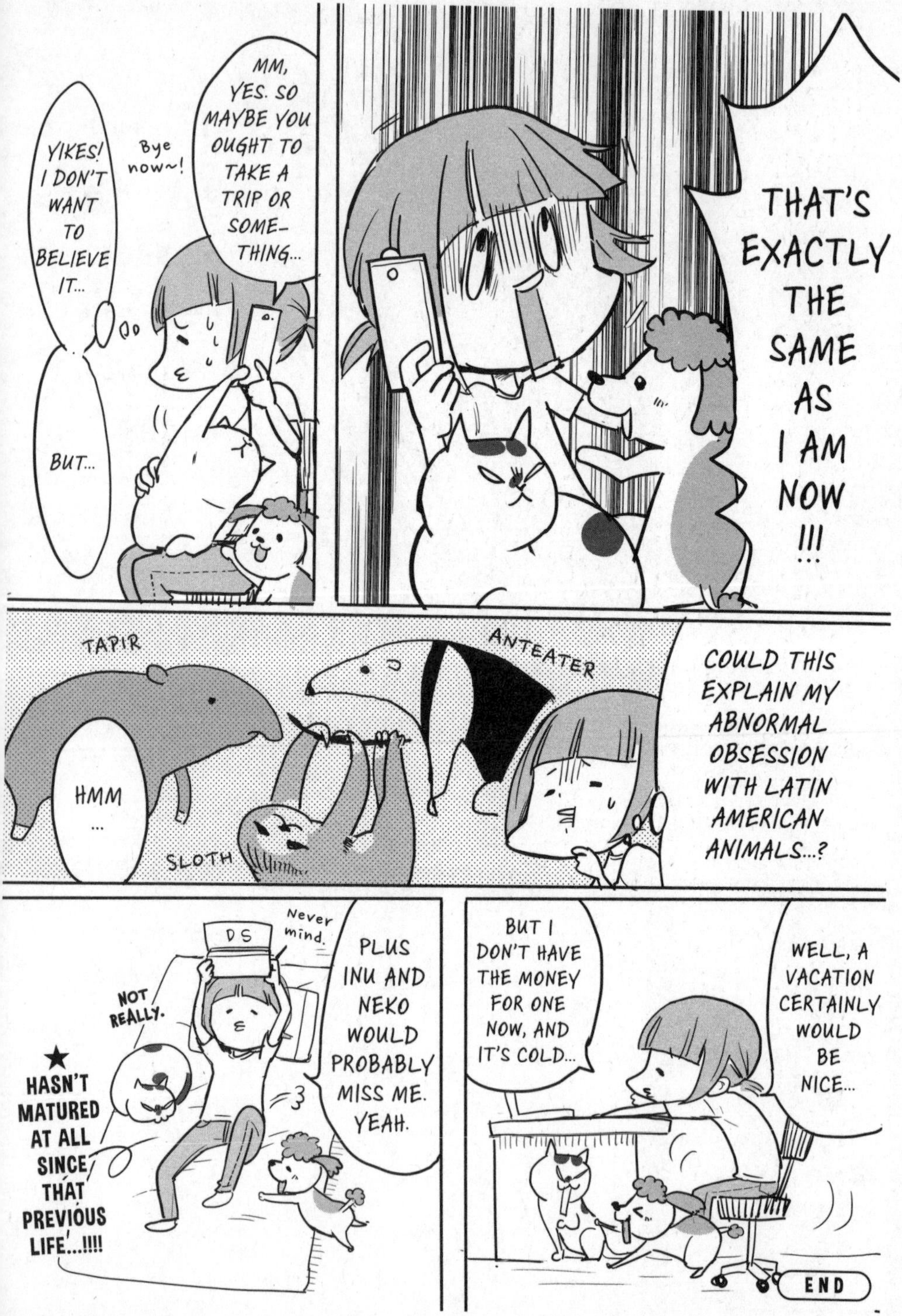
THAT'S EXACTLY THE SAME AS I AM NOW !!!...
MM, YES. SO MAYBE YOU OUGHT TO TAKE A TRIP OR SOME-THING...
Bye now~!
YIKES! I DON'T WANT TO BELIEVE IT...
BUT...
COULD THIS EXPLAIN MY ABNORMAL OBSESSION WITH LATIN AMERICAN ANIMALS...?
ANTEATER
TAPIR
HMM ...
SLOTH
WELL, A VACATION CERTAINLY WOULD BE NICE...
BUT I DON'T HAVE THE MONEY FOR ONE NOW, AND IT'S COLD...
Never mind.
PLUS INU AND NEKO WOULD PROBABLY MISS ME. YEAH.
DS
NOT REALLY.
★ HASN'T MATURED AT ALL SINCE THAT PREVIOUS LIFE...!!!!
END

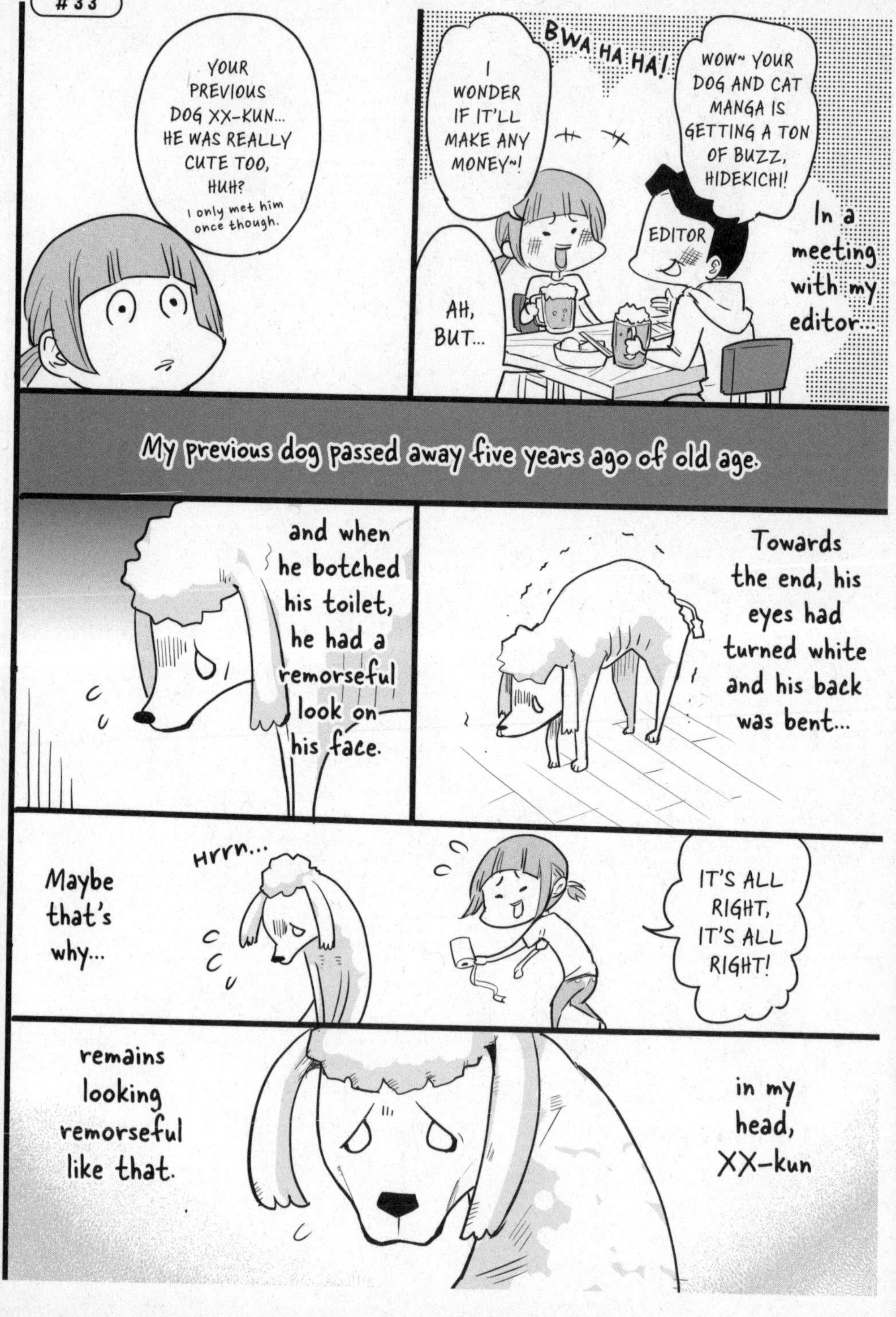
In a meeting with my editor...
WOW~ YOUR DOG AND CAT MANGA IS GETTING A TON OF BUZZ, HIDEKICHI!
BWA HA HA!
I WONDER IF IT'LL MAKE ANY MONEY~!
EDITOR
AH, BUT...
YOUR PREVIOUS DOG XX-KUN... HE WAS REALLY CUTE TOO, HUH?
I only met him once though.
My previous dog passed away five years ago of old age.
Towards the end, his eyes had turned white and his back was bent...
and when he botched his toilet, he had a remorseful look on his face.
IT'S ALL RIGHT, IT'S ALL RIGHT!
Hrrn...
Maybe that's why...
in my head, XX-kun
remains looking remorseful like that.

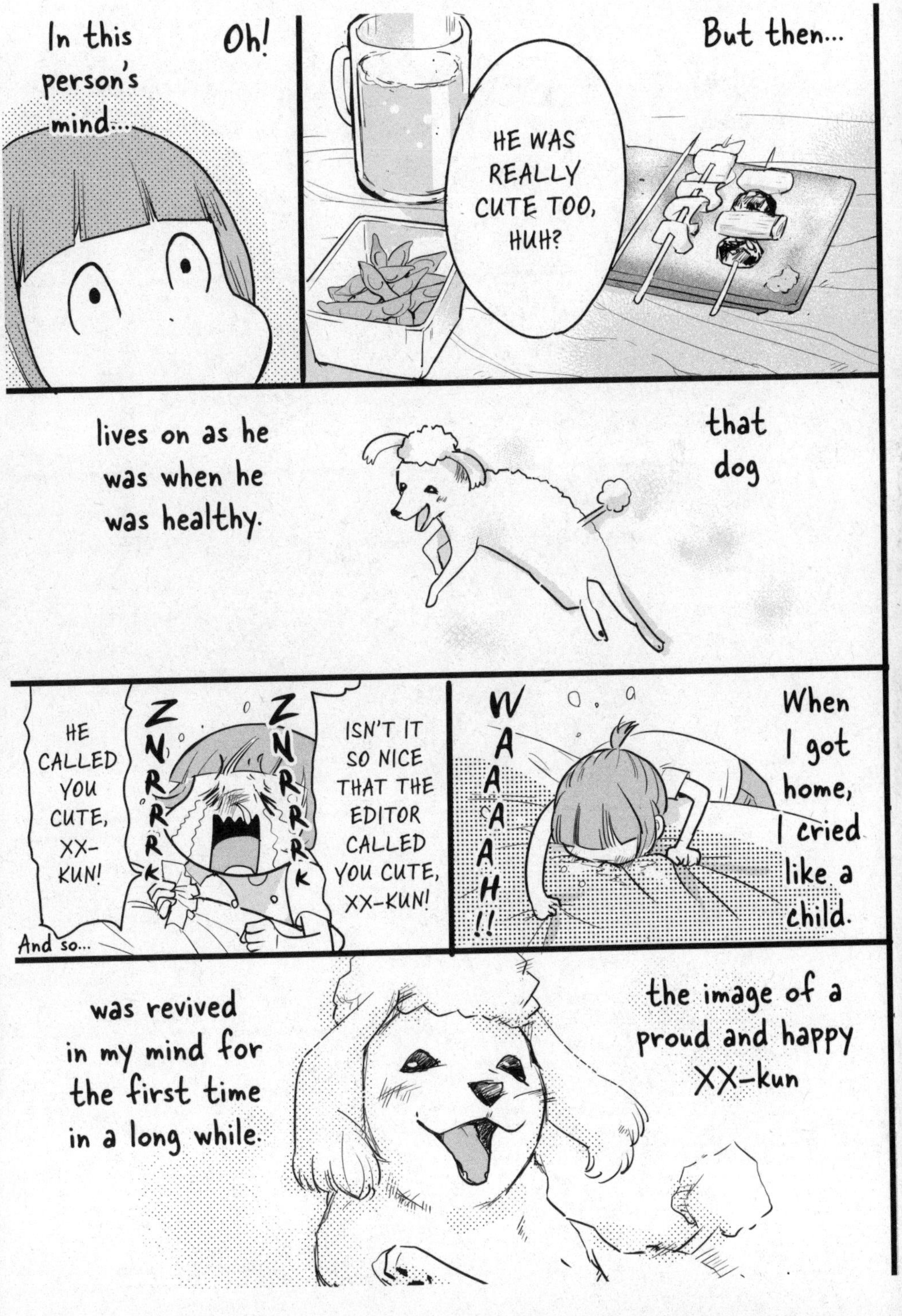
But then...
HE WAS REALLY CUTE TOO, HUH?
Oh!
In this person's mind...
that dog
lives on as he was when he was healthy.
When I got home, I cried like a child.
WAAAAAH!!
ISN'T IT SO NICE THAT THE EDITOR CALLED YOU CUTE, XX-KUN!
ZNRRRRK
HE CALLED YOU CUTE, XX-KUN!
ZNRRRRK
And so...
the image of a proud and happy XX-kun
was revived in my mind for the first time in a long while.

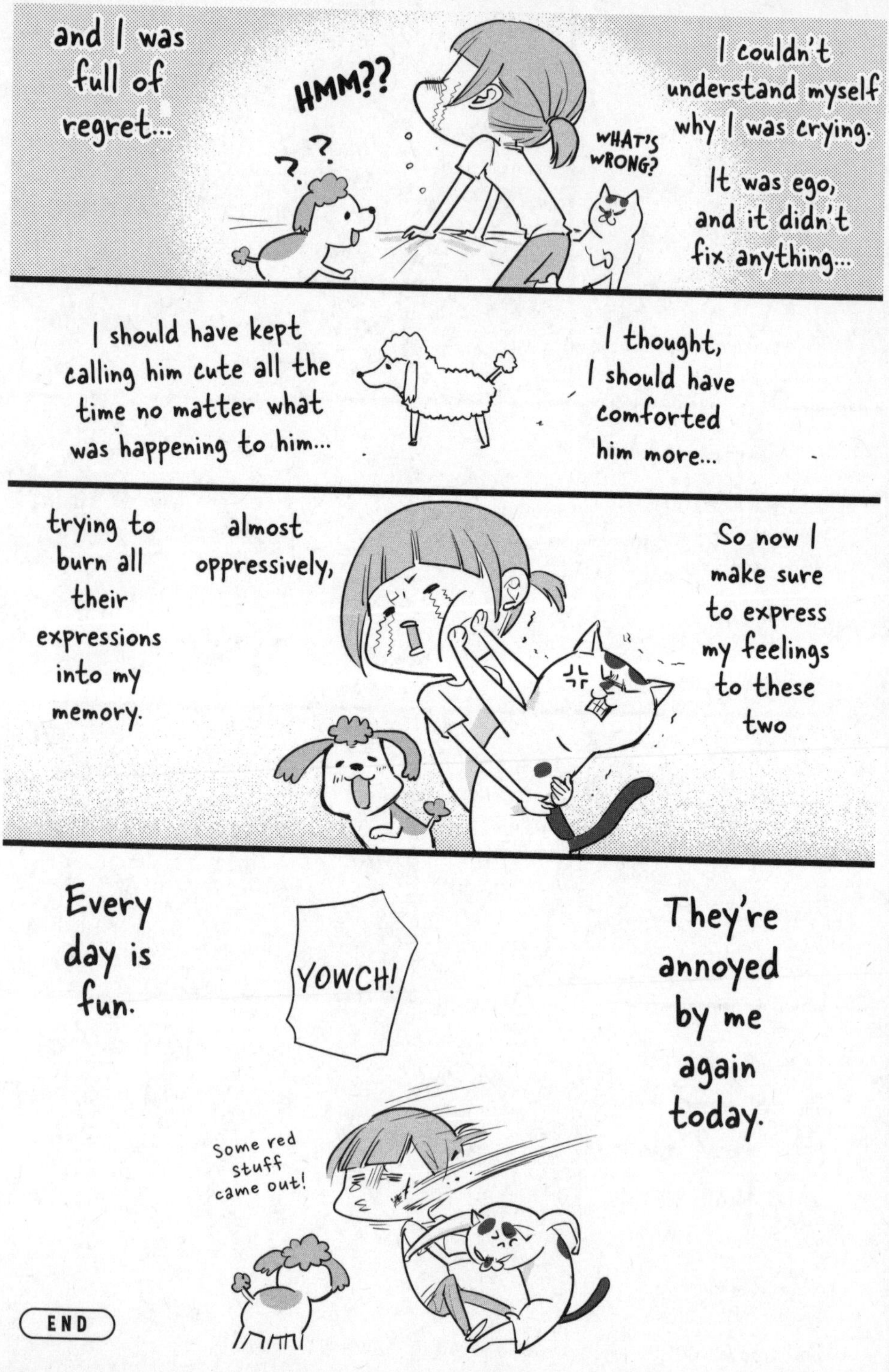
I couldn't understand myself why I was crying.
It was ego, and it didn't fix anything...
WHAT'S WRONG?
HMM??
? ?
and I was full of regret...
I thought, I should have comforted him more...
I should have kept calling him cute all the time no matter what was happening to him...
So now I make sure to express my feelings to these two
almost oppressively,
trying to burn all their expressions into my memory.
They're annoyed by me again today.
YOWCH!
Some red stuff came out!
Every day is fun.
END

Cat appearing to be in a state of enlightenment.

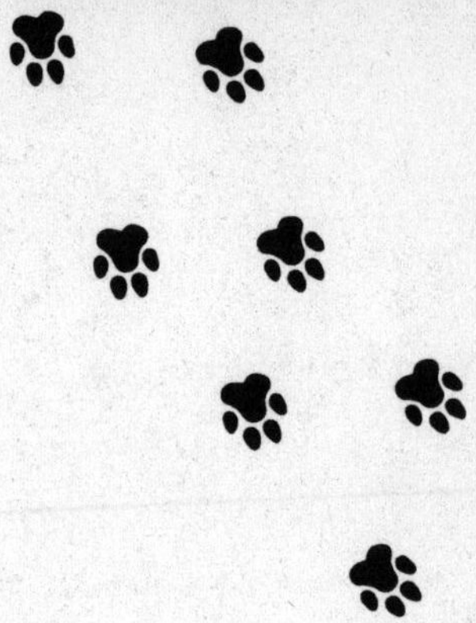

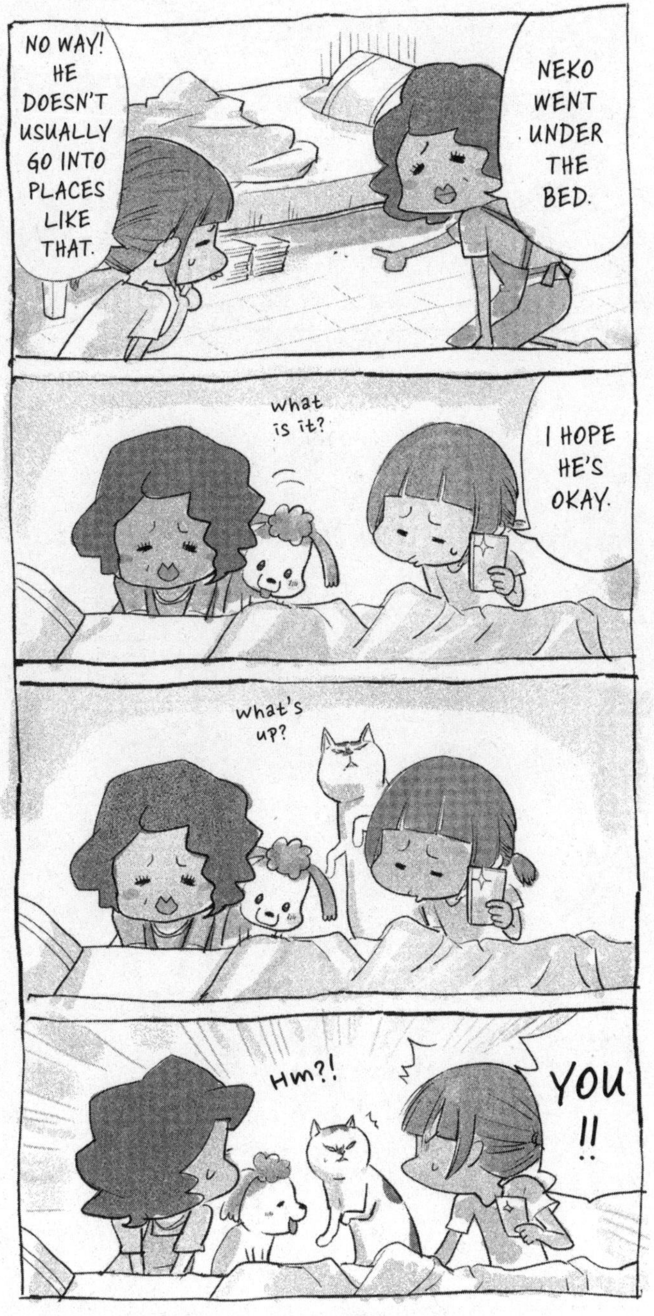
NEKO WENT UNDER THE BED.
NO WAY! HE DOESN'T USUALLY GO INTO PLACES LIKE THAT.
I HOPE HE'S OKAY.
what is it?
what's up?
YOU !!
Hm?!

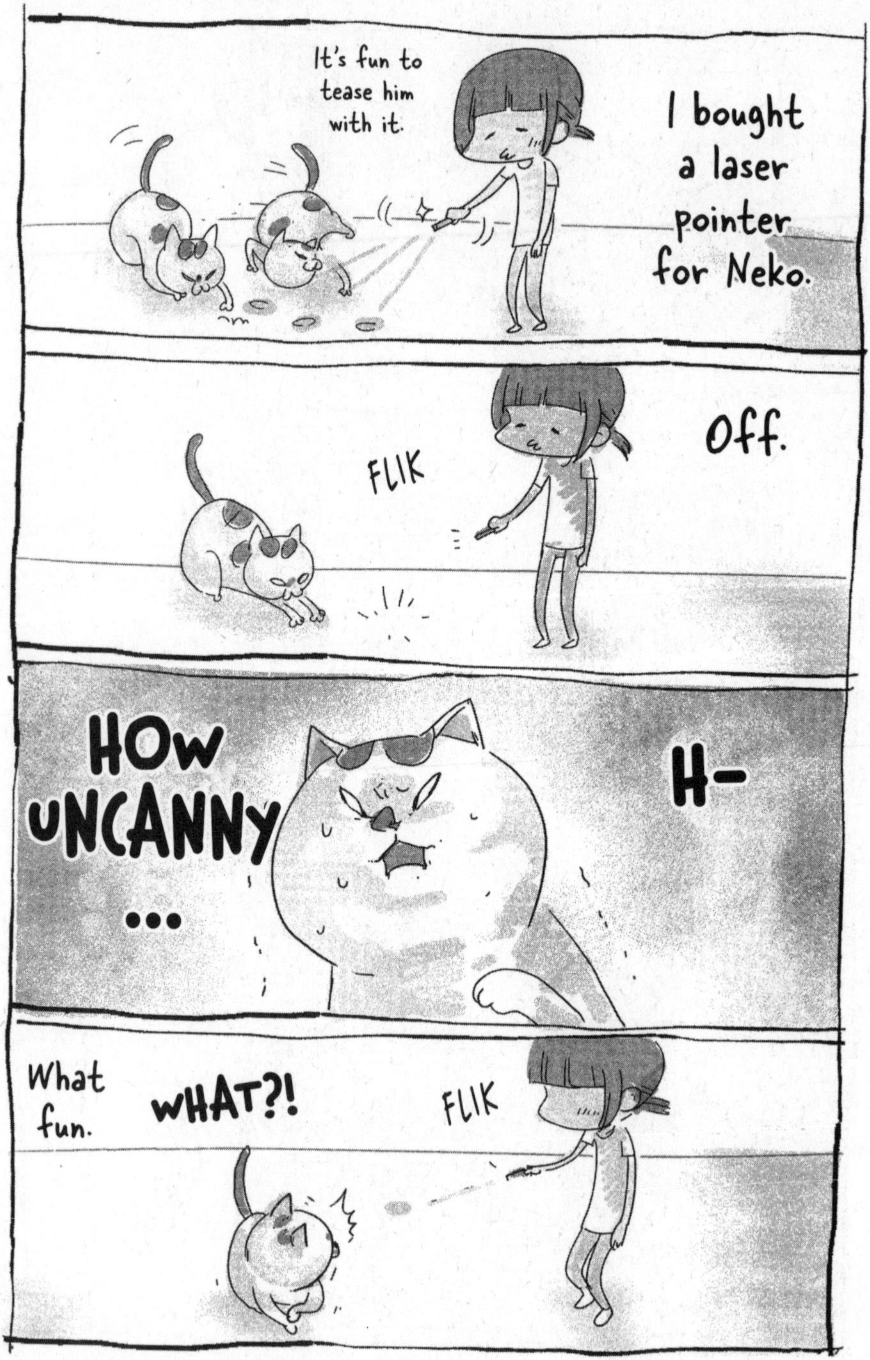
I bought a laser pointer for Neko.
It's fun to tease him with it.
Off.
FLIK
H-
HOW UNCANNY ...
FLIK
WHAT?!
What fun.

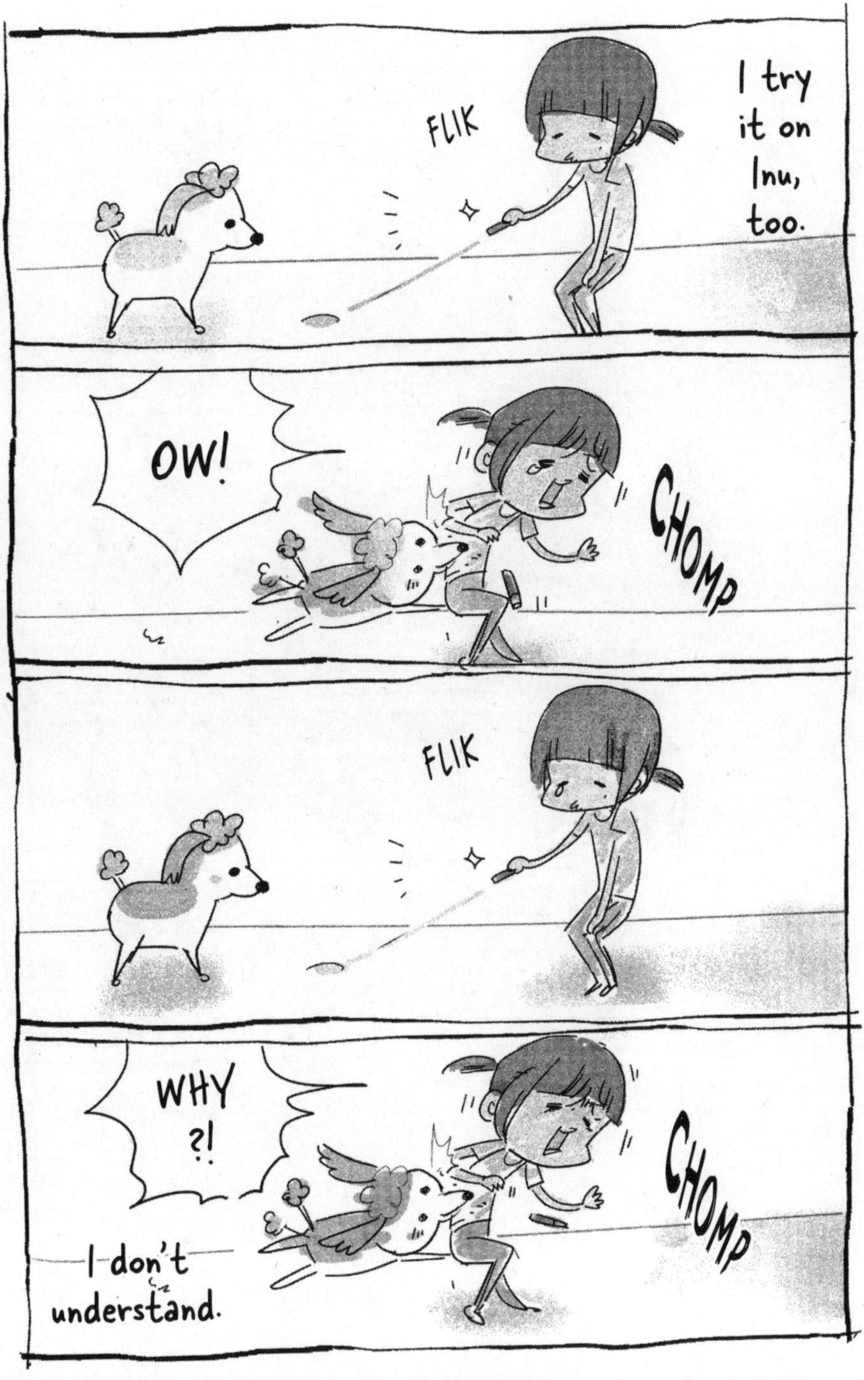
I try it on Inu, too.
FLIK
CHOMP
OW!
FLIK
CHOMP
WHY ?!
I don't understand.

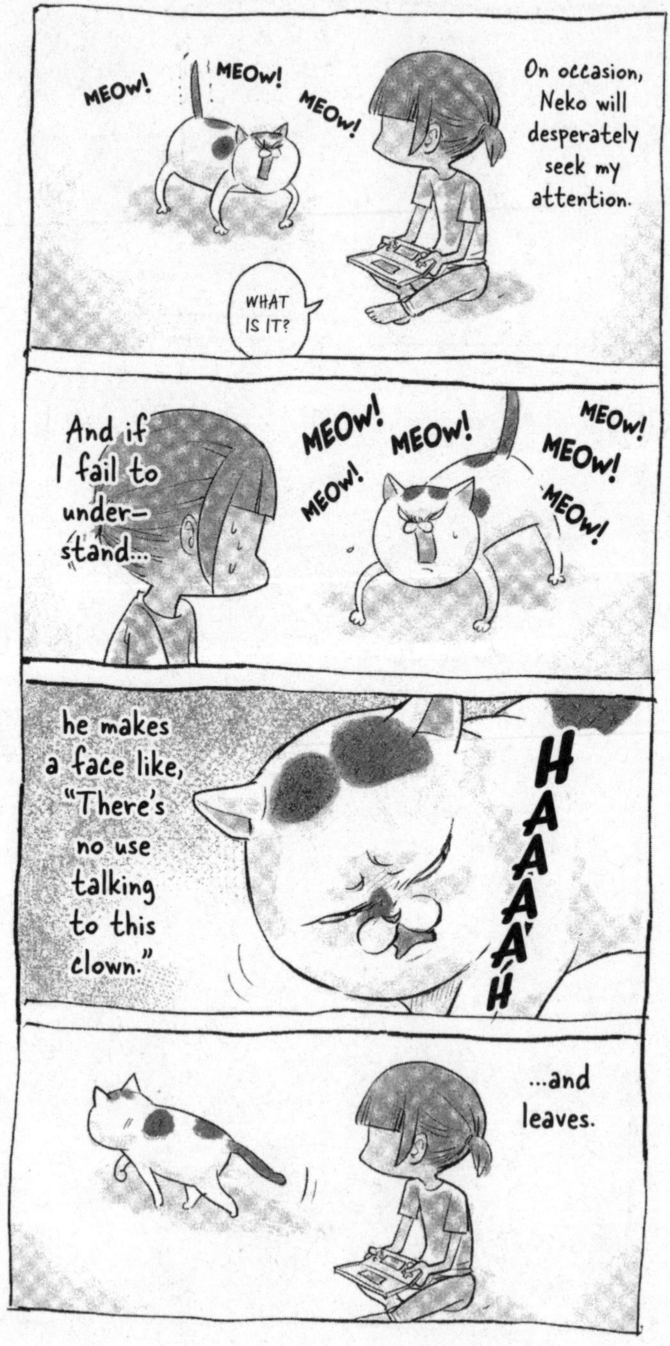
On occasion, Neko will desperately seek my attention.
MEOW!
MEOW!
MEOW!
WHAT IS IT?
MEOW!
MEOW!
MEOW!
MEOW!
MEOW!
MEOW!
And if I fail to under-stand...
HAAAAAH
he makes a face like, "There's no use talking to this clown."
...and leaves.

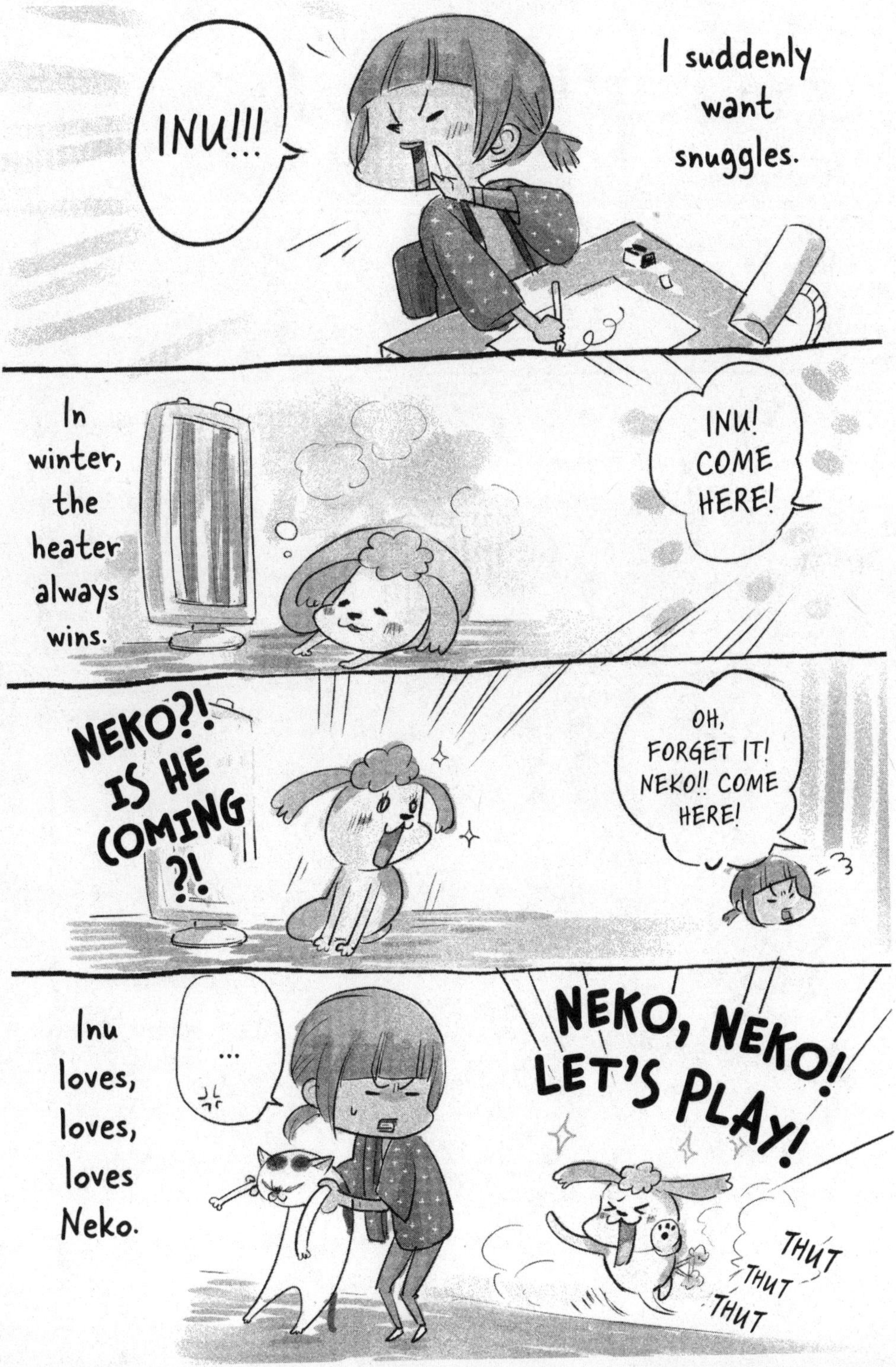
I suddenly want snuggles.
INU!!! ...
INU! COME HERE!
In winter, the heater always wins.
OH, FORGET IT! NEKO!! COME HERE!
NEKO?! IS HE COMING ?!
NEKO, NEKO! LET'S PLAY!
THUT THUT THUT
...
Inu loves, loves, loves Neko.

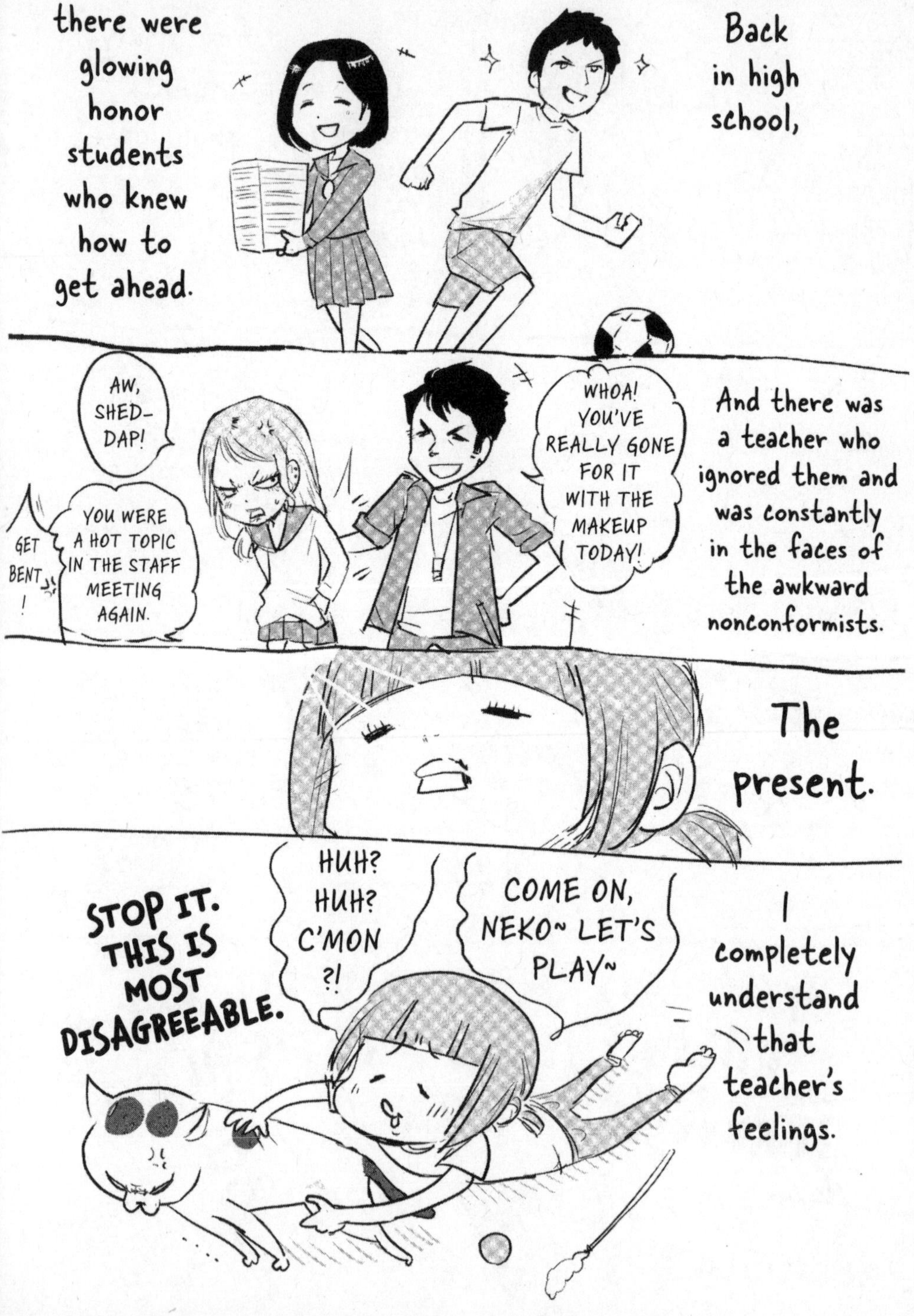

Back in high school,
there were glowing honor students who knew how to get ahead.
And there was a teacher who ignored them and was constantly in the faces of the awkward nonconformists.
WHOA! YOU'VE REALLY GONE FOR IT WITH THE MAKEUP TODAY!
AW, SHED-DAP!
YOU WERE A HOT TOPIC IN THE STAFF MEETING AGAIN.
GET BENT!
The present.
I completely understand that teacher's feelings.
COME ON, NEKO~ LET'S PLAY~
HUH? HUH? C'MON?!
STOP IT. THIS IS MOST DISAGREEABLE.

#34

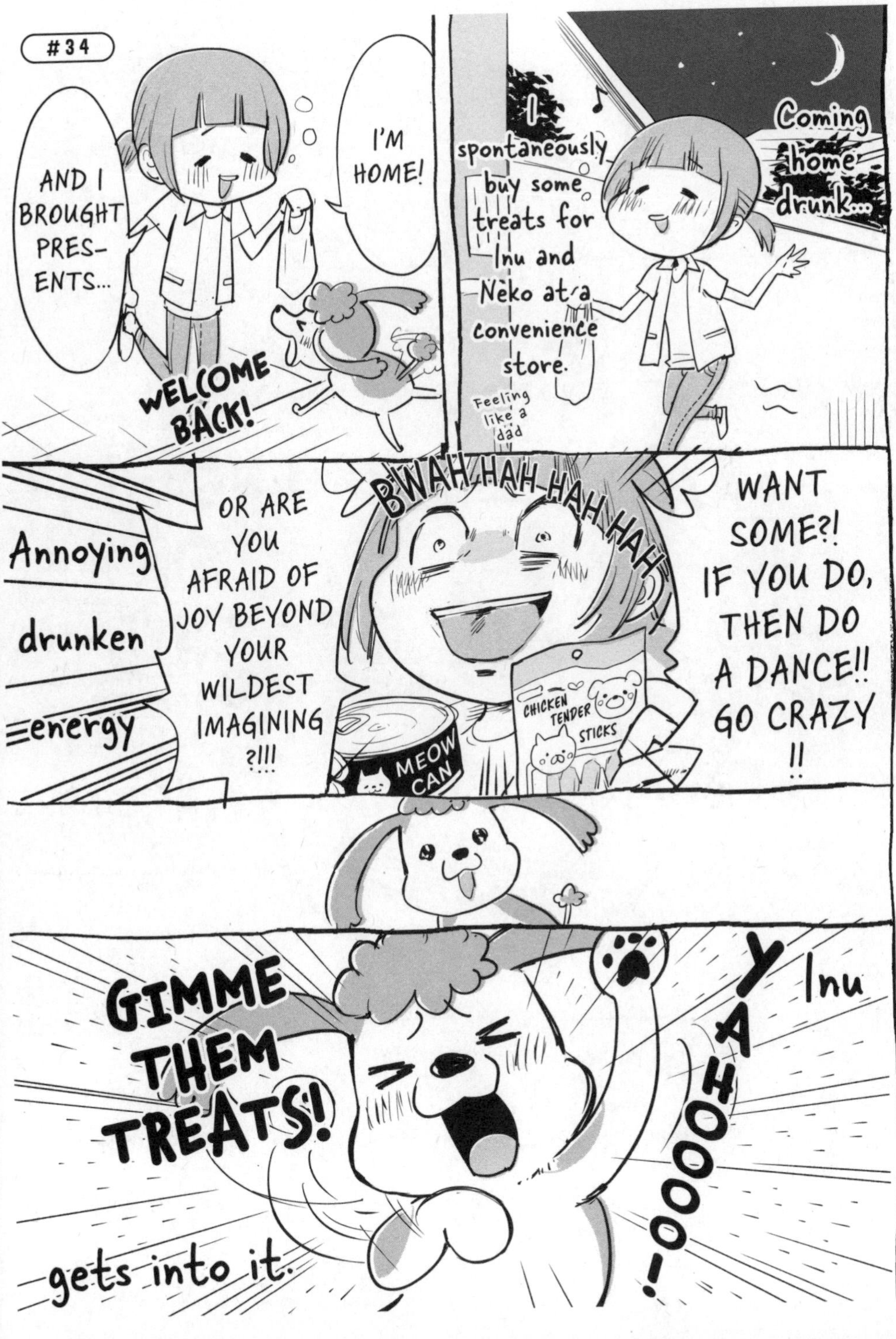
Coming home drunk...
I spontaneously buy some treats for Inu and Neko at a convenience store.
Feeling like a dad
I'M HOME!
AND I BROUGHT PRESENTS...
WELCOME BACK!
BWAH HAH HAH HAH
WANT SOME?! IF YOU DO, THEN DO A DANCE!! GO CRAZY!!
OR ARE YOU AFRAID OF JOY BEYOND YOUR WILDEST IMAGINING?!!!
CHICKEN TENDER STICKS
MEOW CAN
Annoying drunken energy
YAHOOOOOO!
Inu
GIMME THEM TREATS!
gets into it.

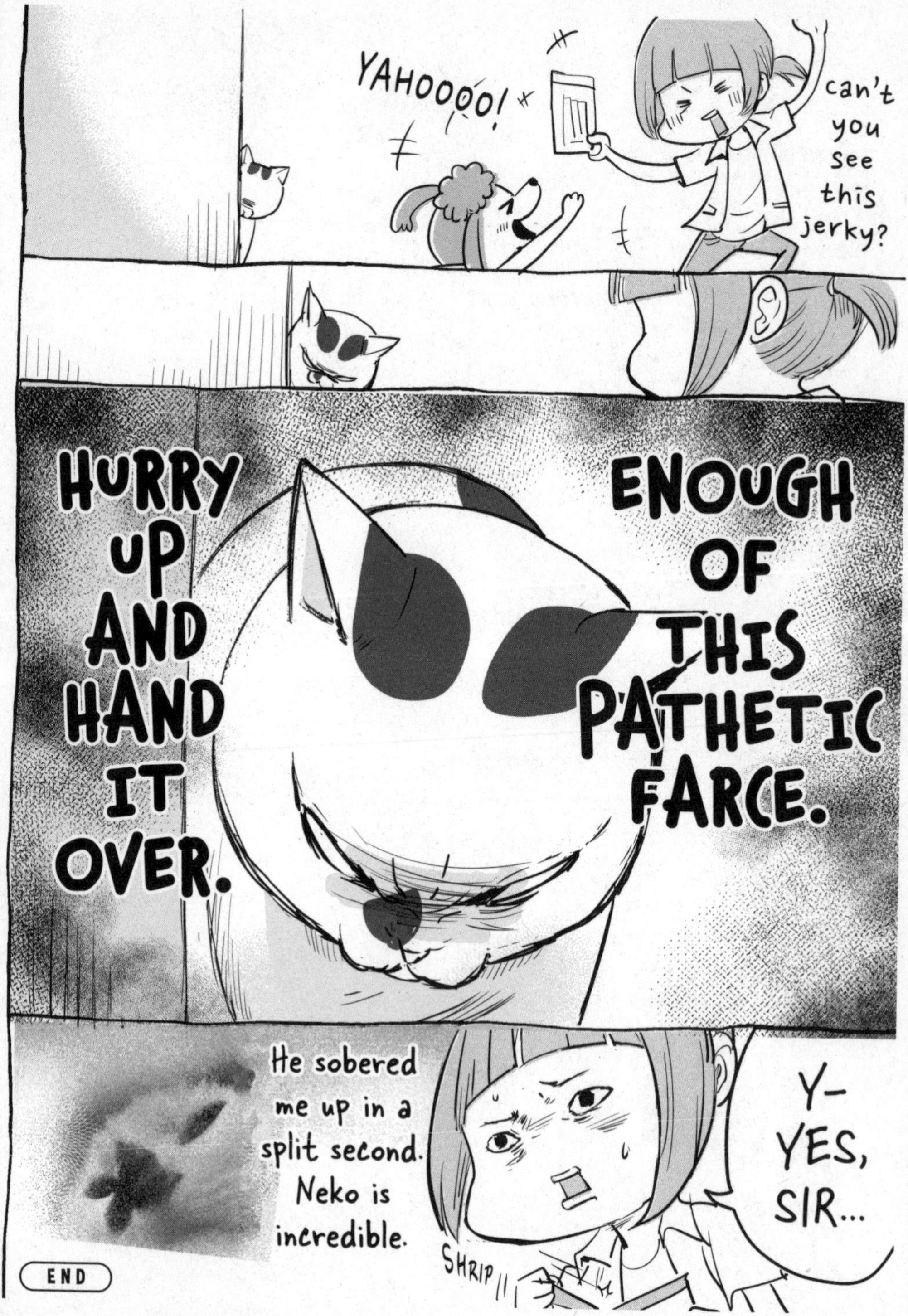
can't you see this jerky?
YAHOOOO!
ENOUGH OF THIS PATHETIC FARCE.
HURRY UP AND HAND IT OVER.
Y-YES, SIR...
SHRIP
He sobered me up in a split second. Neko is incredible.
END

#35

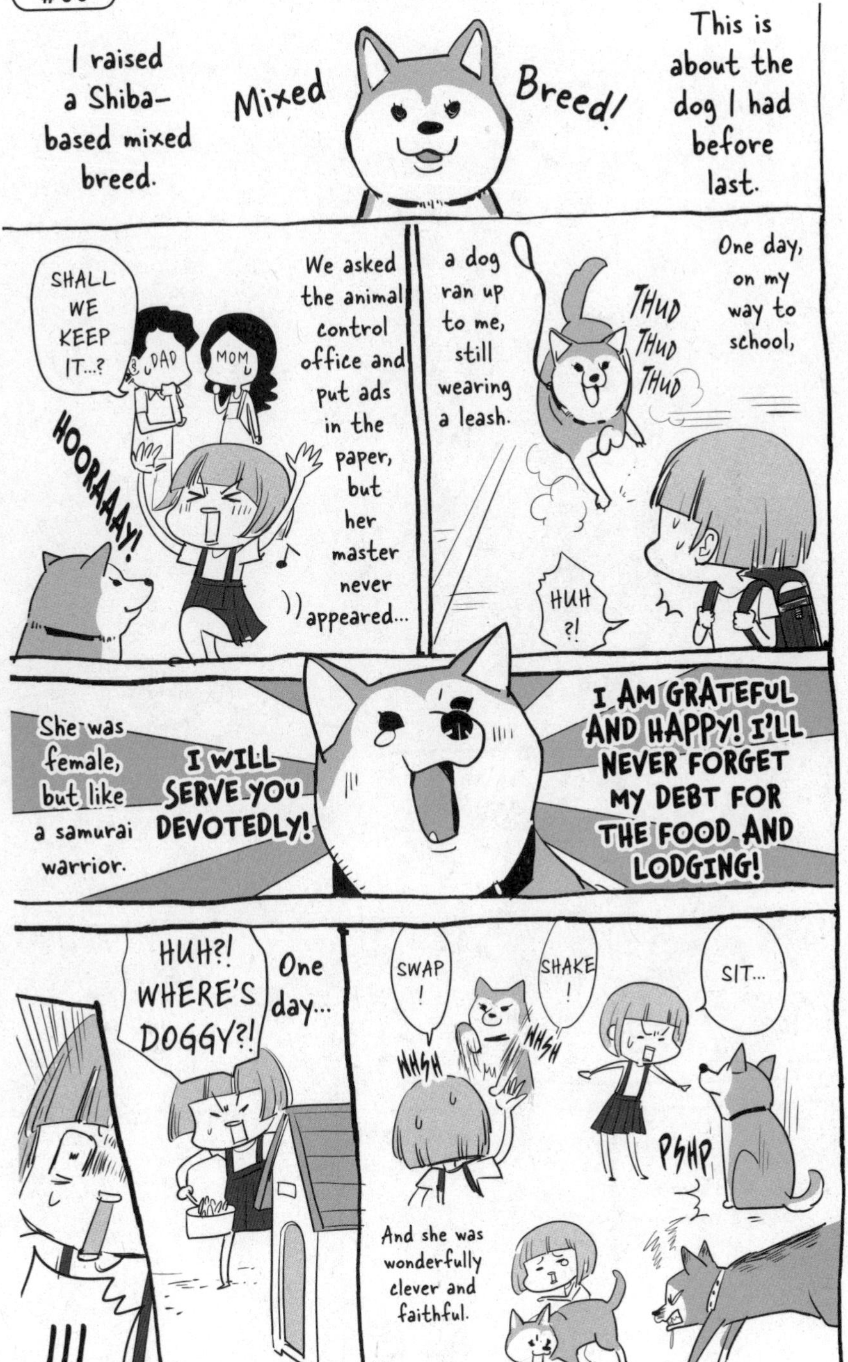

This is about the dog I had before last.
Mixed Breed!
I raised a Shiba-based mixed breed.
One day, on my way to school,
a dog ran up to me, still wearing a leash.
THUD THUD THUD
HUH?!
We asked the animal control office and put ads in the paper, but her master never appeared...
SHALL WE KEEP IT...?
DAD
MOM
HOORAAAY!
I AM GRATEFUL AND HAPPY! I'LL NEVER FORGET MY DEBT FOR THE FOOD AND LODGING!
I WILL SERVE YOU DEVOTEDLY!
She was female, but like a samurai warrior.
SIT...
SHAKE!
SWAP!
WHSH
WHSH
PSHP
And she was wonderfully clever and faithful.
One day...
HUH?! WHERE'S DOGGY?!
!!!
...

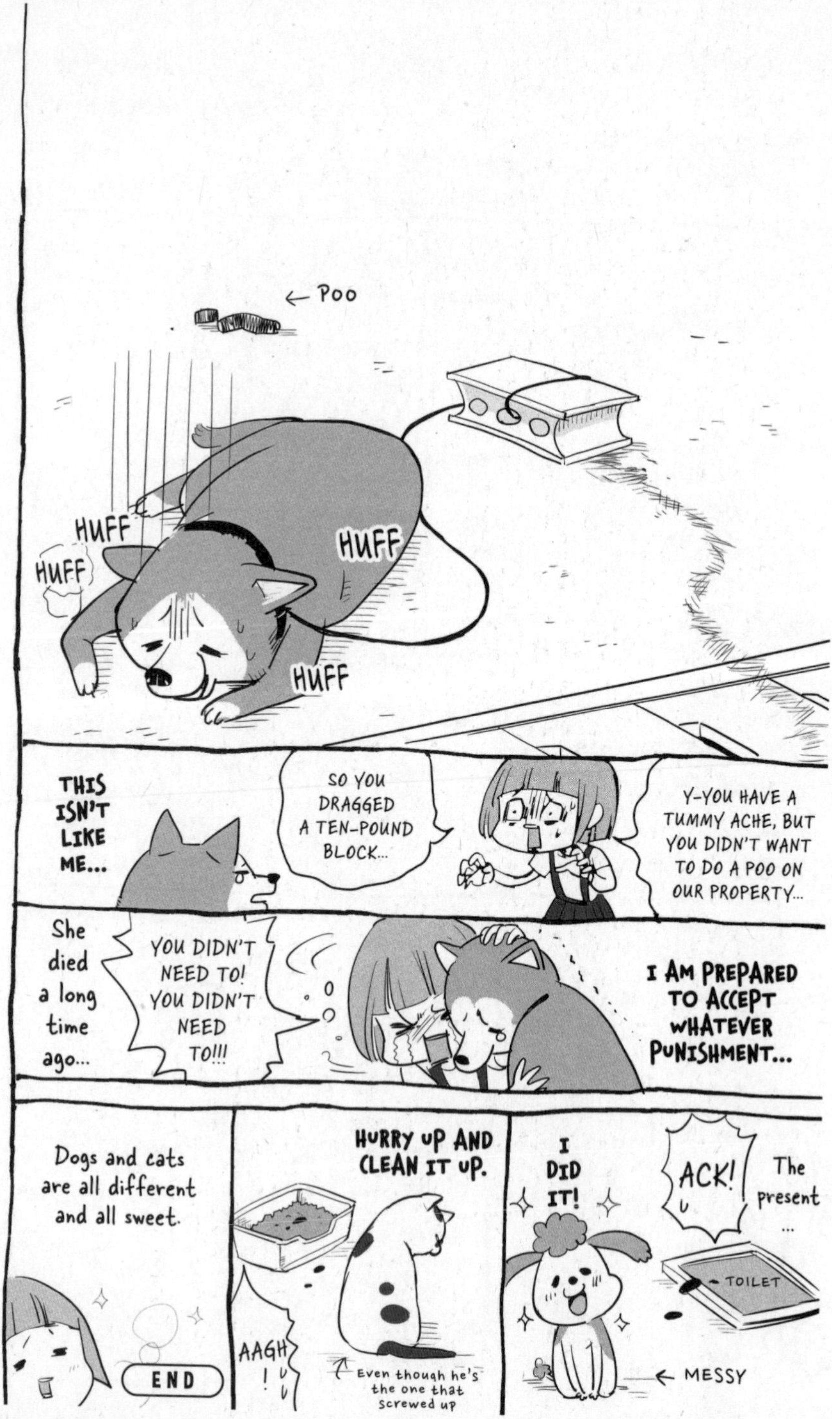
← POO
HUFF
HUFF
HUFF
HUFF
Y-YOU HAVE A TUMMY ACHE, BUT YOU DIDN'T WANT TO DO A POO ON OUR PROPERTY...
SO YOU DRAGGED A TEN-POUND BLOCK...
THIS ISN'T LIKE ME...
I AM PREPARED TO ACCEPT WHATEVER PUNISHMENT...
YOU DIDN'T NEED TO! YOU DIDN'T NEED TO!!!
She died a long time ago...
ACK!
The present ...
TOILET
I DID IT!
← MESSY
HURRY UP AND CLEAN IT UP.
AAGH!
Even though he's the one that screwed up
Dogs and cats are all different and all sweet.
END

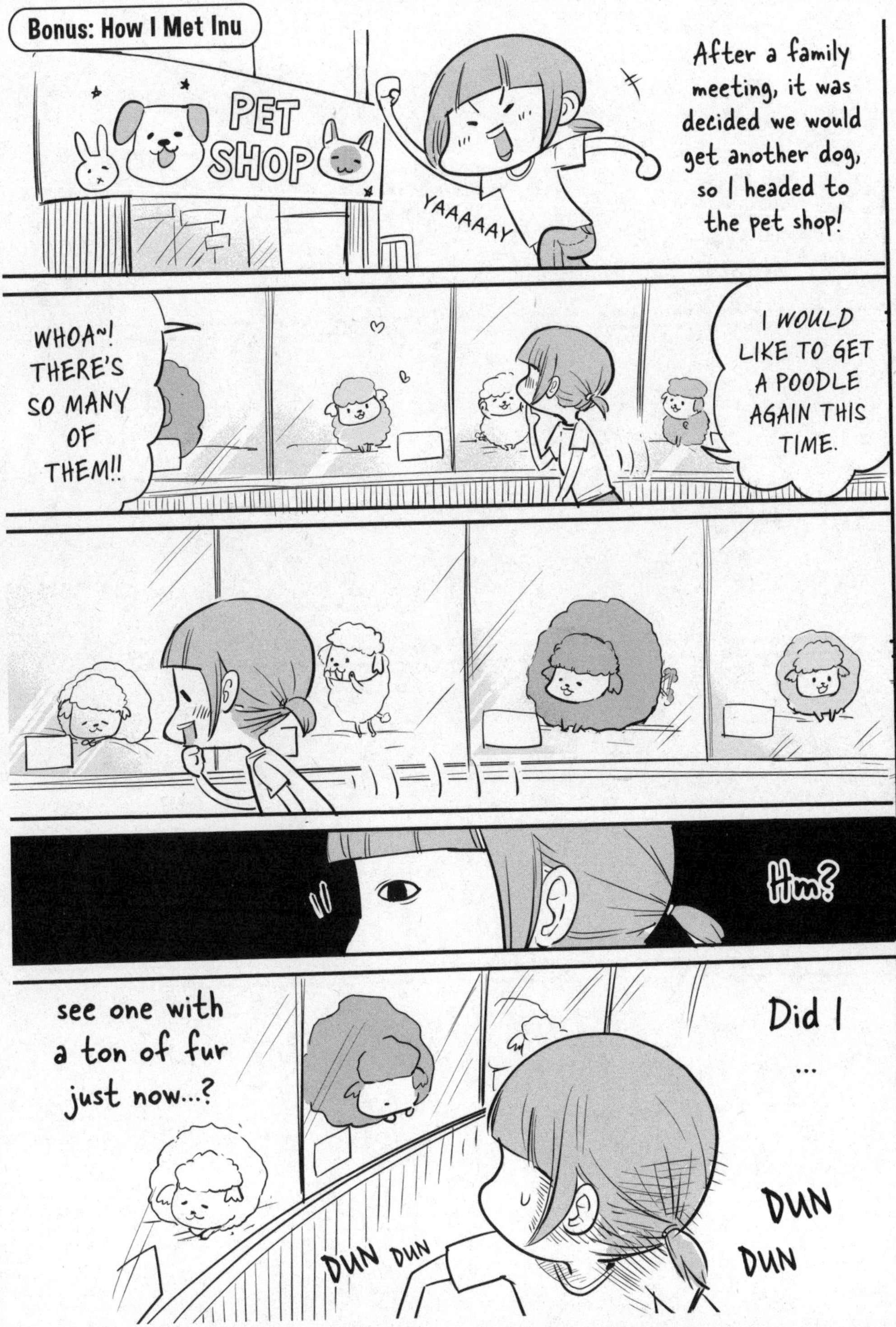
Bonus: How I Met Inu
After a family meeting, it was decided we would get another dog, so I headed to the pet shop!
YAAAAAY
PET SHOP
I WOULD LIKE TO GET A POODLE AGAIN THIS TIME.
WHOA~! THERE'S SO MANY OF THEM!!
Hm?
Did I ...
see one with a ton of fur just now...?
DUN DUN
DUN DUN

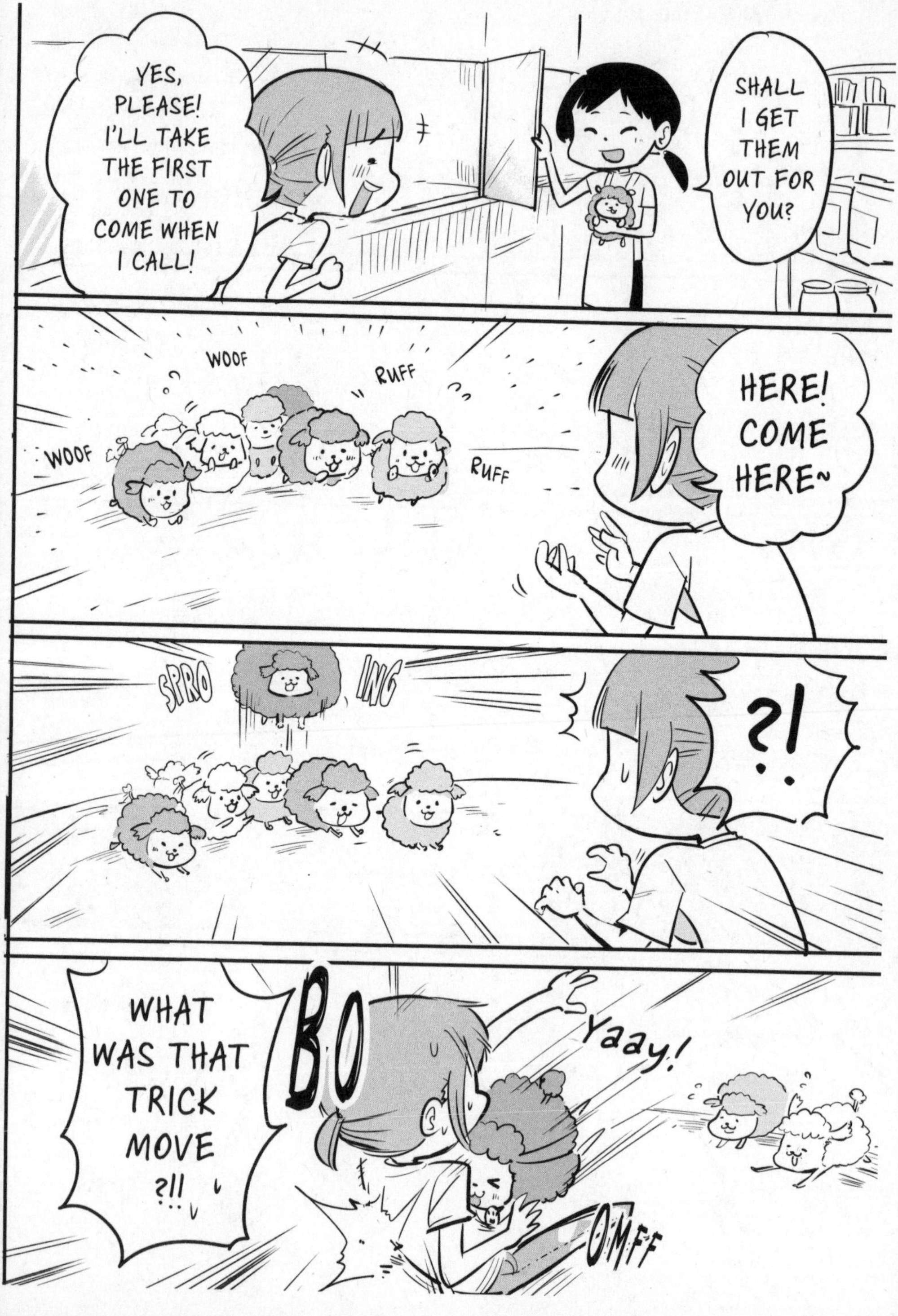
SHALL I GET THEM OUT FOR YOU?
YES, PLEASE! I'LL TAKE THE FIRST ONE TO COME WHEN I CALL!
HERE! COME HERE~
RUFF
WOOF
RUFF
WOOF
?!
SPRO ING
Yaaay!
BO
OMFF
WHAT WAS THAT TRICK MOVE ?!!

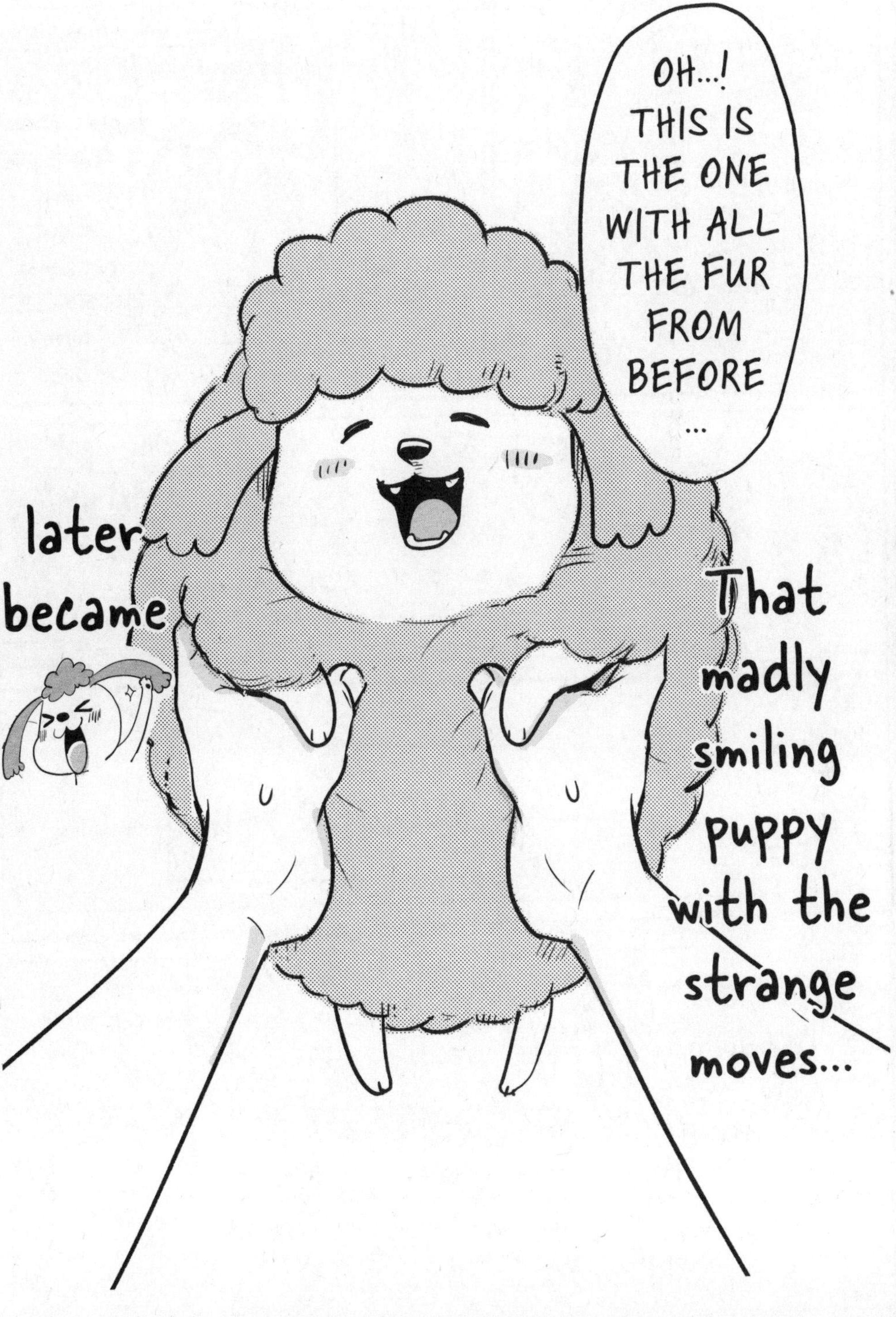
OH...! THIS IS THE ONE WITH ALL THE FUR FROM BEFORE ...
That madly smiling puppy with the strange moves...
later became

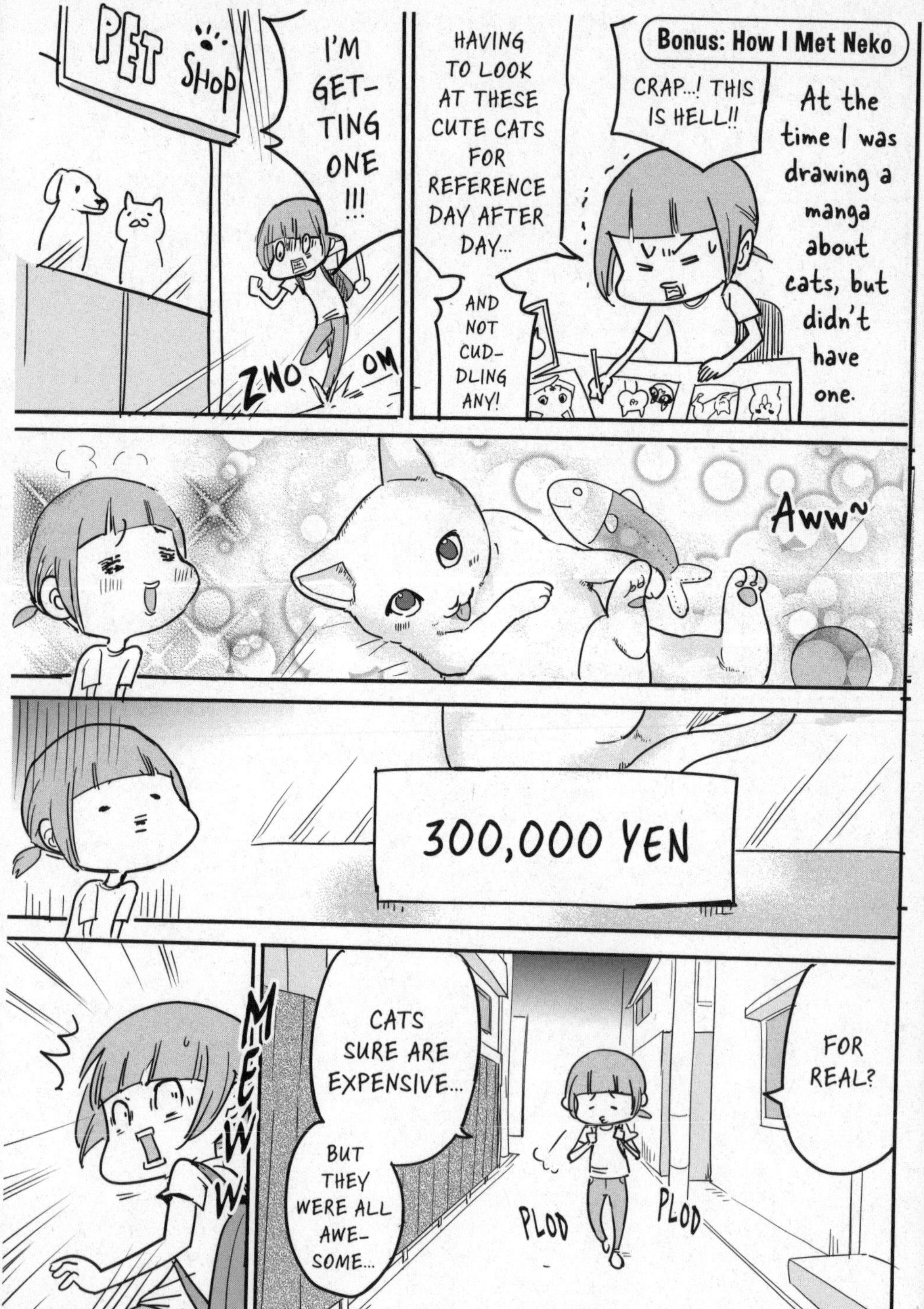
Bonus: How I Met Neko
At the time I was drawing a manga about cats, but didn't have one.
CRAP...! THIS IS HELL!!
HAVING TO LOOK AT THESE CUTE CATS FOR REFERENCE DAY AFTER DAY...
AND NOT CUDDLING ANY!
I'M GETTING ONE!!!
ZWOOM
PET SHOP
Aww~
300,000 YEN
FOR REAL?
PLOD PLOD
CATS SURE ARE EXPENSIVE...
BUT THEY WERE ALL AWESOME...
MEW

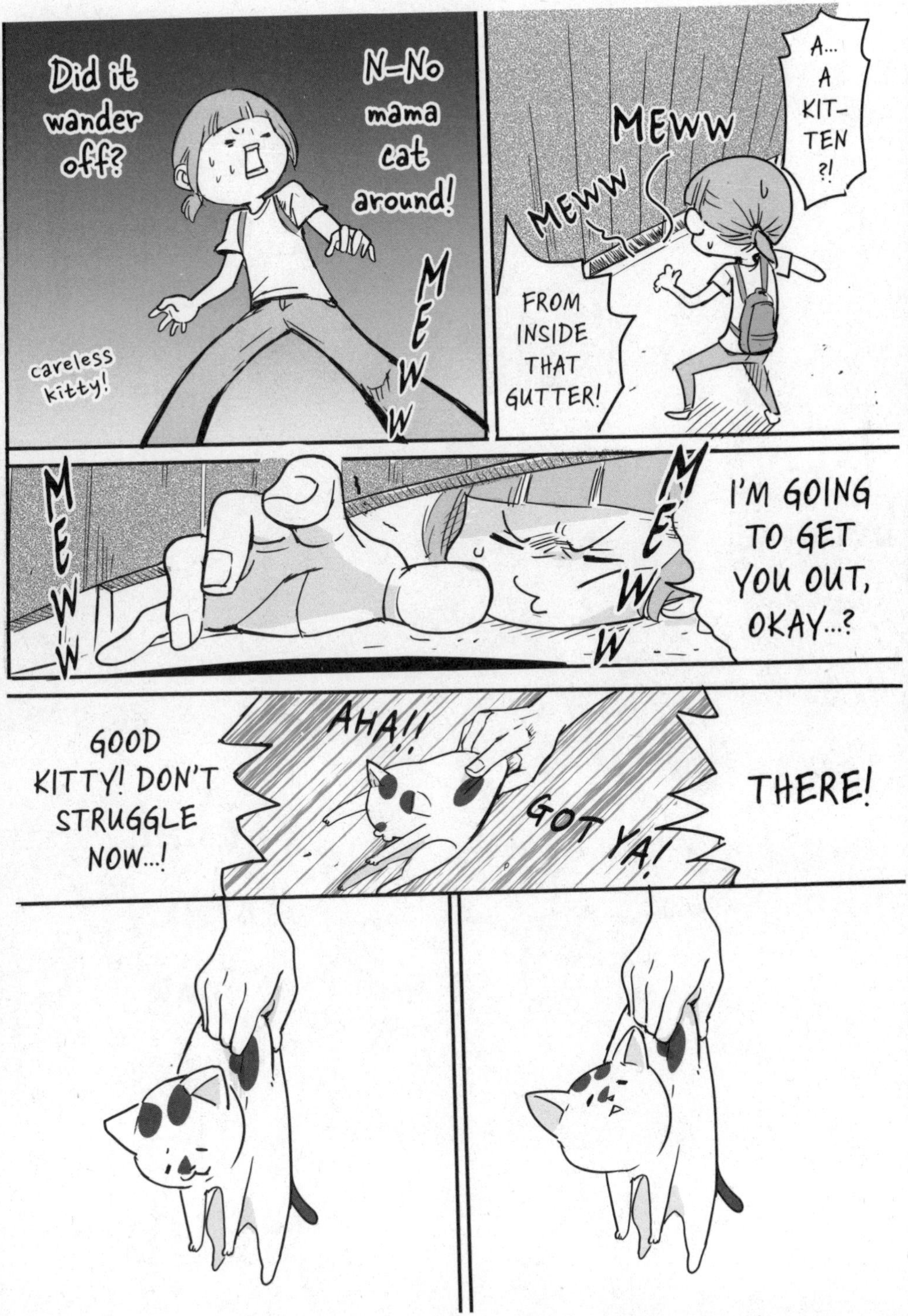
A... A KIT-TEN ?!
MEWW
MEWW
FROM INSIDE THAT GUTTER!
N-No mama cat around!
Did it wander off?
careless kitty!
MEWW
I'M GOING TO GET YOU OUT, OKAY...?
MEWW
MEWW
THERE!
AHA!!
GOT YA!
GOOD KITTY! DON'T STRUGGLE NOW...!

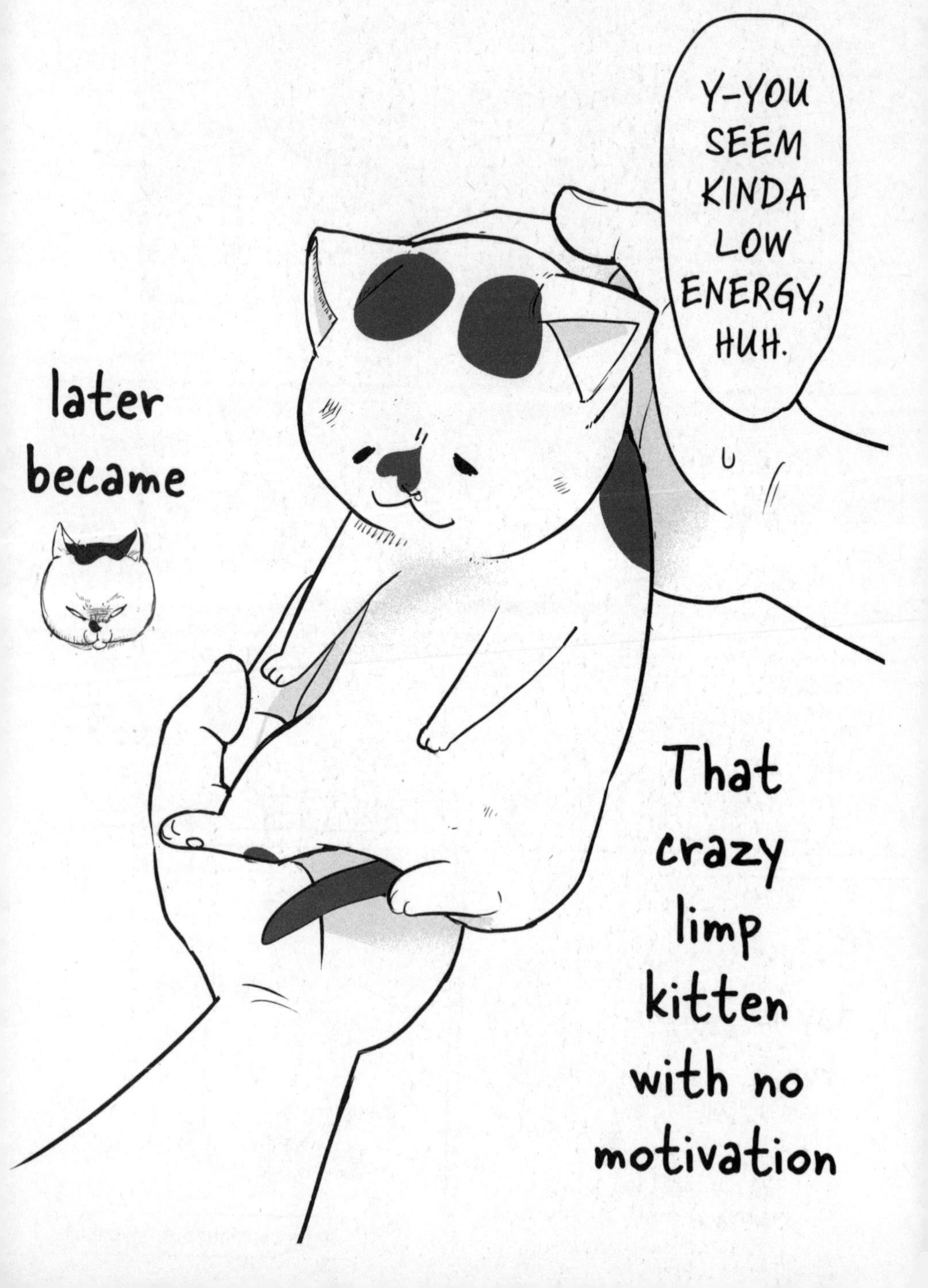
Y-YOU SEEM KINDA LOW ENERGY, HUH.
That crazy limp kitten with no motivation
later became

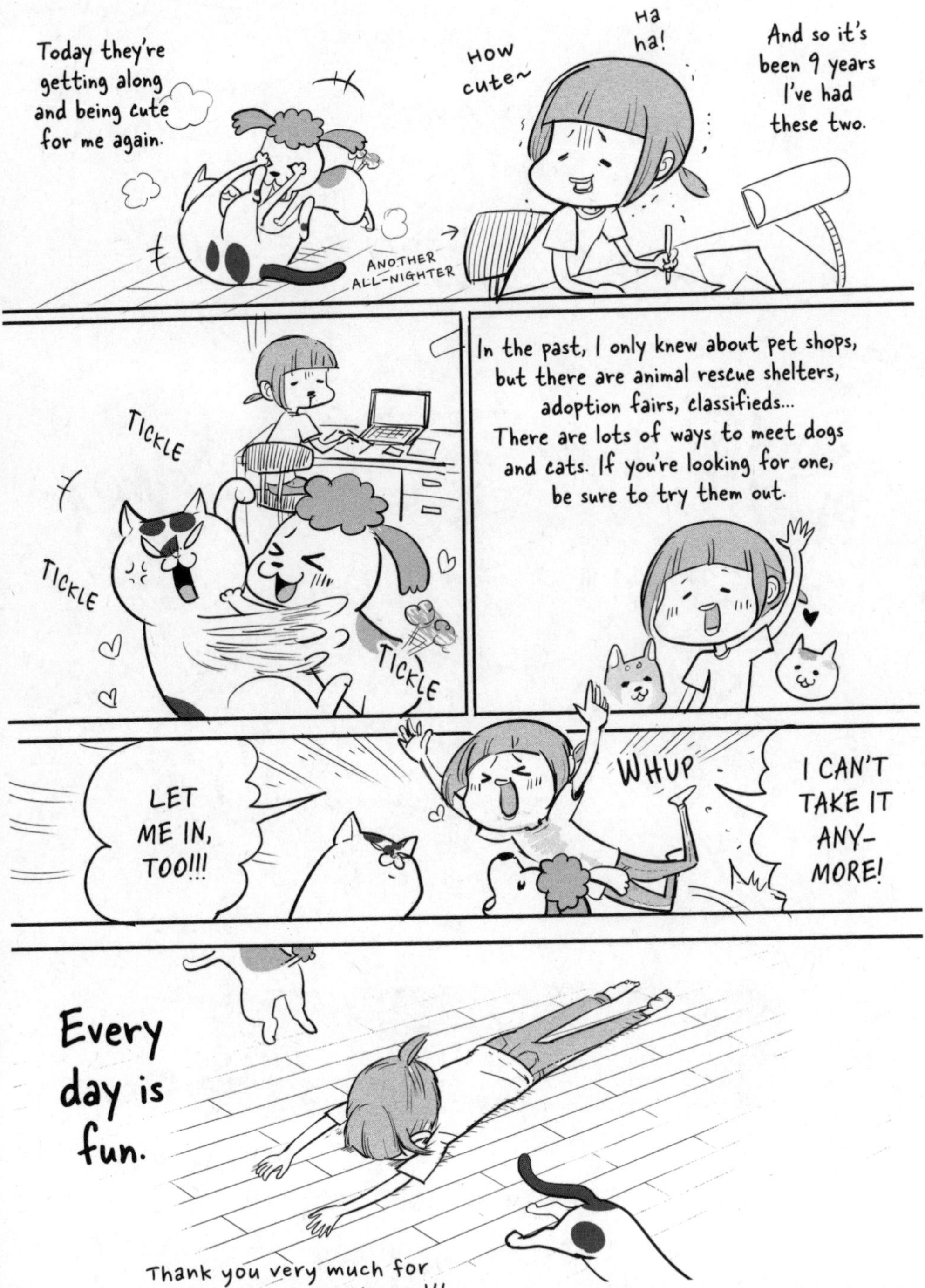

And so it's been 9 years I've had these two.
Ha ha!
HOW cute~
Today they're getting along and being cute for me again.
ANOTHER ALL-NIGHTER
In the past, I only knew about pet shops, but there are animal rescue shelters, adoption fairs, classifieds... There are lots of ways to meet dogs and cats. If you're looking for one, be sure to try them out.
TICKLE
TICKLE
TICKLE
I CAN'T TAKE IT ANY-MORE!
WHUP
LET ME IN, TOO!!!
Every day is fun.
Thank you very much for reading through to the end!!
To be continued in Volume 2

Information

The "With a Dog AND a Cat Every Day is Fun" Series

IS SERIALIZED ON TWITTER!

Twitter @hidekiccan

Thank you for all of your support

New Posts Every Sunday

(with occasional weeks off)

Own this Purr-fect Collection!
The Complete
Chi's Sweet Home
Box Set

The New York Times bestselling cat comic *Chi's Sweet Home* is now available in a complete box set!

Contains all 4 volumes of the series in a cute collector's edition box.

60 cute stickers included!

Available Now!

With a Dog AND a Cat, Every Day is Fun 1

A Vertical Comics Edition

Translation: Kumar Sivasubramanian
Production: Risa Cho
Eve Grandt

First published in Japan in 2018 by Kodansha, Ltd., Tokyo
Publication rights for this English edition arranged through Kodansha, Ltd., Tokyo
English language version produced by Vertical Comics, an imprint of Kodansha USA Publishing, LLC.

Translation provided by Vertical Comics, 2020
Published by Kodansha USA Publishing, LLC., New York

Originally published in Japanese as *Inu to Neko Docchimo Katteru to Mainichi Tanoshii 1* by Kodansha, Ltd., 2018

This is a work of fiction.

ISBN: 978-1-949980-55-4

Manufactured in the United States of America

First Edition

Kodansha USA Publishing, LLC.
451 Park Avenue South
7th Floor
New York, NY 10016
www.readvertical.com

Vertical books are distributed through Penguin-Random House Publisher Services.

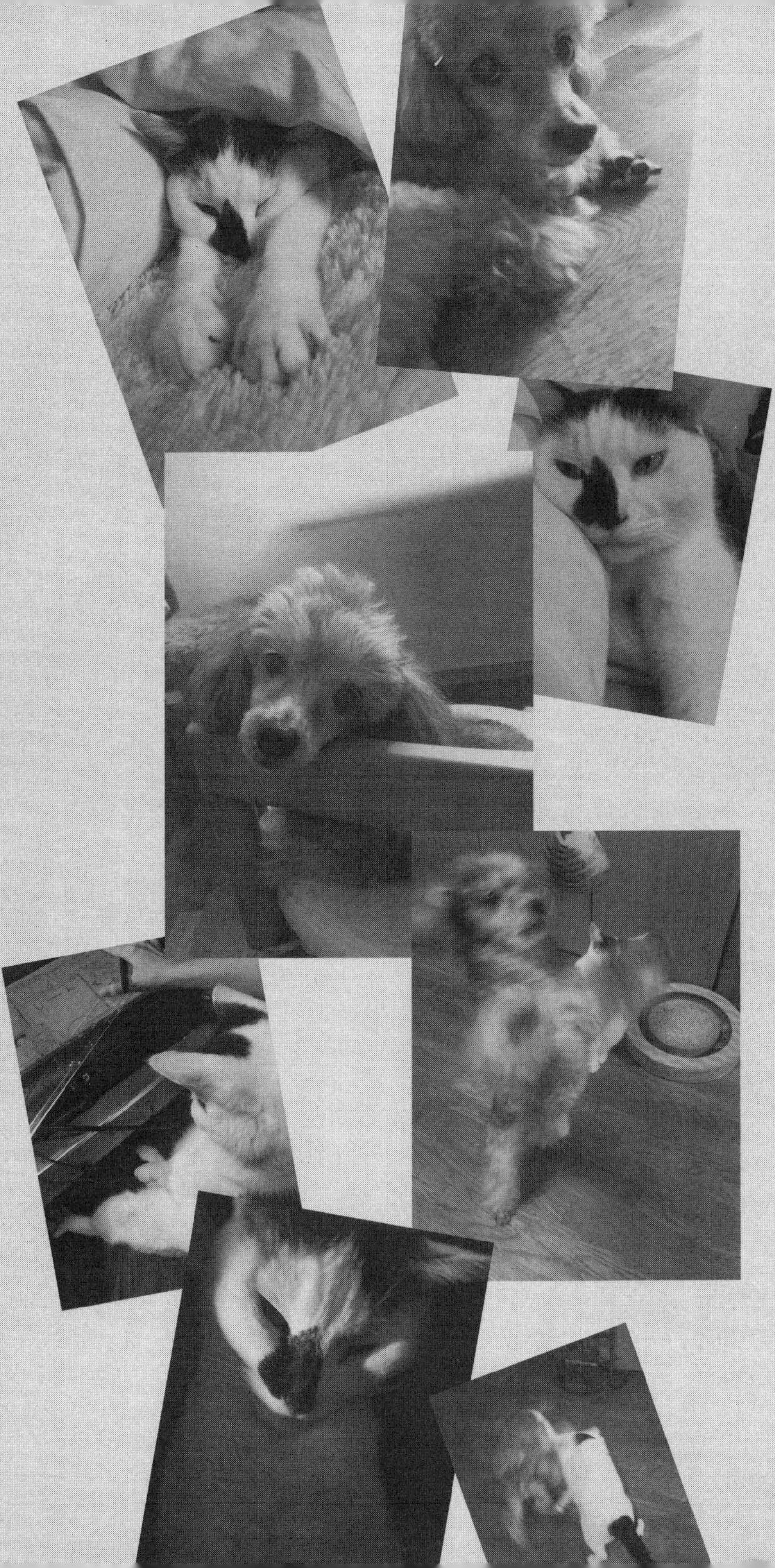

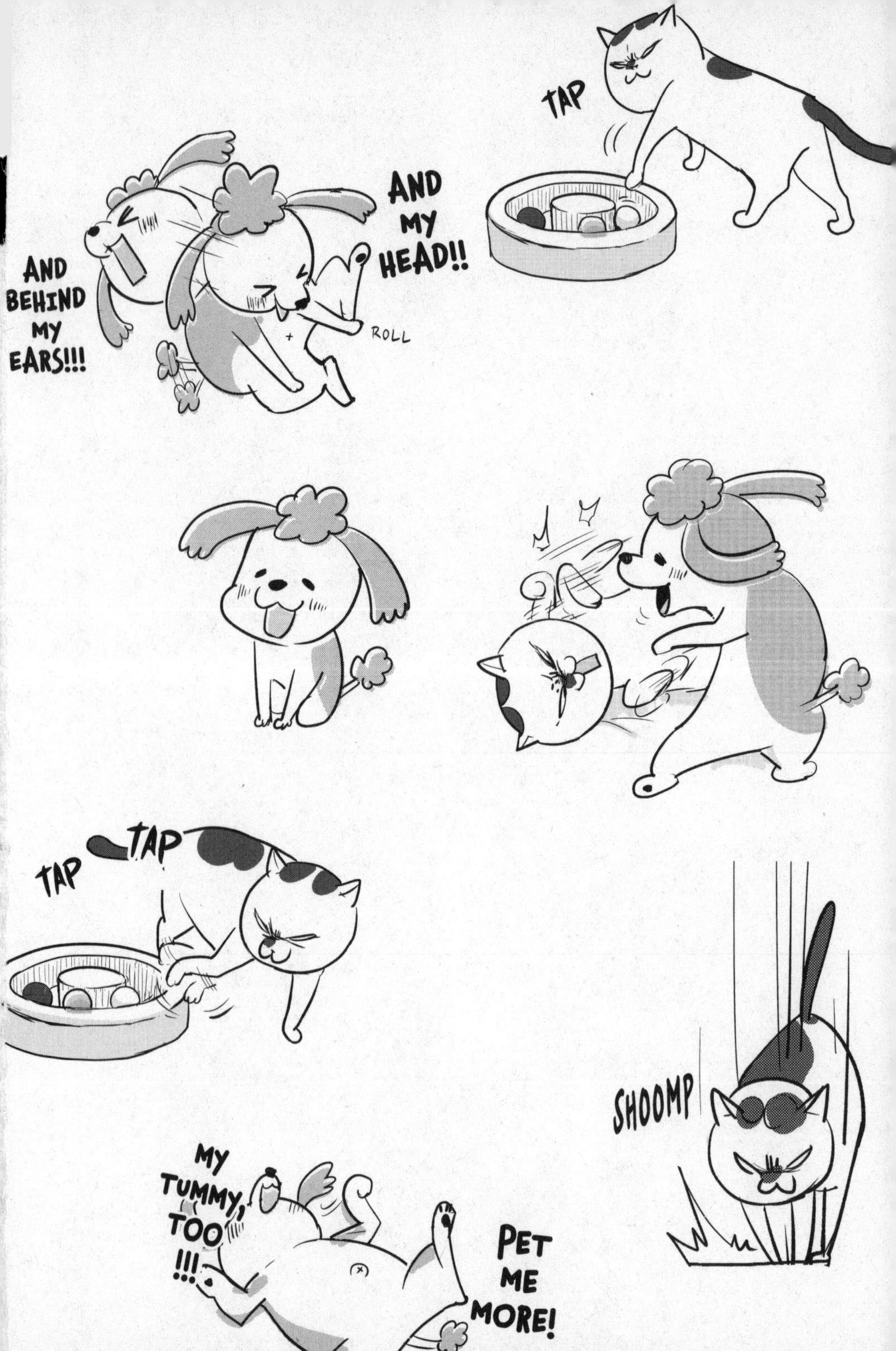
TAP
AND MY HEAD!!
ROLL
AND BEHIND MY EARS!!!
SHOOMP
TAP
TAP
PET ME MORE!
MY TUMMY, TOO!!!